Attachment Theory in Action

Attachment Theory in Action

Building Connections Between Children and Parents

Edited by Karen Doyle Buckwalter
and Debbie Reed

ROWMAN & LITTLEFIELD
Lanham • Boulder • New York • London

Published by Rowman & Littlefield
A wholly owned subsidiary of The Rowman & Littlefield Publishing Group, Inc.
4501 Forbes Boulevard, Suite 200, Lanham, Maryland 20706
www.rowman.com

Unit A, Whitacre Mews, 26-34 Stannary Street, London SE11 4AB

British Library Cataloguing in Publication Information Available

Library of Congress Cataloging-in-Publication Data Available

9781442260122 (cloth : alk. paper)
9781442260146 (pbk. : alk. paper)
9781442260139 (electronic)

♾™ The paper used in this publication meets the minimum requirements of American National Standard for Information Sciences—Permanence of Paper for Printed Library Materials, ANSI/NISO Z39.48-1992.

Printed in the United States of America

Karen Doyle Buckwalter:

In memory of my parents,
Kerry and Violet Doyle

In honor of my siblings,
Angi Doyle Fritz and Tony Doyle

With love and devotion to my husband,
Kirk, and my children, Benjamin and Elizabeth

Debbie Reed:

To my husband, Brennan; our sons, Tanner and Landon;
and my entire family for their unwavering support

And to Gene Simon, who always believed we would find a way

Contents

Prologue

This is a book written for seekers . . . those practitioners, professionals, and parents who refuse to give up on children whom others have deemed beyond hope. Written with clinicians in mind, we are also aware of the assurance a book like this can provide to parents of children struggling with attachment disorders, and the caseworkers, coordinators, and other professionals trying to support them. We have been told time and again that there is both comfort and encouragement in simply knowing there are other children, families, and professionals faced with the same baffling, heartbreaking, and at times frightening behaviors that they, and even the children who display them, don't understand. For those of you on such a quest, it is our hope that the information contained in this book provides you reassurance that there is help, and hope, for children and their families struggling with attachment disorders.

Chaddock is a unique organization in a small Midwestern community. Founded in 1853 by the Methodist Episcopal Church, throughout its history Chaddock has served as a college, an orphanage, a boys' school with a military curriculum, and a home for abused, neglected boys—and girls, starting in 1982. Today, Chaddock offers a full array of residential, community-based, and educational programming for children, birth through age twenty-one, and their families. Chaddock also offers training and consultation to agencies across the country related to attachment-based trauma-informed care. Based on a thirty-acre campus in Quincy, Illinois, Chaddock is nationally accredited by the Council on Accreditation of Services for Children and Families, Inc. (COA), as well as the United Methodist Association of Health and Welfare Ministries. In addition, Chaddock's on-campus special education school is accredited by the North Central Association of Colleges and Schools.

In the past twenty years, Chaddock has served children and their families from more than thirty states, and professionals from five continents have visited our campus to learn about our attachment-based work. We have been, and continue to be, on the journey of building an attachment-based intervention toolbox that will allow us to respond to the individualized needs of each child and family who turns to us for care. It is our hope, through the information provided in this book, that readers will find new paths forward in their own efforts to understand and respond to the needs of hurting children.

We have intentionally tried to make this book read like a conversation with a trusted friend or mentor, not to lessen the importance of the information provided, but rather to make it approachable and provide a big-picture overview of the breadth and depth of knowledge related to attachment-based work, which is often missing from clinical training. We—that is, professionals committed to finding answers for children struggling to attach—have made incredible advances in our understanding of attachment, brain science, and ways to connect with children who resist the very connection they so desperately need. This book is designed to provide a window through which to view those advances, and the resulting treatment strategies and techniques that have provided the key to unlock the hearts of so many children. For added context, each chapter starts with a vignette so you can see how the content may apply to your work.

Entire books have been written about virtually every one of the topics addressed in the coming pages, and we hope the book you hold in your hands will be but one stop on the journey of expanding your understanding of the intricate, and often misunderstood, ways that we humans attach to one another. If a particular concept or technique piques your interest, we encourage you to explore it further. Keep seeking. So many children and families are counting on you to help them find a path forward.

We have organized this book into three distinct sections. Part I, "Attachment Basics," is designed to provide a baseline understanding of attachment theory, a lens through which to apply that theory, and an overview of the brain science that underpins recent advancements in our knowledge of how attachment happens. Chapter 1 specifically focuses on attachment theory, how it was founded and expanded into the rich field it is today. Chapter 2 provides a phase-based framework that has been helpful in guiding our clinicians' thinking about the intent of various interventions and at what point in treatment various interventions can be most effective. Finally, chapter 3, while a bit more technical than the other chapters in this section, provides an explanation of the brain science behind attachment and how such findings support the need for attachment-based interventions.

Building on the fundamentals from part I, part II highlights ten different attachment-based interventions that have proved to be impactful for children and their families challenged by attachment difficulties. For some children, one of these interventions is sufficient to dramatically improve their ability to form reciprocal relationships. For others, it is the combination of two or more interventions, intentionally provided in concert, that provides the most sustainable long-term impact. We believe each of these interventions provides a positive and unique addition to a clinician's attachment toolbox. For those techniques that you find particularly intriguing, we encourage you to seek out more detailed information that is widely available on each of these models. There is an appendix at the back of the book that provides additional resources, including information on where you can learn more about each intervention highlighted in this section.

Part III includes perspectives and information we believe will make your attachment journey a more successful one. While you may be the clinical expert, you will fall short in your efforts if you do not remain open to the insight and experience of those on the healing path with you. First, we are privileged to share the experience, the voice, of two adult adoptees. Unless you yourself were adopted, it is presumptuous for you to believe that you know the lifelong impact of this experience. While each journey is unique, the courageous sharing of these two adoptees, who themselves went on to become attachment-based therapists, provides an additional lens into how our efforts are perceived by those we strive to support. Likewise, we would be remiss if we did not also provide an opportunity for you to hear from an adoptive parent. While you have signed on to support a child for an hour or two a week, these parents live the reality of their child's attachment struggles 24/7. Truly, they have much to teach us about their child, and the resilience and resourcefulness it takes to effectively parent a hurting child.

Finally, and perhaps surprisingly for some, we touch on how to respond to potential systemic and/or financial roadblocks that may impact incorporating these specialized techniques into your organization. We frequently talk to clinicians who are excited about these techniques, and the potential to dramatically impact those in their care, who then feel like they run into a brick wall within their organization. When they call us, they are baffled and frustrated by their inability to gain traction and effect change with the very people who sent them to attachment training in the first place! Most clinicians have little experience with the operational side of their organization. We hope to demystify it a bit and highlight a path for organizational change (sneak preview—you already know how to do it!).

We are grateful to the contributors to this book, and to the many children, families, and professional mentors who have guided us on our journey. Years ago, we made a commitment that we wanted to build a program without an ego, one where we were always seeking and learning, never sitting on our laurels thinking we had arrived at "the" solution. We continue on that journey today, and through this book, we invite you along for the ride.

Karen Doyle Buckwalter
and Debbie Reed

Acknowledgments

Gene Simon, who opened the way for us to "dance our dance."

The children Chaddock serves, who are the reason we are here.

Chaddock's staff and board, past and present, for their willingness to embrace "what if" and think big on behalf of our kids and families.

The clinicians and direct care staff of Chaddock for their energy, bravery, and commitment to putting ideas into action.

Michelle Robison and Marcia Ryan, who never lost heart.

Matt, Amy, Angel, Deb, Kristen, Jeff, Jerry, John, and Molly for their amazing individual and collective gifts and graces that help extend Chaddock's mission reach.

Judy Miller and Katie Powell for their tireless efforts in helping us format the manuscript.

All of the contributors to this book for all they have taught us.

Our tribe of family and friends, who keep us grounded and give us wings.

To the positive disrupters, who color outside the lines and see the world a bit differently, and to the true believers, who have the tenacity to take on and improve "the system"—you will change the world.

Rowman & Littlefield for seeing the potential of this project.

Most important, as caretakers of more than 160 years of ministry at Chaddock, may we always honor and acknowledge the One who guides and sustains us. God is good, all the time.

I

ATTACHMENT BASICS

1

Overview of Attachment Theory and Clinical Application

Karen Doyle Buckwalter

Love is composed of a single soul inhabiting two bodies.

—Aristotle

Often a new way of doing things or a new knowledge base evolves from a desperate quest to find answers. This was how many of the contributors to this book began learning about attachment theory and attachment-based therapy. A clinician's search for answers is frequently born out of feelings of inadequacy and ineffectiveness with some of the families with whom we work. Sometimes there are children who, despite our most earnest attempts, we cannot seem to reach. Often these are children whose hearts are so broken it seems there is nothing we can do to begin to put the pieces back together. These are children who fiercely avoid any kind of caring, trusting relationship with another human being, even their parents. Some of these children are written off as being damaged beyond repair.

Anyone who has any experience working with children from the child welfare system or orphanage care has come across cases such as these. In fact, when I first began working with this group of children one of my fellow therapists gave a name to this feeling of helpless ineffectiveness— "inadequate therapist syndrome." My guess is that some readers will identify with this label.

At first we clinicians were convinced that if we could discover the right combination of therapeutic interventions and parenting techniques, we could penetrate what felt like a wall around the heart of the children we were seeing. We tried many things: traditional play therapy approaches, cognitive behavioral therapy approaches, behavior modification approaches, family therapy, and parent training programs. It felt like each time we managed to help the child take one brick out of the wall around their heart, there was soon another one to take its place, mortared into this figurative wall even more solidly. The

3

behaviors of these children were frustrating, perplexing, and unpredictable. Just when we thought we had a handle on things, and the child was beginning to make progress, the process would become derailed. What could be wrong here? We assumed that nearly all children, particularly young children, could begin to heal if they could work with a skilled team of mental health professionals and had parents who were committed to following treatment recommendations. Again and again, however, these children proved our assumptions wrong.

The contributors to this volume refused to accept that these children were too shattered to be put back together again. Many of us zealously began to read everything we could find regarding children in foster care and children with early losses and traumatic experiences, which was the common denominator in the challenging children we were seeing. As we immersed ourselves in this literature, we began to learn about attachment theory as a theory of human development. It is a theory that, for many of us, was barely mentioned in our formal clinical training. The more we began to understand this theory, the more the children we were treating were demystified. Through the lens of attachment theory, the behaviors we were seeing from these children began to make sense.

We believe that, to gain the most from this book, it is important to have an understanding of the history of attachment theory as a foundation upon which modern advances in this specialized field have developed. This chapter will, in the coming pages, highlight some of the history alongside more recent advances in our understanding of how the brain works and its impact on attachment. We will also discuss the implications of this theory for the daily challenges of working with children and families who present to us with their complex histories.

HISTORY OF ATTACHMENT THEORY

John Bowlby is the founder of attachment theory (Bowlby 1944; 1951; 1953; [1969] 1982) and some would argue the first family therapist (Wood, Klebba, and Miller 2000). While Bowlby laid the foundation for the field of attachment, the path to today's understanding of this theory was a long and winding one.

While attending Cambridge University, Bowlby became drawn to what would later be known as developmental psychology. He went on to study medicine, specializing in psychiatry, and also studied at the British Psychoanalytic Institute. Between finishing his undergraduate degree and medical school, Bowlby spent time working at a home for maladjusted boys (Bowlby 1944). Two boys made a particularly strong impact on him; both had suffered disruptions in their relationships with their mothers (Bowlby 1940). One of the boys was an isolated and affectionless teenager with no experience of a stable mother figure. This child had been expelled from his previous school for stealing. The second child was an anxious boy of seven or eight who trailed Bowlby around so closely he became known as his shadow (Ainsworth 1974). Based on his observations and interactions with these children, Bowlby began to hypothesize about the effect of early experiences upon character development (Bowlby 1944).

Bowlby's thinking was seen as revolutionary by some, but he persisted in his belief that the relationship between the mother and her infant was immensely more complicated than the medical, psychoanalytic, and social theorists were proposing at the time. Bowlby wanted to understand *why* the mother was so important to the child.

The primary accepted theories of the day purported that the infant's relationship with its mother was driven by the need for food (Freud 1977). Bowlby questioned this assumption and found his theories supported by animal research. He became aware of the work of Lorenz (1935), who had been studying imprinting, the term he used to describe how geese became attached to mothers who did not feed them. In addition, he followed the work of Harlow (1958), who discovered that rhesus monkeys, when stressed, preferred a soft cloth monkey to cling to rather than a wire mesh monkey that supplied food. Clearly, the provision of food was not the only factor in the development of the mother-child relationship. There were other factors at play. This confirmation encouraged Bowlby to continue his quest.

As Bowlby continued to expand his understanding of the complexities and importance of the relationship between children with their mother, two associates played a key role in moving the foundational concepts of attachment theory forward to its present place as a rich conceptual framework to understand relationships in families. As part of a grant to study the effects of early separation, Bowlby hired James Robertson to observe one- to three-year-olds in the hospital and record how they reacted. It became clear to Robertson that the hospital stays and ongoing separation from parents was having a grave impact on the children. He noticed three stages the children seemed to go through: (1) *protest*, being upset, crying, and clinging in response to their parent leaving them after weekly visits; (2) *despair*, where the children became listless and withdrawn, losing interest in what was around them; and finally (3) *detachment*. The child in the final stage began to interact more and regain an appetite, but he was a different child, one who did not seem to recognize or care about his mother when she came to visit (Robertson 1970).

Robertson, hoping to add impact to the observations he was making, captured these stages through a film of one of his subjects (Robertson 1952). That film, *A Two-Year-Old Goes to Hospital*, which would later become famous in the world of child development, provided evidence for Bowlby's theory about the impact that separation from parents has on children. Still, British psychoanalysts refused to accept what the data was revealing. A good lesson for all of us: when we begin to think we are infallible, we lose the ability to learn from the story unfolding before us.

Once again undeterred, Bowlby undertook more formal research to prove his theories, which included hiring research assistant Mary Ainsworth to work with him on a project commissioned by the World Health Organization. After spending time in Uganda observing mothers and babies in naturalistic settings, she returned to the United States and initiated an innovative research project involving extensive home observations of infants and their mothers. On the basis of what she learned from these home observations, she developed a laboratory protocol to observe babies with their mothers that would become known as the Strange Situation, which has been replicated countless times by developmental psychologists. This procedure involves a series of separations and reunions with a child between twelve and twenty-four months of age and a parent, typically the child's mother (Ainsworth and Bell 1970).

The twenty-minute procedure entails a series of separation-reunion sequences between parent and infant and the introduction of a stranger—namely, someone unfamiliar to the child. The Strange Situation is video-filmed and trained coders rate each of the eight episodes for proximity seeking, contact maintenance, avoidance, resistance, and disorganized attachment behaviors. Researchers are most focused on the two reunions of the baby with the parent. The procedure is meant to stress the babies to a level that their "coping strategies" are evident, particularly how they use (or don't use) their mothers to regain safety in times of distress.

Ainsworth was able to identify distinct patterns in how babies respond to the return of their mothers into the room. *Secure babies* went to their mother and were able to be calmed down by her. There were other babies who did not seem interested in the mother when she came back into the room. It was as though these *avoidant* babies seemed to convey that they could get along with or without their mother. A third category of babies seemed to want the mother, but when she tried to soothe them, they remained fussy. In this case, they got what they wanted—their mother—but then they didn't want her. These babies were labeled *ambivalent or resistant* (Ainsworth et al. 1978).

Bowlby believed that all babies had a drive toward attachment, and that they were wired at birth to seek their mother for safety and comfort. So why didn't all the babies behave like the secure babies? Some babies had to adjust to how their mother responded to their neediness. For example, when mothers did not like the neediness and clinginess of a frightened or upset newborn, those babies learned to be more avoidant, to show that they did not need their mothers. It is important to note that even though these babies outwardly appeared not to need their mothers, researchers have now discovered that internally, as measured by physiological factors such as cortisol (Spangler and Grossmann 1993) and heart rate (Hill-Soderlund et al. 2008), these babies are stressed!

Ambivalent/resistant babies had mothers who were inconsistently available to them. Hence they, too, were ambivalent about the connection and tended to express distress to demand that inconsistent caregivers be there when needed. The secure children expressed their needs indicating that they expected those needs would consistently be met. By contrast, the insecure babies had the same needs but had to also "consider" what approach would work best for their type of mother. That's a lot to be concerned with for a baby. Additional research in this area has also shown that the babies who are assessed secure are less stressed than babies in other categories during additional tough baby events like getting inoculated. Gunnar and colleagues (1996) found lower levels of stress in these babies as measured by cortisol levels, a hormone that elevates when humans are under stress.

Eventually, Mary Main came on board to code the Strange Situation data. Main's first love was linguistics, but she was unable to get in the linguistic program due to poor grades (Main and Hesse 2009), so she had to "settle" for working with Ainsworth. Little did she know the groundbreaking work that was ahead in this collaboration.

As Main was coding Strange Situation data, she began to see behavior from children that did not fit into the three original categories Ainsworth had identified. She observed behaviors in this group of children such as turning in circles while approaching the parent or becoming disoriented and freezing into a trance-like state (Main and Solomon 1986). She called these babies' behaviors *disorganized/ disoriented*. And so a fourth and very important category was added, one that would later be shown to be most predictive of adult psychopathology. These strange and contradictory strategies exhibited at the parent's return were found to come from babies who experienced their caregiver as either frightened or frightening. This created a state in the baby of "fright without solution" (Hesse and Main 2000) because the same person who was supposed to protect the baby was, at the same time, a person the child feared. These behaviors were observed to be more prevalent in children living in maltreating caregiving contexts and also those with parents who had unresolved trauma and loss in their own background. This new category was a watershed moment in that those babies most at risk for problems later could be identified.

It is important to make note of the cross-cultural studies related to attachment. Bowlby's ([1969] 1982) contention was that attachment was a biological need and evolutionary construct across the species. If this was so, evidence of it must be found universally across cultures The three basic attachment patterns—secure, avoidant, and ambivalent—have been observed in every culture in which attachment studies have been conducted. In fact, Ainsworth first began to notice these patterns in her Ganda study in Uganda (Ainsworth 1967), not in her Baltimore sample, as is often cited. The strategies that children use to deal with attachment challenges may vary across cultures, but it appears the patterning is the same (Hinde and Stevenson-Hinde 1990). In addition, cross-cultural studies have helped deepen the understanding of the wider social networks that children develop within (Harkness and Super 1996; Nsamemang 1992) and the need to change from a dyadic view of attachment to a network approach (Tavecchio and van IJzendoorn 1987).

In keeping with her love of language and background in linguistics, Main later went on to develop an interview for adults, the Adult Attachment Interview, or AAI, which asked questions about the adult's history of being parented and any traumatic experiences in their past. Incredibly, when recordings of the interview were transcribed, she and her colleagues (George, Kaplan, and Main 1985) were able to identify patterns in how the adults spoke about their own histories that would correlate with their babies' patterns in the Strange Situation. This was a total shift in how to assess attachment. Instead of looking at actual behaviors, as in the Strange Situation, the interview was examining adult narratives about attachment relationships as they were represented in the mind of the subject. Main (Main and Hesse 2009) noted that the AAI stresses the adult subject in a similar way that the Strange Situation stresses a baby, and so defensive patterns of each subject can be evaluated.

According to the coding system developed for the AAI, the classifications for adults included the following: secure, dismissing, preoccupied, and unresolved. *Secure adults* can speak about their history in a coherent and clear way, and they tend to have secure babies. *Dismissing parents* are less coherent, avoid talking about attachment relationships, and are seemingly cut off from feelings about their early relationships with caregivers. These parents most often have babies who exhibit an avoidant attachment pattern. *Preoccupied parents* also tend to be less coherent, but in a different way. They are preoccupied with past attachment relationships and display angry, conflictual feelings. These parents tend to have babies who show the resistant/ambivalent attachment pattern. Individuals whose narratives are classified as *unresolved* tend to show striking lapses in reasoning and monitoring, such as noting a person was dead in one part of the interview but later speaking as if they were alive. It is almost as though the person being interviewed became disoriented. The babies of these parents most often display the disorganized behaviors described earlier. The baby's behaviors reflected the mind of the parents. These researchers could give a twenty-question, hour-long interview and, without seeing the parent with the child, predict the quality of the attachment relationship in the next generation. Later it was found that this correlation between the AAI and the Strange Situation held true even if the parents were given the interview before their children were born (Fonagy, Steele, and Steele 1991). Perhaps equally compelling is that the parent's actual history was not as important as how they spoke about it. Main states the following in a 2009 lecture:

> Although a person's life history cannot change it can be told in many differing conversational forms. These forms predict with 75–80% accuracy how a young infant will be treated by the speaker and consequently how the infant will respond to the speaker in the strange situation. The parents of the insecure avoidant infant tried to avoid discussion of their own attachment related histories and the parents of the ambivalent resistant infants got all mixed up and had an underlying anger.

The importance of this research cannot be over emphasized. Clearly there is an intergenerational transmission of attachment patterns (van IJzendoorn 1995) *and* the old maxim is true: "You can't give what you haven't got." Most fascinating is that in a nonclinical sample of adults (meaning people who are not seeking mental health treatment) only about 56 percent will be coded secure in an AAI (Bakermans-Kranenburg and van IJzendoorn 2009). Translating that research to our work today, that means nearly half of the parents we work with may not themselves be secure. And, in the limited amount of research that has been done gathering AAI data from adoptive parents (Howard 2016), the rate of security is actually significantly lower with these parents. So, regardless of what you try to do for the child, unless you can bring the parents along and move them toward security as well, lasting change and attachment security for the child may be elusive. In fact, it may be that in many cases clinical work with the parents will have a greater impact on the child than the actual work with the child. The idea that the parent's attachment history will impact children's behavior has been demonstrated in research (Cowan et al. 1996). Selma Fraiberg and her colleagues (1975), in the seminal article "Ghosts in the Nursery," write of a visit with a high-risk mother who did not respond to her child's cries. It was like she could not hear her baby crying. What was the matter here? Their clinical hypothesis was that the mother needed for them to hear and understand her own painful story—and they were right! "When this mother's own cries are heard she will hear her child's cries" (Fraiberg et al. 1975, 396).

INTERNAL WORKING MODELS, ATTACHMENT, AND THE SCULPTING OF A BRAIN

As a result of Bowlby's work, and later that of Ainsworth and Main, we know that children form a view of the world, an "internal working model," or a blueprint for other relationships at a very young age (Bowlby 1979). These early mental representations of the self and others—formed within the child-caregiver relationship—carry forward and influence thoughts, feelings, and behaviors in other relationships. Thus these child-caregiver relationships, when they go well, give the child a sense of "felt security" and safety (Bretherton 1985; Sroufe and Waters 1977).

The internal working models of the children many of us work with are very different from the internal working models of children who feel safe and connected to caregivers. Children with early attachment losses, often compounded with other traumatic experiences, learn the world is unsafe and adults cannot be trusted. Such children are operating from a completely different frame of reference, which is why we, looking at them with many typical (yet incorrect) assumptions, can be baffled by their behaviors and persistent difficulties.

Bowlby's work highlights that the attachment relationship is not just a parent and child feeling close and connected to each other. Attachment is a biological need for our species with major ramifications for human brain development. This is critical because our brain controls our emotions and behaviors. Equally important in this equation is the fact that certain attachment-promoting behaviors must come from the parent in response to the baby's attachment-seeking behaviors (Schore 2000). Many of these behaviors may just seem to be the cute little things that babies do, but there is actually a survival function embedded in the baby's smiling, cooing, clinging, sucking, and gazing. These behaviors from infants attract caregivers to them (Bowlby [1969] 1982) not only for protection but also to organize their little brains. An infant nervous system, which is quite disorganized at birth, becomes organized in a manner that allows for her to adapt or respond to a wide range of internal and external systems she encounters. How does this happen? It happens by the guidance and sensory feedback provided by the infant's primary caregiver. Schore (2001) calls these interactions *psychobiological* in nature. The mother's right brain directly influences and shapes the baby's right brain, as each limbic system interacts with the other.

When a child with an immature, unorganized nervous system is aroused, an infant needs the primary caregiver to provide coherent, consistent sensory feedback that can be processed by the baby's brain. The child incorporates this feedback into his sensory experience and begins to learn how to move from an unpleasant aroused state to a more favorable experience.

The infant does not initially have the capacity to distinguish between sensory stimulation that originates from internal and external sources. A baby simply experiences what his sensory-motor system communicates to the brain. It is the caregiver who provides stimulation that counters unpleasant stimulation within the infant. Incredible that a mother rocking and speaking softly to her baby when he's upset is sculpting the child's brain. With enough repetition, the child develops the neuropathways that allow him to intentionally move from unpleasant to pleasant states of arousal (Schore 2001).

Over time, as the child continues to grow and as brain structures become more clearly defined in their interconnections, the capacity for self-regulation of emotional states increases. This is why some experts describe the brain as experience-dependent and use-dependent (Perry et al. 1995) and go so far as to say that the "states" the brain is in the most, good or bad, will later become "traits" as neuropathways for these states become more and more defined. Another way some have described this (Schore 2001) based on Hebbian Theory (Hebb 1949) is that "neurons that fire together wire together." Some (Trevarthen 1979) have even written about the special ways that mothers communicate with babies prior to language acquisition (using a higher-pitched voice, singing, rocking, and swaying) as "motherese," a special language a baby's brain understands.

The bottom line is that a baby's brain will be shaped by, and resemble in some ways, the brain that cares for it. A good example of how a mother regulates her baby is from an experiment called the still-face paradigm, where a mother who is looking at her baby is told to hold a still face and not move or talk after a period of normal interaction with the infant (Tronick 2007). This upsets the baby! He needs mom's face to show him how he is feeling. She is his emotional mirror until he's old enough to better regulate his own emotions. Once the mother "comes back" to her normally expressive face and voice, the baby settles.

Attachment is not just a theory about a connection between a baby and parent, but rather an entirely different way of understanding the brain and what underlies human behavior in relationships. This is why in therapy we can't just look at behaviors and try to get rid of them. That's about as effective as cutting dandelions off at the stem. We need to understand the root of the behavior and what is fueling it. The context of attachment theory helps us do that.

Contributor Jonathan Baylin, in his upcoming chapter about the brain, will go into great detail about how the clinical models reviewed in this book impact the brain. Nonetheless, here it is useful to discuss a few ideas that have been elucidated over the 1990–2000 "Decade of the Brain" (Schore 2001), when so much more was learned about brain functioning.

APPLICATION OF ATTACHMENT THEORY TO CLINICAL PRACTICE: WHAT EVERY THERAPIST SHOULD KNOW

Toward the end of his career, John Bowlby noted, "It is a little unexpected that, whereas attachment theory was formulated by a clinician for use in the diagnosis and treatment of emotionally disturbed patients and families, its usage hitherto has been mainly to promote research in developmental psychology. Whilst I welcome the findings of this research as enormously extending our understanding of personality development and psychopathology, and thus as of the greatest clinical relevance, it has none the less been disappointing that clinicians have been so slow to test the theory's uses" (Bowlby 1988, ix–x). Obviously, the developer of attachment theory meant for it to be relevant to clinical practice.

Approaching this work through the lens of attachment theory connects us to our clients in a different way. Children who may seem difficult, unlikable, and unappealing become more delightful, joyful, and easier to be around—even though their behaviors did not change—simply because we are able to view, understand, and respond to them in a different way. Once we are able to view our clients differently, we can better support their healing, helping chip away at their negative internal working models by giving them a new and different experience with adults and caretakers. In a sense, the children heal by getting what they don't expect—safe and need-fulfilling relationships with parents and others. While critically important, this is not a simple or straightforward thing to accomplish, because by the time these children come to us, their brains and bodies have learned to reject that which they desperately need. They have learned, in effect, to protect themselves in relationships.

Bowlby (1988) identified five therapeutic tasks or responsibilities of a clinician adhering to his model. Just as a mother becomes the secure base from which her baby can explore the world, we need to offer ourselves to our clients as a secure base. Bowlby describes this as becoming a trusted companion who is willing to provide support, encouragement, and empathy as the client explores painful aspects of life both past and present, some that he or she would find difficult or even impossible to think about without our support. While Bowlby was speaking of work with adult clients, this process is strikingly similar to what we are also attempting to do with the children with whom we work. In addition, we often must become the secure base for parents so they can be the same for their child as the painful past of the child is explored.

Second, Bowlby noted that we need to assist clients in their own exploration by encouraging them to consider the ways they engage in current relationships, expectations for behavior, and unconscious biases in relationships that create undesired situations. Here again, the relevance to working with children with attachment difficulties and traumatic backgrounds can't be missed. Not only do such children expect caregivers to be unavailable and misattuned, but in a sense they create such a circumstance to gain predictability. It's the "I will reject you before you reject me" scenario, or "I will, with my behavior, get you to behave like other parent figures I have had so I can be in control of what happens to me."

It's interesting to note that prior to working with parents struggling with a child's attachment difficulties, I had never before heard parents say things like "I don't know what is wrong with me. I have never felt like harming any child before, but with this child I have feelings of wanting to hurt him." Parents are guilt-ridden and horrified by these unfamiliar impulses, which are an indication of how powerful the unconscious drives of the child are in creating situations that feel familiar to him.

This phenomenon is supported in science by what neuroscientists call *limbic attractors*, which means that because of the way our neurons are wired, our brain tends to see things the way we have seen and experienced them before (Lewis, Amini, and Lannon 2000). Even more remarkable, our brain will impact the limbic network of others, meaning their behavior can be impacted by the way we expect them to behave. Children who are expecting rejection and abuse from parents can actually influence the brains of their parents in this direction.

The third point Bowlby makes is that the clinician needs to help the client recognize what is going on between the two of them (meaning between the client and the clinician). The internal working models of the children we work with will impact not only their relationship with their parents but also their relationship with the clinician. Basic therapy principles require the therapist to form a trusting relationship with a client. When you are working with a child who cannot let his or her guard down to trust anyone, it makes accomplishing this task much more difficult. These are kids who will push every button you have. They will tell you your breath stinks, that you are fat, that you are ugly, that you are stupid and boring. They will poop their pants in your office and pee on your furniture. Just as they do with their parents, they will have an almost eerie sixth sense of how to get to you. It is important to first understand that much of this is unconscious for the child, and they are not just being master manipulators. They are driven to protect themselves from closeness in any way they can.

Which brings us to another point: Don't take their rejection personally. You must become the person who won't reject them or give up on them no matter what, and you must support their parents in this same endeavor. This is what will slowly but surely begin to change a child's internal working model. If you intend to be in this line of clinical work, get some support for yourself. Find a way to receive good reflective supervision (Heffron and Murch 2010) where you have the safety to look deeply at how this work is impacting you. This is not the same as administrative supervision, where you talk about whether you have your case notes up to date, or clinical supervision, where you talk about what's going on with your cases and current treatment strategies. It is not a question of whether you will be triggered by doing this kind of work, but rather whether you will be conscious of how you are being triggered or unconsciously responding and reacting in the same way the children you work with do. Take care of yourself physically, emotionally, and spiritually. Get a therapist yourself. Do whatever it takes to keep you in a healthy place to be open, curious, and strong enough to hold the intense pain and suffering of your clients.

The fourth and fifth clinical applications Bowlby wrote about are closely linked. He described the need to help clients identify current perceptions and expectations that result from early experiences with their parents. Once they recognize these, clients can then better understand how such perceptions have contributed to their models or images of self, others, and the world that may be impacting their current relationships. What does this look like when you are working with children and adolescents? Help them link their current behavior to their history. In attachment terms, this is sometimes called creating a *coherent autobiographical narrative* (Siegel 2001). Help the children you work with make sense of their story. Be honest and real about what happened to them. They already hold in their minds and bodies the lasting impact of these experiences (van der Kolk 2014), so you are not doing them any favors by trying to sugarcoat what their early life was like. In fact, you may be making matters worse because the more you try to gloss over how things were, the more confused and shamed the child will be about why they think, feel, and behave the way they do.

Your job is to help the child understand that the way he feels and how he behaves make sense. Of course this work needs to be paced in a way that does not overwhelm but rather helps clients understand the story of their life and the impact it had on them. A coherent narrative of one's history is linked to secure attachment in adulthood (Main 1991; Oppenheim 2006). This means knowing your story and the impact it has had on you and how it influences your life now. It's not about what happened to you but rather how you make sense of what happened to you that matters in the end. It is only by knowing your story in a deep and painfully honest way that you can truly be free from having that past drive your behavior.

A few more tips for clinicians starting this work:

1. Recognize that internal working models of children are not easy to change (Hamilton 2000). However, with persistence and appropriate clinical intervention, including with parents, they can change.
2. An awareness that the parents' own history of being parented and their "state of mind with regard to attachment" will directly impact the child's ability to move toward healing and security in the parent-child relationship (Dozier et al. 2001; Steele et al. 2003).Working with parents is key.
3. This work does not require perfect parents. Winnicott's (1964) term "good enough parenting" gives us all a sigh of relief. Parents don't have to do it all right all of the time for kids to be psychologically healthy.
4. The clinician's own history of being parented matters greatly and will impact the treatment process. As we often say at Chaddock, "If you don't work your issues, the kids will work them for you."
5. Once you think you are an expert, you are sunk. Always be ready to change your mind, to be wrong. Remain open and be curious. You will feel confused, overwhelmed, and inadequate working with tough cases day in and day out. Be secure enough to not be afraid of the confusion, because the alternative is convincing ourselves we have it all figured out. Listen to the story before you, whether it is being told by word or behavior, while at the same time never taking it at face value. Trust the process.

6. Above all else, remember that knowing how to be with someone is the most important thing and will always trump employing a technique correctly (Trout 2010).

THE JOURNEY BEGINS

It is with this foundation of attachment theory that we invite you, in the coming chapters, to gain a broader understanding of specific techniques for carrying out this critical work. There is no a magic wand or single technique that works in every situation. All of the techniques included in this book are ones we have found to be helpful in our efforts to change a child's internal working model, allowing them to risk trusting their parents and us. This work takes patience, fortitude, and a willingness to hear a child's story and respond. It is in equal measures incredibly challenging and incredibly rewarding. If you have the passion to never give up on a child, and the determination to follow his or her story, you can change the course of a child's life.

BIBLIOGRAPHY

Ainsworth, M. D. S. 1967. *Infancy in Uganda: Infant Care and the Growth of Love*. Baltimore: Johns Hopkins University Press.

———. 1974. Citation for the G. Stanley Hall Award to John Bowlby. Unpublished manuscript.

Ainsworth, M. D. S., and Silvia M. Bell. 1970. "Attachment, Exploration, and Separation: Illustrated by the Behavior of One-Year-Olds in a Strange Situation." *Child Development* 41 (1): 49–67.

Ainsworth, M. D. S., M. C. Blehar, E. Waters, and S. Wall. 1978. *Patterns of Attachment: A Psychological Study of the Strange Situation*. Hillsdale, NJ: Erlbaum.

Bakermans-Kranenburg, Marian J., and Marinus H. van IJzendoorn. 2009. "The First 10,000 Adult Attachment Interviews: Distributions of Adult Attachment Representations in Clinical and Non-clinical Groups." *Attachment & Human Development* 11 (3): 223–63.

Bowlby, John. 1940. "The Influence of Early Environment in the Development of Neurosis and Neurotic Character." *International Journal of Psycho-Analysis* 21: 154.

———. 1944. "Forty-Four Juvenile Thieves: Their Characters and Home Life." *International Journal of Psychoanalysis* 25: 107–27.

———. 1951. *Maternal Care and Mental Health*. Geneva: World Health Organization.

———. 1953. *Child Care and the Growth of Love*. London: Penguin Books.

———. 1956. Mother-Child Separation. *Mental Health and Infant Development* 1: 117–22.

———. (1969) 1982. *Attachment and Loss: Attachment*. New York: Basic Books.

———. 1979. *The Making and Breaking of Affectional Bonds*. London: Tavistock.

———. 1988. *A Secure Base: Parent-Child Attachment and Healthy Human Development*. New York: Basic Books.

Bretherton, Inge. 1985. "Attachment Theory: Retrospect and Prospect." *Monographs of the Society for Research in Child Development* 50 (1–2): 3–35.

Cowan, Philip A., Deborah A. Cohn, Carolyn Pape Cowan, and Jane L. Pearson. 1996. "Parents' Attachment Histories and Children's Externalizing and Internalizing Behaviors:

Exploring Family Systems Models of Linkage." *Journal of Consulting and Clinical Psychology* 64 (1): 53.

Dozier, Mary, K. Chase Stoval, Kathleen E. Albus, and Brady Bates. 2001. "Attachment for Infants in Foster Care: The Role of Caregiver State of Mind."*Child Development* 72 (5): 1467–77.

Fonagy, Peter, Howard Steele, and Miriam Steele. 1991. "Maternal Representations of Attachment during Pregnancy Predict the Organization of Infant-Mother Attachment at One Year of Age." *Child Development* 62 (5): 891–905.

Fraiberg, Selma, Edna Adelson, and Vivian Shapiro. 1975. "Ghosts in the Nursery: A Psychoanalytic Approach to the Problems of Impaired Infant-Mother Relationships." *Journal of the American Academy of Child Psychiatry* 14 (3): 387–421.

Freud, Sigmund. 1977. *Five Lectures on Psycho-Analysis*. New York: W. W. Norton.

George, Carol, Nancy Kaplan, and Mary Main. 1985. The Adult Attachment Interview. Unpublished manuscript. University of California at Berkeley.

Gunnar, Megan R., Laurie Brodersen, Melissa Nachmias, Kristin Buss, and Joseph Rigatuso. 1996. "Stress Reactivity and Attachment Security." *Developmental Psychobiology* 29 (3): 191–204.

Hamilton, Claire E. 2000. "Continuity and Discontinuity of Attachment from Infancy through Adolescence." *Child Development* 71 (3): 690–94.

Harkness, S., and C. M. Super, eds. 1996. *Parents' Cultural Belief Systems: Their Origins, Expressions, and Consequences*. New York: Guilford Press.

Harlow, Harry F. 1958. "The Nature of Love." *American Psychologist* 13 (12): 673.

Hebb, Donald Olding. 1949. *The Organization of Behavior: A Neuropsychological Theory*. New York: Wiley.

Heffron, Mary Claire, and Trudi Murch. 2010. *Reflective Supervision and Leadership in Infant and Early Childhood Programs*. Washington, DC: Zero to Three.

Hesse, Erik, and Mary Main. 2000. "Disorganized Infant, Child, and Adult Attachment: Collapse in Behavioral and Attentional Strategies." *Journal of the American Psychoanalytic Association* 48 (4): 1097–127.

Hill-Soderlund, Ashley L., W. Roger Mills-Koonce, Cathi Propper, Susan D. Calkins, Douglas A. Granger, Ginger A. Moore, Jean-Louis Gariepy, and Martha J. Cox. 2008. "Parasympathetic and Sympathetic Responses to the Strange Situation in Infants and Mothers from Avoidant and Securely Attached Dyads."*Developmental Psychobiology* 50 (4): 361–76.

Hinde, R. A., and J. Stevenson-Hinde. 1990. "Attachment: Biological, Cultural, and Individual Desiderata." *Human Development* 33: 62–72.

Howard, Amanda R. Hiles. 2016. Email with author, July 27.

Lewis, Thomas, Fari Amini, and Richard Lannon. 2000. *A General Theory of Love*. New York: Vintage.

Lorenz, K. Z. 1935. "Der Kumpan in der Umwelt des Vogels" (The companion in the bird's world). *Journal für Ornithologie* 83: 137–213. (Abbreviated English translation published 1937 in *Auk* 54: 245–73.)

Main, Mary. 1991. "Metacognitive Knowledge, Metacognitive Monitoring, and Singular (Coherent) vs. Multiple (Incoherent) Models of Attachment." In *Attachment across the Life Cycle*, edited by C. M. Parkes, J. Stevenson-Hinde, and Peter Marris, 127–59. New York: Routledge.

Main, Mary, and Erik Hesse. 2009. "Adult Attachment and the Adult Attachment Interview." Lecture at the Life Span Learning Institute and UCLA, Los Angeles, California.

Main, Mary, and Judith Solomon. 1986. "Discovery of an Insecure-Disorganized/Disoriented Attachment Pattern." In *Affective Development in Infancy*, edited by T. B. Brazelton and M. Yogman, 95–124. Norwood, NJ: Ablex.

Nsamemang, A. B. 1992. *Human Development in Cultural Context: A Third World Perspective*. Newbury Park, CA: Sage.

Oppenheim, David. 2006. "Child, Parent, and Parent–Child Emotion Narratives: Implications for Developmental Psychopathology." *Development and Psychopathology* 18 (3): 771–90.

Perry, Bruce D., Ronnie A. Pollard, Toi L. Blakley, William L. Baker, and Domenico Vigilante. 1995. "Childhood Trauma, the Neurobiology of Adaptation, and Use Dependent Development of the Brain: How States Become Traits. "*Infant Mental Health Journal* 16 (4): 271–91.

Robertson, James. 1952. *A Two-Year-Old Goes to Hospital* (Film). London: Tavistock.

———. 1970. *Young Children in Hospital*. London: Routledge & Kegan Paul.

Schore, Allan N. 2000. "Attachment and the Regulation of the Right Brain." *Attachment & Human Development* 2 (1): 23–47.

———. 2001. "Contributions from the Decade of the Brain to Infant Mental Health: An Overview." *Infant Mental Health Journal* 22 (1–2): 1–6.

Siegel, Daniel J. 2001. "Toward an Interpersonal Neurobiology of the Developing Mind: Attachment Relationships, 'Mindsight,' and Neural Integration." *Infant Mental Health Journal* 22 (1–2): 67–94.

Spangler, G., and K. E. Grossmann. 1993. "Biobehavioral Organization in Securely and Insecurely Attached Infants." *Child Development* 64 (5): 1439–50.

Sroufe, L. Alan, and Everett Waters. 1977. "Attachment as an Organizational Construct." *Child Development* 48 (4): 1184–99.

Steele, Miriam, Jill Hodges, Jeanne Kaniuk, Saul Hillman, and Kay Henderson. 2003. "Attachment Representations and Adoption: Associations between Maternal States of Mind and Emotion Narratives in Previously Maltreated Children." *Journal of Child Psychotherapy* 29 (2): 187–205.

Tavecchio, Louis W. C., and Marinus H. van IJzendoorn, eds. 1987. *Attachment in Social Networks: Contributions to the Bowlby-Ainsworth Attachment Theory*. Amsterdam: North Holland.

Trevarthen, Colwyn. 1979. "Communication and Cooperation in Early Infancy: A Description of Primary Intersubjectivity." In *Before Speech: The Beginning of Interpersonal Communication*, edited by Margaret Bullowa, 321–47. Cambridge: Cambridge University Press.

Tronick, Edward. 2007. *The Neurobehavioral and Social-Emotional Development of Infants and Children*. New York: W. W. Norton.

Trout, Michael. 2010. *A Brief Course in Infant Mental Health*. Champaign, IL: Infant Parent Institute.

van der Kolk, Bessel. 2014. *The Body Keeps the Score*. New York: Viking.

van IJzendoorn, Marinus. 1995. "Adult Attachment Representations, Parental Responsiveness, and Infant Attachment: A Meta-Analysis on the Predictive Validity of the Adult Attachment Interview." *Psychological Bulletin* 117 (3): 387.

Winnicott, Donald. 1964. *The Child, the Family, and the Outside World*. London: Penguin.

Wood, Beatrice L., Kendra B. Klebba, and Bruce D. Miller. 2000. "Evolving the Biobehavioral Family Model: The Fit of Attachment." *Family Process* 39 (3): 319–44.

2

Chaddock's Journey to Discover What Works

Developmental Trauma and Attachment Program (DTAP) Treatment Model

Karen Doyle Buckwalter, Michelle Robison, Marcia Ryan, and Angel Knoverek

> Sometimes you put walls up not to keep people out but to see who cares enough to break them down.
>
> —Socrates

After more than twenty years of working with children and adolescents who have endured attachment disruptions and extreme and repeated traumatic experiences, we can say one thing for sure—what works in healing one child often does not work in healing another! Because of this experience, we have taken the approach of "leaving no stone unturned" as we seek to find answers about how to help each child with whom we have worked. We believe that older youth, including adolescents, who have attachment disruptions are not doomed and benefit from attachment-focused treatment. While there are a number of excellent attachment-based models, many of which are highlighted in this book, we have not found one model that can be used exclusively and successfully with every child. Our quest to find what works for different children at different points in treatment has led to us learning and benefiting from many others who work with clinically complex situations. This book is a collection of treatment approaches we have found to be effective with some of the most severe cases in our residential treatment program.

As we continued to add to our therapeutic toolbox, however, we found that we needed a way to frame our thinking regarding what intervention would be most effective with a child at specific points in the treatment. To develop such a framework, we drew on our knowledge of brain science, recognizing we had to be cognizant of always starting with a child's most basic developmental needs. Even though the adolescents with whom we were working might have "big-kid bodies" we needed to consider that developmentally they might have the security or impulse control needs of a toddler. Thus, we began development of the DTAP Treatment Model as a way of organizing our thinking about a child's individualized treatment needs without locking our clinicians into a single intervention.

In this way, we would remain seekers, always looking for new research, interventions, or activities that could meet a child's sensory needs or improve their impulse control. This way of thinking provides a framework to build on, while also allowing the flexibility to identify new ways to meet a specific child's identified needs.

During the journey of evolving Chaddock's treatment approach, we found that there were several unwritten rules that served as essential, nonnegotiable guiding principles for optimizing the impact of our model. These were key concepts that helped our clinicians move from simply being skilled in the mechanics of a model to knowing how to effectively engage and connect with a child. While these concepts may seem obvious to someone who has worked in the field for years, we found that, unless explicitly addressed, they can easily be overlooked.

The guiding principles that underpin the DTAP Treatment Model, each of which we will discuss later in the chapter, include the following:

1. Attachment theory and trauma-informed approaches must be interconnected in treatment.
2. Parent involvement in the treatment process is paramount when working with children, and the parent's own history of attachment and/or trauma-related experiences must be understood and considered.
3. The therapist's way of "being" is just as important, if not more so, as their method of "doing."
4. Therapists must be open to learning from their client not only early on but all throughout treatment.
5. Interventions should be targeted to the different levels of functioning of the child's brain.
6. Numerous effective interventions that prioritize safety and engagement must be "in the toolbox."
7. Treatment interventions must be used with accuracy and consistency.
8. Ongoing training, supervision, and personal reflection are required.
9. The therapist needs to know when a particular intervention will be most helpful during the various phases of the treatment process.

This is a book about attachment-based interventions, so all the models in this book have been influenced by attachment theory and research. However, because many of the children and adolescents we work with have also had traumatic experiences, we need to also have a working knowledge of trauma-informed practice. Thus, *attachment theory and trauma-informed approaches must be interconnected in treatment.* An entire book could be written on each of these topics, and many have been! Our goal here is to cover some of the basics of each and how they intersect.

To recap a critical concept from chapter 1, attachment has been defined as an "inborn system in the brain that evolves in ways that influence and organize motivational, emotional and memory processes with significant caregiving figures" (Siegel

1999, 67). Through this relationship, children form what Bowlby (1969) called an "internal working model" of themselves, their caregivers, and the world that will impact all future relationships. Internal working models are not psychiatric diagnoses but rather ways a child has learned to manage a relationship with a specific caregiver. However, these models do impact a child's behavior.

In looking at both attachment and trauma together, it is helpful to keep in mind the following three points: (1) Attachment theory is a theory of human development, whereas (2) trauma is an experience that can impact development, and (3) a secure attachment relationship is a buffer for stressful or traumatic experiences (Gunnar et al. 1996). Ogden and Fisher (2015) tease out some differences in attachment-related core beliefs and trauma-related core beliefs by giving examples of each. Some attachment beliefs they describe are "I'll always be alone" or "My needs are not important" versus trauma beliefs: "I'll die if I am left alone" or "I am completely helpless." They explain emotions that accompany beliefs with trauma as "animal defenses" such as panic, rage, and terror (Ogden and Fisher 2015). In our work we speak of these as "back brain" emotional reactions, meaning they come from the more primitive reactionary part of the brain. These arise out of instinctive survival mechanisms in the brain. These are different from emotions related to attachment relationships such as sadness, loneliness, and anger.

Another point of intersection between the attachment theory and trauma theory is relational trauma. This is when interactions with others are frightening enough to evoke primitive fears. The disorganized attachment classification in the Strange Situation (described in chapter 1) is an example of this. Here a child is experiencing the caregiver as a source of fear. In this case, the person who is to protect you is also a source of fear, as with an abusive parent. This "fright without solution" (Hesse and Main 2000) is a no-win situation for a baby, and this is why the baby cannot develop an organized way of coping. Trauma can also impact attachment security even when a caregiver is not the source of the trauma by virtue of the fact that the child may no longer believe the attachment figure is a source of protection.

All of this complexity is why children with attachment disruptions layered with other traumatic experiences are often given many different diagnoses, including attention deficit/hyperactivity disorder, oppositional defiant disorder, conduct disorder, mood disorders, and bipolar disorder, to name a few. Do the children we work with meet the criteria of behaviors and symptoms listed for each of these diagnoses? Yes, they do. However, our approach has been to recognize and seek to treat the root of the child's problem behavior rather than the behavior or symptom itself. The children we work with have the "double whammy"—lack of secure attachment (therefore lacking a buffer against trauma) and repeated traumatic experiences. This is why our treatment approach addresses both attachment and trauma issues.

It seems obvious when working from an attachment-based perspective that work with parents would be essential. In addition, we know that the parents' reactions to a child's trauma can influence the child's own reactions. Hence, *parent involvement in the treatment process is paramount when working with children.* Someone who is working with children from birth to three years old would seldom, if ever, consider working with the child alone, but parents are often excluded from therapy with older children. In our work, we have latched on to the idea from family systems theory that the client is the "relationship" (Lieberman and Pawl 1993; Pawl and Lieberman 1997) between the parent and the child rather than the client being the individual child or parent.

Unfortunately, many therapists who work with children lack experience—and often lack interest—in working with adults, and this may contribute to reticence in involving parents in treatment. Many therapists are not trained to see the client as the relationship and so may not know how to intervene in a relationship. Sometimes the therapist might see the parents as the problem or as impeding the child's progress, so they leave them out. Some research indicates that even when parents are in therapy sessions with their child, the therapist actively engages them in parent-focused skill-building strategies less than 25 percent of the time (Garland et al. 2010). Whatever the reason, our contention is that if you cannot work with adults (parents), you cannot be an effective child therapist, particularly if the child's primary issues are related to relational trauma and disrupted attachments. Another issue is that some therapists may think their work with the child or adolescent should be kept confidential and not shared with the parent. Parents, and the safety and comfort they provide, are the primary healing agents for children. Even with adolescents who have attachment insecurity and traumatic histories, the therapist's role is to orchestrate a deeper connection between parent and child. This is impossible to do if there is a disconnection between parents and their child in the treatment process and if there are secrets between the child and therapist. While therapy may occur with the child without the parents present, as we have to do in residential treatment, there are still numerous ways to connect the child with his or her parents through family therapy sessions, daily conversations, and so forth, while also maintaining our ethical obligation of confidentiality.

We recognize that the health of the parent can have a great impact on the child's progress in therapy (Hughes and Baylin 2012), so our care of and respect for parents cannot be emphasized enough. There may be certain circumstances where a parent is not emotionally available to the child or is unsafe for some reason, and this needs to be evaluated. However, in general it should be the exception to not involve parents in their child's treatment. Even in such cases, the therapist may be able to work with the parent on these issues or refer the parent for individual therapy for a designated time in the child's treatment rather than abandon altogether the idea of having the parent involved in the child's therapy.

While specific techniques and interventions can be helpful, we believe that *the therapist's way of "being" is just as important, if not more so, as their method of doing.* Most of us learned Carl Rogers's (1961) three facilitative growth factors of genuineness, acceptance (unconditional positive regard), and empathy, which can be foundational in developing therapeutic rapport with clients. In Dyadic Developmental Psychotherapy, Hughes (2007) shares the "attitude" of PACE—playful, accepting, curious, and empathic. We have found this "attitude" improves our presence with the youth. In addition, Koloroutis and Trout (2012) talk about "wondering," "following," and "holding" when in therapy sessions with children and their parents. Approaches such as these convey your interest in what is being shared and help the client sense you are completely present in the therapy session. When you can just "be" with a client, instead of always focusing on fixing a problem, the child can sense the difference and it may open the door for new levels of engagement.

Building on this focus on their way of being with a child or parent, *therapists must be open to learning from their client.* We believe the most effective therapists strike a balance between feeling competent in their expertise to help the children and families while simultaneously being willing to follow unexpected developments that may unfold during treatment. Michael Trout's notion of "wondering" encourages clinicians to be open to the possibility that their assumptions, hunches, and beliefs about the individuals they are working with may be inaccurate, and to trust the client to clarify and help them better understand their experiences, thoughts, or feelings. We should never start to believe we have all the answers or know what will work for every child. We need to be "brilliantly stupid," open to new information unfolding before us and remain curious (Koloroutis and Trout 2012).

When we are open to the client's experiences, we can be better attuned to where the client is at any given moment in treatment. This is important because therapeutic *interventions should be targeted to the different levels of functioning of the child's brain.* Perry (2009) discusses how the brain develops sequentially and is use-dependent. Sequential development means the brain develops from the brainstem, to the midbrain region and limbic system, and finally to the cortical region. This brain development is aided by the attachment process and sensory-rich experiences. Conversely, when a child is exposed to a traumatic event, then the brain development can be stunted, delayed, or altered. This is why when a child is stressed or feeling less secure, he can go into "back brain," causing behaviors to regress. As for brain development being use-dependent, this follows the old adage "use it or lose it." We have seen the images of a "normal" three-year-old child's brain versus the image of a three-year-old child who has experienced extreme neglect. The neglected child's brain is so much smaller, and there are not as many areas activated in the brain. This is why we strongly believe that the interventions used with children who have attachment disruptions and other traumatic experiences have to be targeted to the different parts of the brain.

When we open ourselves up to understanding the client's experiences, we have an increased awareness of their expressed needs. We quickly recognized in our efforts to help children that "one size does not fit all" when it comes to successfully treating children with attachment disruptions. For this reason, we found that *numerous effective interventions that prioritize safety and engagement must be available in our "toolbox"* when providing treatment in complex cases. We obviously want to use interventions that are going to be effective with children, although we admit that the term "effective" has different meanings for different therapists.

To researchers, using the term "effective" has implied that rigorous research studies have been conducted in a controlled study. While using the more rigorously studied intervention may be ideal, we also recognize that many interventions do not have the resources required for this high level of research. Although we use a variety of evidence-based approaches at Chaddock, the body of research on a model is not our only litmus test for use. The broader category of evidence-based practice has included scientific evidence as well as clinical expertise and client preference (Trull and Prinstein 2012). Certainly having had clinicians, parents, and children claim that the therapy worked, meaning that the intervention helped them address the issues, has offered a measure of effectiveness. Also, effectiveness can be noted in treatment by comparing the data collected from assessments at the beginning and end of treatment. We have shared this to let you know that when we are seeking interventions to add to our "toolbox" to help clients, we are an equal-opportunity explorer in that we have a broad definition of effective since our experience has been that no one thing will work for all of our clients.

If an approach does not have a strong evidence base, we ask ourselves: Are the principles of the model consistent with attachment theory and trauma-informed care? Does the model incorporate current findings in brain research related to attachment and trauma? Does the model involve the caregiver? We want "yes" answers to these questions. We also ask ourselves: Is there any potential that this therapy could re-traumatize a child? Is the model harsh, punitive, coercive, or compliance-based in any way? Since we prioritize safety and child and family engagement in treatment, then obviously we want these answers to be "no."

Another factor that impacts effectiveness is that *treatment interventions must be used with accuracy and consistency.* We refer to this as using the intervention with fidelity. Do you remember that there was a period of time when describing your therapy style as "eclectic" was considered a good thing? Well, today when we hear this it often means that the therapist is either unable to clearly articulate their preferred theoretical orientation or relying on their own knowledge and skills to essentially do whatever they think will work best for a client. We want clinicians trained in various treatment interventions who then intentionally implement the intervention with fidelity. We also seek supervision and external consultation from an expert or master trainer in that particular intervention. In addition, we encourage clinicians to achieve certification in numerous models, which can be a lengthy, arduous process that is rewarding both to the clinician for professional growth and to our children and families who benefit from the clinician's increased competence.

Providing specialized care, especially to a vulnerable and volatile population, often requires advanced knowledge and skills for therapists, so *ongoing training, supervision, and personal reflection are required.* Many therapists seek additional information to help in their work with clients, just like you are doing by reading this book! It can be helpful to read articles and books by others in the field who share their experiences, including successes as well as those experiences where we learned we would do something differently in the future.

In addition to reading everything we can get our hands on, we know that attending training can further advance our knowledge and clinical skills. Training can be eye-opening to new thoughts or methods for working with our clients. There have been occasions when we found that even though we attended exceptional training, it was difficult to come back and implement the information into our daily work. There were many reasons—we were too busy getting through our days at work, we slipped back into doing what was more comfortable, or when we tried (or thought we tried) the new skill, it didn't work the first time, so efforts to try again dwindled. This is why, no matter how many years we have been working as therapists, we have found that supervision by experienced clinicians is extremely important.

Supervision looks different depending on whether you are in a larger agency or in private practice, yet the essential feature is that you are connecting with a qualified licensed clinician to gain additional insights about your work. Clinical supervision helps therapists conceptualize the case through the trauma and attachment lens and helps the clinician gain a deeper understanding of trauma and attachment and its impact on the child and family. It also provides opportunities for the clinician to strengthen skills in assessing clients as well as providing individual and family therapy.

Reflective supervision (Parlakian 2001; Gilkerson 2004; Heffron and Murch 2010) is also essential and, unfortunately, may be a luxury not many clinicians experience. However, we have found that having a safe place to explore parallel processes and issues of countertransference is an important component in offering support and decreasing burnout, which many professionals working with this vulnerable population experience. It also encourages reflection to address those issues outlined above when implementing a new skill or intervention. A reflective supervisor might ask, "What are the aspects of what is going on with this case that challenge you, or even scare or worry you?"

Another way we help our therapists increase their skills is by video recording therapy sessions and reviewing the recording in individual as well as group supervision. This allows clinicians to get both clinical and reflective supervision on their sessions in a more effective manner. We believe video review of clinical work is far superior to simply talking about cases because it allows all that occurred in the session to be seen, not just what the clinician is conscious of to share with a supervisor. In addition to the impact of using videos in clinical supervision, in chapter 10 we will share how impactful Video Intervention Therapy can be when working with children struggling with attachment disruptions.

Through ongoing training, supervision, and consultation, we want therapists to develop strong clinical decision-making skills, as *the therapist needs to know when a particular intervention will be most helpful during the various phases of the treatment process.* With the foundational knowledge that attachment impacts brain development, we understand that when there are attachment disruptions compounded by repeated traumatic events, the individual may be accessing, or "stuck in," different parts of the brain. It is essential for therapists to keep this in mind when choosing which therapeutic interventions to use at a particular point in treatment. An integration of treatment models based on the needs of individualized cases is quite common. Each of the authors in this book was selected to write about a specific area of treatment he or she developed or has expertise in. Many of these authors also use a variety of other treatment approaches or have incorporated a range of treatment approaches into their own model. For example, you will see Eye Movement Desensitization Reprocessing (EMDR) is used in both the Family Attachment Narrative chapter and the EMDR Integrative Model chapter.

Building on these guiding principles as a foundation, we are now ready to look specifically at how a clinician might select certain interventions using the DTAP Treatment Model as a framework for decision making.

THE DEVELOPMENTAL TRAUMA AND ATTACHMENT PROGRAM (DTAP) TREATMENT MODEL

As Chaddock began to incorporate and integrate a variety of treatment approaches into our work with children and adolescents and their families, there was a need to have a way to organize our thinking about the various models and where each fit into the overall treatment plan for each child. The DTAP Treatment Model graphic (figure 2.1) is an effort to do this in a visual way. The three levels of the pyramid

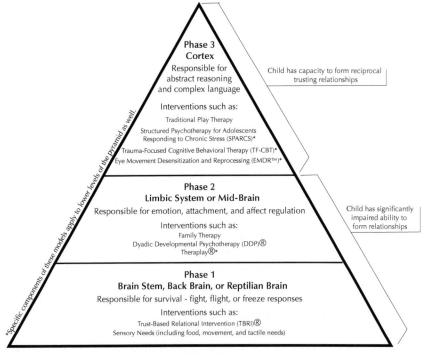

Figure 2.1. Developmental Trauma and Attachment Program (DTAP) Treatment Model®

represent the three levels of the triune brain (MacLean 1990)—the brain stem and back brain, the midbrain and limbic system, and the cortex of the brain.

We are aware that this is a simplistic model of how the brain works. It is meant to be a tool to help organize one's thinking, not a diagram for a neuroscience article. Chapter 3 will go into much greater detail about the brain and how it responds to the treatment models discussed in this book. This treatment model references clinical interventions that we have used most frequently. Some of them do not neatly fit into one of the three different brain levels. Indeed, some models may be used at all three levels. In such cases, we list the intervention in the level it is most frequently used. Because of the multiple interventions often used in our most challenging cases, we have found the pyramid pictorial to be an invaluable tool in our treatment planning process and a way to conceptualize thinking about complex cases.

Not every treatment intervention used at Chaddock is written on the pyramid of our treatment model. The model is intentionally designed to encourage us to remain open to new interventions. However, each intervention that is delivered is used in the context of the pyramid. Thus, we believe the most useful aspect of the model is that it can be used generically as a conceptual framework by anyone who is working with this population. Individual therapists and agencies can choose to adopt whatever therapy approaches make the most sense to them provided they address all three levels of the brain in some manner.

The DTAP Treatment Model also reflects recent developments in the field of trauma related to phase-based treatment (Courtois and Ford 2009; Cook et al. 2005; Brand et al. 2012) and "child readiness" (Bernet et al. 1998) for treatment. In phase-based treatment of trauma there are three overarching levels described: stabilization and safety, trauma processing, and reconnection. When children have experienced multiple traumatic events beginning at a very young age within the caretaking system, which is referred to as complex trauma (Cook et al. 2003), a great deal of time needs to be spent on stabilization and safety. Many of the children we work with have experienced complex trauma, so this type of stabilization and safety is one of the goals of the first two phases of the treatment pyramid.

A child-readiness approach (Bernet et al. 1998) reminds us that we need to wait for children to be ready to talk about traumatic experiences. Some children will find the major part of their healing occurs at the lower two phases of the pyramid. The main message here is that we have not had success starting at the top of the pyramid when beginning treatment. We start at the bottom and work up (Perry 2006). Another way of thinking about this is that we must match treatment to a child's developmental level rather than their chronological age. At times this may require giving the same amount of attention, structure, and nurturing we would with a two-year-old to a fifteen-year-old. It is not a linear process, in that when children become anxious or stressed enough to lead to dysregulation, we need to drop back down to the bottom of the pyramid for a time. However, this is required less and less as treatment continues and children's ability to self-regulate improves.

Phases 1 and 2 are where we form a therapeutic alliance with children through right-brain-oriented therapies (Schore 2003) that involve not only talking but also nonverbal experiences, including movement and appropriate levels of touch, as in Theraplay (Booth and Jernberg 2009). Attachment does not develop by words (although quality of voice such as cadence, tone, and prosody matter), so it follows that we cannot use words alone to develop a relationship and establish safety. Many of the kids we work with have had many hours of "talk therapy," so if that were the solution for them, they would not have ended up in our residential treatment center.

In fact, because the brain stores traumatic experiences in implicit memory (Siegel 1999), or what is sometimes referred to as body memory (van der Kolk 2014), language-based therapy may not be helpful regardless of when the trauma occurred. Implicit memory is about sights, sounds, smells, and touch. This is why sensory experiences that are similar to the ones experienced during the traumatic event can trigger an intense fear that seems to not fit the current situation, such as a child having overwhelming fear about a teacher who has a beard because the child had been abused by someone with a beard. Implicit memory is very different from explicit or conscious memory that a person can talk about. The challenging part of this is that, for example, children like the one mentioned above may act out behaviorally, and when asked why they are doing what they are doing, they may become even more defiant or say, "I don't know." The truth is, they really don't know and can't explain their behavior. They are being driven by a fear they can't even name.

It is important to note that in many cases each of the models mentioned on the Treatment Model's pyramid have utility when used alone. This pyramid framework was developed for the kids for whom that was *not* the case, and as a result they were placed into residential treatment. However, through the process of developing the DTAP Treatment Model, we discovered that this way of thinking was helpful to some degree with all the children with whom we have worked. Children with less severe difficulties were simply able to move to Phase 3 more quickly.

DTAP MODEL BASICS

DTAP Treatment Model: Phase 1

The bottom of the three-part pyramid represents the most primitive part of the brain, the brain stem and back brain, also sometimes called the reptilian part of the brain. This is where automatic reactions to danger such as fight, flight, or freeze responses originate. An example of this part of the brain would be that if someone is standing in the middle of a road and a big truck is speeding toward them, they will quickly jump out of the way. They don't think about how they are feeling about the truck or evaluate what would be the best course of action; they just automatically jump out of the way.

The lower part of the brain, also called the brain stem, regulates body states such as heart rate and body temperature, but it also stores anxiety and arousal states from traumatic experiences. Treatment needs to start at the bottom of the brain and go upward (Perry 2009). As noted previously, current research on both attachment and trauma has a great deal to say about implicit and explicit memory (Siegel 1999) and the idea that our physical body can "hold" experiences with caretakers and experiences of trauma that we cannot name with words (van der Kolk 2014). Trauma is not about thinking. It is stored in a much deeper level in the brain. We cannot talk ourselves out of how we feel. In a sense all trauma is nonverbal because the language system in the brain shuts down during a traumatic experience. This is why many times when a trauma victim describes what happened to them, rather than a clear narrative it may sound more like a list of sensory experiences such as the way the perpetrator smelled or a mark they saw on their skin or a sound they heard in the environment. If the somatic memories that remain from trauma will not go away by talking about them (Wylie 2004), the question becomes how to work through these kinds of experiences that are "trapped" in the body.

In recent years there has been a great deal of support for the idea that body therapies that calm physiology can help traumatized individuals. Yoga (van der Kolk et al. 2014) and massage are examples of body work that helps our bodies feel safe and calm in a way that words never will. The groundbreaking work being done with Sensorimotor Therapy (Ogden, Minton, and Pain 2006), which is discussed in chapter 5, expounds upon how the body has been left out of the "talking cure." The use of Healing Touch (Wilkinson et al. 2002) has been helpful to many children who come to Chaddock in the early stages of treatment. These are all approaches that would fit into Phase 1 of treatment.

Another issue to be considered in Phase 1 is something called Sensory Processing Disorder, or SPD (Kranowitz 2005). Our first sensory experiences shape our neural networks (Perry 2002). *Sensory processing* is a term that refers to the way in which people sense, or take in and receive, information and input from the outside world. It is the process by which the senses carry signals to the nervous system. Any activity that a person completes, including walking across the room, chewing a piece of gum, feeling lotion on their hands, or smelling soap, all involve sensory processing (Ayers and Robbins 2005). SPD is when these signals to the brain and nervous system are not organized optimally. The model of Trust-Based Relational Invention has been critical in our understanding of the impact of SPD on children we work with (Purvis et al. 2013).

Many children with a background of neglect and deprivation, such as what may have been experienced by children who were in the foster care system or orphanage care, have sensory processing issues (Purvis, Cross, and Pennings 2009). These children have not had appropriate amounts of healthy attuned sensory stimulation. When babies are held, rocked, sung to, and met with a loving gaze, brain circuitry grows and develops. Conversely, if a child does not experience this from a loving and consistent caregiver, brain circuitry becomes impaired (Purvis, Cross, and Sunshine 2007). SPD is treated by occupational therapists; however, we have found that having a basic awareness of sensory issues in our environment (in addition to a more specific plan to address individual children) can have a positive impact and enhance treatment outcomes.

In case this has not been said enough, in this first phase of treatment, remember the basic tenet of therapy: First develop a relationship and rapport with your client. Don't assume the client will be able to form a relationship with you through talking. If the client doesn't have basic feelings of safety, then you need to communicate safety in ways other than just through language.

DTAP Treatment Model: Phase 2

The next part of the Treatment Model's pyramid represents the limbic system. This is a complicated system involving many parts of the brain, but in the DTAP Treatment Model's pyramid we focus on emotional regulation and certain aspects of memory. One of the primary goals at this stage of treatment is to have attachment relationships move toward security. A model we use heavily in this stage of treatment is Theraplay. Theraplay is a model that still involves the body and a great deal of physical movement, building on Phase 1 of the pyramid, but the Theraplay model also works extensively with regulation of the body, impulse control, and feeling states. For example, in Theraplay we might do a hand stack activity with the child and parent. Here we are using movement and touch, and then we also might add a signal given from the therapist to the child to move her hand from the bottom to the top of the hand stack. This simple addition of a signal helps the child's body and brain learn to hold the impulse to move and wait for the signal. We may also go through multiple cycles of stacking hands slow, then faster, then really fast, then slower and slower, bringing the child's excitement back down to a state of calm. Now the child is getting an experience of what it feels like to be really excited but then be able to calm down. Many of the kids we work with could use some help with that! Through repeated activities similar to this, we begin to expand the child's window of tolerance (Perry and Szalavitz 2007).

In Theraplay we also use a lot of descriptive language, much like a mother does with her baby who is learning about his feeling states, not only describing with words what is happening but also using facial expressions and voice tone, volume, and cadence to interpret and join in what the child is experiencing. This is an experience referred to as attunement (Stern et al. 1985). Going back to the hand stack, during the very fast part we might be saying, "Oh this is very exciting for you! I see a big smile and you are really ready for your turn!" Next we might say in a slower and lower tone, "Now it's time to slow down." For many of the children we work with, that might be hard to do, and we can then comment on that: "Oh, it is hard to slow down after so much excitement! We will keep trying." We can then give the child whatever is needed from us to slow down. This may be our verbal commentary on what is happening, and we may even add holding on to the child's hand and allowing our movement to regulate the child's movement by slowly moving his hand to the next position in the hand stack. The first step in learning to name emotion is being aware of what emotions feel like in your body. Often therapists who don't understand the need to work differently in different phases of treatment skip this step and go right to helping children learn feeling words and how to use them. This will not be successful because children must have the experience identified and reflected back to them first. When you have no awareness of your emotional states and how they actually feel in your body, it's pretty hard to choose a feeling word for them!

Another model that has worked well for the children we work with at this stage of treatment is Hughes's (2007) Dyadic Developmental Psychotherapy (DDP). With the increased capacity to regulate both body and emotions as a result of the work we have done in Phase 1 of the pyramid, using DDP can be more fruitful. DDP is a powerful model for helping children put additional words to their inner experience and develop a coherent narrative of their story in a safe and empathic way. This trauma processing begins in Phase 2 of the pyramid with DDP techniques, but it continues in the upper level of the pyramid where a trauma narrative may be developed using Trauma-Focused Cognitive Behavioral Therapy (TF-CBT). Certain aspects of EMDR have also been helpful at Phase 2 of treatment, particularly resource development and installation (Korn and Leeds 2002); development of an internal safe place (Shapiro 2001); and, as described in chapter 12, attachment resource development (Wesselmann, Schweitzer, and Armstrong 2014).

DTAP Treatment Model: Phase 3

The top part of the pyramid represents the cortex and higher cognitive functioning, including abstract thinking. A good way to remember this part of the brain is when a teacher says to the class, "Put on your thinking caps!" In other words, get your cortex ready! It's time for some learning!

Effective therapeutic work is possible only when children feel safe in both the environment they are in (Knoverek et al. 2013) and the therapeutic relationship (Gellar and Porges 2014). Thus, in the top level, building on the foundation of the first two phases of the pyramid, a clinician can choose from a number of models to continue treatment. With basic safety established, attachment relationships moving toward security, and a strong therapeutic alliance, many approaches will be effective. After all, as noted earlier, there is much research to suggest that it is the therapeutic relationship rather than a specific technique that is the agent of change (Duncan and Moynihan 1994; Lambert et al. 1993; Orlinsky, Grawe, and Parks 1994).

Techniques such as Traditional Play Therapy and Family Therapy Approaches, Trauma-Focused Cognitive Behavior Therapy (Cohen, Mannarino, and Deblinger 2006), and Structured Psychotherapy for Adolescents Responding to Chronic Stress (De Rosa et al. 2006) have been more effective in our work when used further along in treatment, following the use of other models in the lower parts of the pyramid. There is much that can be said about this top level of our treatment; however, this book is about attachment-based therapy, which is more specifically emphasized in the bottom two levels of our treatment model.

We believe the power of this framework is in its simplicity and adaptability. It provides fundamental questions for a therapist to consider when selecting the best intervention for a specific point in treatment. It offers a way of thinking that does not become outdated or obsolete as we learn more about the nuances of brain functioning and/or develop new interventions based on that knowledge. It is flexible enough to accommodate each of the interventions highlighted in this book, as well as many others. At the same time, it provides enough structure to make sure a therapist does not overlook a critical step on a child's road to healing. It is our hope that you will see it, as we do, as a road map for your journey.

BIBLIOGRAPHY

Ayres, A. Jean, and Jeff Robbins. 2005. *Sensory Integration and the Child: Understanding Hidden Sensory Challenges*. Los Angeles: Western Psychological Services.

Bernet, William, John E. Dunne, Maureen Adair, Valerie Arnold, R. Scott Benson, Oscar Bukstein, Joan Kinlan, Jon M. McClellan, David Rue, and L. Elizabeth Sloan. 1998. "Summary of The Practice Parameters for the Assessment and Treatment of Children and Adolescents with Posttraumatic Stress Disorder." *Journal of the American Academy of Child and Adolescent Psychiatry* 37 (9): 997–1001.

Booth, Phyllis B., and Ann M. Jernberg. 2009. *Theraplay: Helping Parents and Children Build Better Relationships through Attachment-Based Play*. San Francisco: Jossey-Bass.

Bowlby, John. 1969. *Attachment: Vol. 1 of Attachment and Loss*. New York: Basic Books.

Brand, Bethany L., Amie C. Myrick, Richard J. Loewenstein, Catherine C. Classen, Ruth Lanius, Scot W. McNary, Clare Pain, and Frank W. Putnam. 2012. "A Survey of Practices and Recommended Treatment Interventions among Expert Therapists Treating Patients with Dissociative Identity Disorder and Dissociative Disorder Not Otherwise Specified." *Psychological Trauma: Theory, Research, Practice, and Policy* 4 (5): 490.

Cohen, Judith A., Anthony P. Mannarino, and Esther Deblinger. 2006. *Treating Trauma and Traumatic Grief in Children and Adolescents*. New York: Guilford Press.

Cook, A., M. Blaustein, J. Spinazzola, and B. van der Kolk. 2003. "Complex Trauma in Children and Adolescents: White Paper from the National Child Traumatic Stress Network Complex Trauma Task Force." Los Angeles: National Center for Child Traumatic Stress.

Cook, Alexandra, Joseph Spinazzola, Julian Ford, Cheryl Lanktree, Margaret Blaustein, Marylene Cloitre, and B. van der Kolk. 2005. "Complex Trauma." *Psychiatric Annals* 35 (5): 390–98.

Courtois, Christine A., and Julian D. Ford, eds. 2009. *Treating Complex Traumatic Stress Disorders: An Evidence-Based Guide*. New York: Guilford Press.

DeRosa, Ruth, Mandy Habib, David Pelcovitz, Jill Rathus, Jill Sonnenklar, Julian Ford, Suzanne Sunday, et al. 2006. *Structured Psychotherapy for Adolescents Responding to Chronic Stress*. Unpublished manual.

Duncan, Barry L., and Dorothy W. Moynihan. 1994. "Applying Outcome Research: Intentional Utilization of the Client's Frame of Reference." *Psychotherapy: Theory, Research, Practice, Training* 31 (2): 294.

Garland A. F., M. S. Hurlburt, L. Brookman-Frazee, R. M. Taylor, and E. C. Accurso. 2010. "Methodological Challenges of Characterizing Usual Care Psychotherapeutic Practice." *Administration and Policy in Mental Health and Mental Health Services Research* 37 (3): 208–20.

Geller, Shari M., and Stephen W. Porges. 2014. "Therapeutic Presence: Neurophysiological Mechanisms Mediating Feeling Safe in Therapeutic Relationships." *Journal of Psychotherapy Integration* 24 (3): 178.

Gilkerson, L. 2004. "Reflective Supervision in Infant–Family Programs: Adding Clinical Process to Nonclinical Settings" (Irving B. Harris distinguished lecture). *Infant Mental Health Journal* 25 (5): 424–39.

Gunnar, Megan R., Laurie Brodersen, Melissa Nachmias, Kristin Buss, and Joseph Rigatuso. 1996. "Stress Reactivity and Attachment Security." *Developmental Psychobiology* 29 (3): 191–204.

Heffron, M. C., and T. Murch. 2010. *Reflective Supervision and Leadership in Infant and Early Childhood Programs.* Washington, DC: Zero to Three.

Hesse, Erik, and Mary Main. 2000. "Disorganized Infant, Child, and Adult Attachment: Collapse in Behavioral and Attentional Strategies." *Journal of the American Psychoanalytic Association* 48 (4): 1097–127.

Hughes, Daniel A. *Attachment-Focused Family Therapy.* 2007. New York: W. W. Norton.

Hughes, Daniel A., and Jonathan Baylin. 2012. *Brain-Based Parenting: The Neuroscience of Caregiving for Healthy Attachment* (Norton Series on Interpersonal Neurobiology). New York: W. W. Norton.

Knoverek, Angel M., Ernestine C. Briggs, Lee A. Underwood, and Robert L. Hartman. 2013. "Clinical Considerations for the Treatment of Latency Age Children in Residential Care." *Journal of Family Violence* 28 (7): 653–63.

Koloroutis, Mary, and Michael Trout. 2012. *See Me as a Person.* Minneapolis, MN: Creative Health Care Management.

Korn, Deborah L., and Andrew M. Leeds. 2002. "Preliminary Evidence of Efficacy for EMDR Resource Development and Installation in the Stabilization Phase of Treatment of Complex Posttraumatic Stress Disorder." *Journal of Clinical Psychology* 58 (12): 1465–87.

Kranowitz, Carol Stock. 2005. *The Out-of-Sync Child: Recognizing and Coping with Sensory Processing Disorder.* New York: Berkley.

Lambert, Michael J., A. E. Bergin, and S. L. Garfield. 1993. *Handbook of Psychotherapy and Behavior Change.* Hoboken, NJ: John Wiley & Sons.

Lieberman, A. F., and J. H. Pawl. 1993. "Infant-Parent Psychotherapy." In *Handbook of Infant Mental Health,* edited by Charles H. Zeanah, 427–42. New York: Guilford Press.

MacLean, Paul D. 1990. *The Triune Brain in Evolution: Role in Paleocerebral Functions.* New York: Springer Science & Business Media.

Ogden, Pat, and Janina Fisher. 2015. *Sensorimotor Psychotherapy: Interventions for Trauma and Attachment* (Norton Series on Interpersonal Neurobiology). New York: W. W. Norton.

Ogden, Pat, Kekuni Minton, and Clare Pain. 2006. *Trauma and the Body: A Sensorimotor Approach to Psychotherapy* (Norton Series on Interpersonal Neurobiology). New York: W. W. Norton.

Orlinsky, David E., Klaus Grawe, and Barbara K. Parks. 1994. "Process and Outcome in Psychotherapy: Noch Einmal." In *Handbook of Psychotherapy and Behavior Change,* edited by A. Bergin and J. S. Garfield, 270–378. Fourth edition. New York: Wiley.

Parlakian, R. 2001. *Look, Listen, and Learn: Reflective Supervision and Relationship-Based Work.* Washington, DC: Zero to Three.

Pawl, J. H., and A. F. Lieberman. 1997. "Infant-Parent Psychotherapy." In *Handbook of Child and Adolescent Psychiatry, Volume 1: Infants and Preschoolers: Development and Syndromes,* edited by Stanley Greenspan, Serena Wieder, and Joy Osofsky, 339–51. New York: Wiley.

Perry, Bruce D. 2002. "Childhood Experience and the Expression of Genetic Potential: What Childhood Neglect Tells Us about Nature and Nurture." *Brain and Mind* 3 (1): 79–100.

———. 2006. "Applying Principles of Neurodevelopment to Clinical Work with Maltreated and Traumatized Children: The Neurosequential Model of Therapeutics." In *Working with Traumatized Youth in Child Welfare*, edited by Nancy Boyd Webb, 27–52. New York: Guilford Press.

———. 2009. "Examining Child Maltreatment through a Neurodevelopmental Lens: Clinical Applications of the Neurosequential Model of Therapeutics." *Journal of Loss and Trauma* 14 (4): 240–55.

Perry, Bruce Duncan, and Maia Szalavitz. 2007. *The Boy Who Was Raised as a Dog: And Other Stories from a Child Psychiatrist's Notebook—What Traumatized Children Can Teach Us about Loss, Love and Healing*. New York: Basic Books.

Purvis, Karyn B., David R. Cross, Donald F. Dansereau, and Sheri R. Parris. 2013. "Trust-Based Relational Intervention (TBRI): A Systemic Approach to Complex Developmental Trauma." *Child & Youth Services* 34 (4): 360–86.

Purvis, Karyn B., David R. Cross, and Jacquelyn S. Pennings. 2009. "Trust-Based Relational Intervention™: Interactive Principles for Adopted Children with Special Social-Emotional Needs." *Journal of Humanistic Counseling* 48 (1): 3.

Purvis, Karyn Brand, David R. Cross, and Wendy Lyons Sunshine. 2007. *The Connected Child: Bring Hope and Healing to Your Adoptive Family*. New York: McGraw-Hill.

Rogers, Carl. 1961. *On Becoming a Person*. New York: Houghton Mifflin Company.

Schore, Allan N. 2003. *Affect Regulation and the Repair of the Self*. New York: W. W. Norton.

Shapiro, F. 2001. *Eye Movement Desensitization and Reprocessing: Basic Principles, Protocols, and Procedures*. Second edition. New York: Guilford Press.

Siegel, Daniel J. 1999. *The Developing Mind*. New York: Guilford Press.

Stern, Daniel N., Lynne Hofer, Wendy Haft, and John Dore. 1985. "Affect Attunement: The Sharing of Feeling States between Mother and Infant by Means of Inter-Modal Fluency." In *Social Perception in Infants*, edited by Tiffany Field and Nathan A. Fox, 249–68. New York: Ablex.

Trull, Timothy J., and Mitch Prinstein. 2012. *Clinical Psychology*. Belmont, CA: Cengage Learning.

van der Kolk, Bessel. 2014. *The Body Keeps the Score*. New York: Viking.

van der Kolk, Bessel A., Robert S. Pynoos, Dante Cicchetti, Marylene Cloitre, Wendy D'Andrea, Julian D. Ford, Alicia F. Lieberman, et al. 2009. "Proposal to Include a Developmental Trauma Disorder Diagnosis for Children and Adolescents in DSM-V." Unpublished manuscript.

van der Kolk, Bessel A., Laura Stone, Jennifer West, Alison Rhodes, David Emerson, Michael Suvak, and Joseph Spinazzola. 2014. "Yoga as an Adjunctive Treatment for Posttraumatic Stress Disorder: A Randomized Controlled Trial." *Journal of Clinical Psychiatry* 75 (6): 559–65.

Wesselmann, Debra, Cathy Schweitzer, and Stefanie Armstrong. 2014. *Integrative Team Treatment for Attachment Trauma in Children: Family Therapy and EMDR*. New York: W. W. Norton.

Wilkinson, Dawn S., Pamela L. Knox, James E. Chatman, Terrance L. Johnson, Nilufer Barbour, Yvonne Myles, and Antonio Reel. 2002. "The Clinical Effectiveness of Healing Touch." *Journal of Alternative and Complementary Medicine* 8 (1): 33–47.

Wylie, Mary Sykes. 2004. "The Limits of Talk." *Psychotherapy Networker* 28 (1): 30–36.

3

Attachment-Focused Treatment and the Brain

A Neuroscience Perspective

Jonathan Baylin

> The mammalian nervous system did not evolve solely to survive in dangerous and life-threatening contexts, but it evolved to promote social interactions and social bonds in safe environments.
>
> —Porges (2011, 256)

What happens to a child's brain development when the child is initially exposed to an uncaring, unnurturing environment? To respond to this critical question, this chapter will move away from the conversational tone of the rest of this book in order to dive deeply into the neuroscience of developmental trauma and its impact on the attachment system.

The core task of the infant is to learn about the nature of the social world, about the nature of other humans, in order to build a brain suited for surviving among one's first caregivers. As part of this process, the child is learning how to feel about himself, learning whether he is a source of delight and joy for the adults taking care of him or a source of frustration, anger, disgust. Is he a person of high value or of little or no value? Is it safe to live expansively, taking up interpersonal space and engaging fully with others? Or is it necessary to rein in "vitality affects" (Stern 2000) and attachment-based needs and to live by hiding from others and depending on oneself?

The neuroscience of developmental trauma reveals that the child's defense system gets turned on by maltreatment and then develops much more robustly than the social engagement system (De Bellis 2001; Teicher et al. 2003). Once this system kicks into overdrive it is difficult for the child to even perceive messages of safety and trustworthiness in other people's voices, faces, and movements. With a brain dedicated to self-defense and self-reliance, the child has "safety blindness," perceiving other people through the filter of a chronically hyperactive threat-detection system. This developmental trajectory biases brain development toward (1) chronic hypervigilance for threats; (2) suppression of prosocial emotions in favor of asocial, self-protective emotions; (3) low self-esteem supporting the need to keep a low profile around others; and (4) self-provisioning to ensure one gets enough food, water, shelter, and thermoregulation to survive physically while forgoing the comfort and joy of safe relationships. In essence that child adapts in ways to increase the likelihood of survival.

THE JOURNEY FROM MISTRUST TO TRUST

The goal of attachment-focused treatment, from a brain-based perspective, is to help a child recover from this "blocked trust" (Baylin and Hughes 2016). How can we lead this fear-driven brain to reclaim its birthright to experience the comfort and joy of safe relationships with caring others? Attachment-focused therapy for children focuses on changing this core of mistrust wired into the child's brain to one capable of trust.

From a brain-based perspective, the different processes described in this book co-construct new meaning to counter old, trauma-based narratives through here-and-now sensory-based experiences, rather than using only words. Specific attachment figure–based methods—such as co-regulation of affect with playfulness, acceptance, curiosity, and empathy (PACE); bilateral stimulation; video feedback; somatic awareness and a focus on movement and rhythm; and strategic use of voice tone, volume, and cadence—help disarm the child's defense system and promote the awakening of the child's social engagement system. While emphasizing different processes, all of these models "work" by ultimately helping quiet the child's chronically active defense system and promoting a brain-awakening journey upward to the prefrontal regions of the brain. The child needs to engage these regions of the brain to achieve emotion regulation and construction of new autobiographical narratives.

Safety Messengers and Amygdala Whisperers: Targeting the Child's Defense System

When caregivers are consistent messengers of safety, they function as "social bufferers" (Tottenham et al. 2012) and co-regulators of the child's emotions, which deactivates the child's stress response and self-defense systems. In contrast, children in the care of untrustworthy adults are dysregulated by the presence of these caregivers and fail to experience the social buffering effects that promote trust and protect their brains from excessive stress reactivity. Rather than receiving consistent safety messages, the maltreated child receives consistent messages that are threatening, painful, and distressing. These messages come into the child's brain from the facial expressions, tones of voice, and qualities of touch provided by caregivers. Rapidly, in less than a tenth of a second, these sensory experiences reach the midbrain "salience network." This brain system is dedicated to rapid appraisal of the emotional impact and importance of all sensory experiences. Sensory inputs rapidly activate the deep-brain limbic system, especially the child's amygdala, the first filter for appraising safety and danger. Here, in the subcortical regions of the child's brain, is where the process of learning to trust or mistrust caregivers begins.

A major goal of attachment-focused treatment is to promote the social buffering process between adults and children. Indeed, the social buffering effect is now being used as a measure of the effectiveness of interventions aimed at promoting more secure attachments in young children through the use of pre- and post-measures of stress reactivity (Dozier et al. 2014; Tottenham et al. 2012). Social buffering works primarily through nonverbal communication between an adult and a child. Facial expressions, tones of voice, and touch are key to sending the necessary safety messages to the child's amygdala to disarm the child's defense system.

In order to send these safety messages, the adult has to be in a state of mind conducive to safety messaging: a state of openness and compassion toward the child,

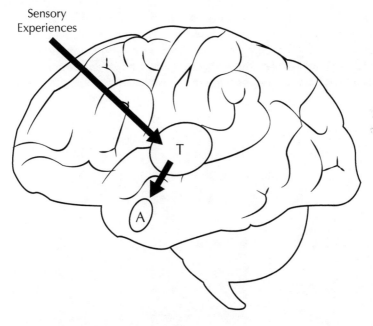

A: amygdala
T: thalamus

Figure 3.1.   Sensory Input and Rapid Appraisal of Safety and Threat

especially when the child is in "defense brain." In this sense, the key issue in attachment-focused treatment is the state of mind of a therapist or caregiver toward the child, especially toward the child's chronic defensiveness. To avoid "mutual defense societies" from developing in response to the child's mistrust, the adults have to be mindful of where they are holding the child in their mind, the goal being to hold the child in a compassionate place, not in the adult's defense system.

Therapists and caregivers ultimately help mistrusting children recover from the effects of maltreatment by being "amygdala-whispering safety messengers"—reliable social buffers who can disarm the child's defense system with kind eyes, kind voice, and good touch. For this to consistently happen, parents and therapists must not take what the "amygdala does" personally and realize this is an automatic survival mechanism built into the child's brain. The child needs to be surprised by kindness in the caregiver. Being punitive and rigid will have the opposite effect, sending the child deeper into defenses. Both therapists and parents need to be "amygdala whisperers."

EPICENTER OF DEVELOPMENTAL TRAUMA: THE MIDBRAIN ALARM SYSTEM

Treatment for attachment disorders rooted in early life exposure to extremely poor care needs to target the brain system at the "epicenter" of complex trauma: the midbrain alarm system (Fisher 2014; Liddell et al. 2005). The midbrain alarm system centers around the functioning of the amygdala, especially in the right hemisphere of the brain. The amygdala is dedicated to the rapid appraisal of all sensory experiences for safety and threat, an unconscious process that neuroscientist Stephen Porges calls

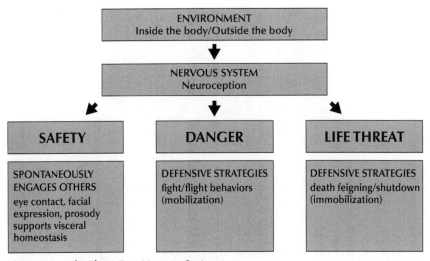

Figure 3.2. The Three-Part Nervous System

"neuroception" to distinguish it from the slower process of perception and the much slower process of conscious thought.

Neuroception is working from the time of birth in infants and perhaps prior to birth. The amygdala has strong connections with three key systems that together comprise the midbrain alarm system: (1) the vigilance system; (2) the fight, flight, or freeze defensive behaviors; and (3) the stress response system—the hypothalamic-pituitary-adrenal (HPA) axis that regulates the functioning of stress hormones like cortisol and corticotropin-releasing hormone (CPA).

When a young child is exposed to poor care in the form of neglect and/or abuse, the amygdala rapidly appraises the facial expressions, tones of voice, and tactile sensations experienced during interactions with caregivers, and then it activates these three neural systems to support a process of self-defense. Through repeated exposure to threatening care, this brain system promotes chronic defensiveness.

Maltreated children deploy this brain circuit automatically, mindlessly, in response to adults who try to come close to them, not waiting to process more information about the other person. This is the brain system that has to be calmed in treatment by providing the child with "enriched care," a consistently compassionate way of relating to the child's defensiveness that helps to awaken the child's brain to the news of a difference: I am safe now!

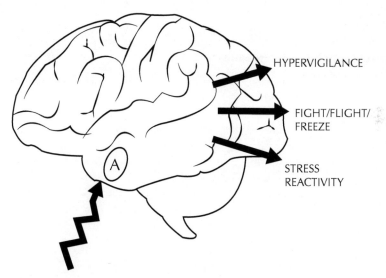

EXPOSURE TO VERY POOR CARE:
faces, voices, touch

A: amygdala

Figure 3.3.   The Midbrain Alarm System

Suppression of the Higher Brain Regions

Hyperactivation of the midbrain alarm system suppresses the development of connectivity in the child's brain, keeping the child in "survival brain" mode. When a child is in survival mode, higher regions of the brain, including the hippocampus and prefrontal cortex, are suppressed in favor of activation of the midbrain defense system. Suppression of hippocampal and prefrontal functions helps keep the child in a state of constant readiness for self-defense—an initially adaptive response to poor care that then becomes a chronically maladaptive way of relating to safer caregivers. Over time, this neurodynamic scenario puts the child's brain development on a trajectory dedicated to survival through mistrust and self-reliance rather than a trajectory dedicated to living in trust and depending on the care of an attachment figure. These parts of the brain, in effect, hijack other parts of the child's brain that would allow feeling safe enough to be vulnerable to connection with caregivers.

Treatment has to give the child's brain a chance to utilize the hippocampal and prefrontal regions of the brain that are essential to the process of "contextualizing" experiences and changing one's mind and behavior in response to changes in the environment of care. Trauma is not actually about being stuck in the past, it's about not being able to be in the present. This is why "here-and-now" playful experiences that engage the child's brain and body, such as in Theraplay (described in chapters 7 and 8), are so effective. These models begin to revise the child's internal working models by giving them new experiences in the present.

Suppression of Bilateral Integration

In addition to suppressing the vertical integration of the developing brain— through the growth of connections between the amygdala, hippocampus, and prefrontal cortex—early life adversity suppresses the development of horizontal or bilateral integration, which is the connectivity between the right and left hemispheres. Neuroscientific studies of developmental trauma in humans reveal that the corpus callosum, the main connective fibers between the two hemispheres, is smaller in certain regions in people exposed to early life abuse and neglect (De Bellis 2001;Teicher et al. 2003). This makes it harder for the person to use both sides of the brain efficiently when processing information, which in turn interferes with meaning making—the process of making sense of life experiences and developing a coherent narrative to support positive self-esteem—and the capacity to trust another human being.

Since traumatic experiences tend to overactivate the right hemisphere limbic system while suppressing left hemisphere functioning, treatment needs to promote bilateral activity to help the child's brain reprocess memories of traumatic experiences productively. This is necessary, for example, to help the child put emotions into words rather than being stuck in wordless states of fear (van der Kolk 2014). This is also the science behind the effectiveness of Eye Movement Desensitization Reprocessing (EMDR), which will be discussed in chapter 12 of this book.

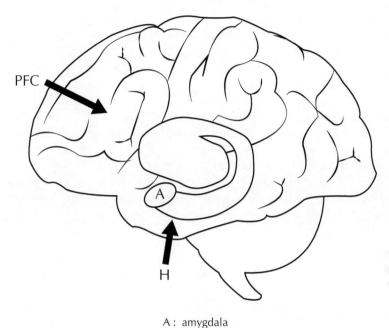

A : amygdala
H : hippocampus
PFC : prefrontal cortex

Figure 3.4. Amygdala Suppresses Hippocampus and Prefrontal Cortex Development

Dissociation: The Opioid Block and Management of Social Pain

In addition to hyperactivation of the self-defense system to prepare the child for rapid defensive action, the young child's brain has a mechanism for reducing the pain of not having a trustworthy "go to" comforter. This mechanism is the opioid system, the brain's natural chemistry that gets automatically released whenever children, including infants, experience pain, be it physical pain or "social pain," such as the pain of rejection (Eisenberger et al. 2011; Lieberman 2013). Developmental traumatologists now think that the opioid system, involving the massive release of opioids in response to the pain of neglect and abuse, is the core mechanism of dissociation (Lanius 2014).

Once the child starts using this system to survive the pain of being neglected and abused, this becomes a chronic neurobiological strategy for disengaging affectively from other people, a way of being physically present while being emotionally detached. Treatment has to address this dissociative process and lower the opioid blocking system in the child to help the child be present to experience what it is like to have a trustworthy caregiver. Maltreated children typically avoid social pain, especially the separation distress and sadness that would lead to the urge to cry and seek comfort.

Treatment has to help these children recover the capacity to feel these essential "social emotions" if they are going to recover the ability to seek comfort from trustworthy adults. In essence, treatment needs to address the suppressed "call and response" system in a parent-child dyad, enabling the child to feel the need for care and the caregiver to feel the need to provide this care. This means that treatment needs to target interpersonal processes, to address both the child's blocked trust and the caregiver's capacity to stay open and compassionate toward the mistrusting child.

In order to help the child safely recover the capacity to feel the pain of disconnection and the need for comfort, therapists have to both follow the child's affect and gently lead the child into affective states that have been blocked. This has to be done with close monitoring of the child's "window" of affective tolerance, ensuring that caregivers are ready and able to comfort the child as the child starts to experience the emotions that he or she has historically had to suppress to survive without the comfort of a safe caregiver.

STATE-DEPENDENT FUNCTIONING: THE POLYVAGAL MODEL OF DEVELOPMENTAL TRAUMA AND ATTACHMENT-FOCUSED TREATMENT

Traumatization is a "state-dependent process," generating bad memories that get stored in the brain/body states in which the traumatic experiences are first processed. The model of the nervous system described by Stephen Porges in his polyvagal theory is very helpful for understanding the state-dependent nature of developmental trauma and trauma-focused treatment. Porges (2011) describes three core neural systems that together comprise the human social, emotional brain. This model helps therapists understand the state-dependent nature of cognitions, emotions, and behavior and, in so doing, helps us see treatment as a process of "interstate travel," of helping maltreated children shift their brains from defensiveness to openness.

The polyvagal model is a three-part view of the nervous system that focuses on the key differences between states of defensiveness and the state of social engagement. The most recently evolved and neurobiogically complex system is the social engagement system, which is supported by an upper branch of the vagus nerve that Porges calls the "smart vagus." This neural network supports the uniquely human ability to sustain social engagement with other people without shifting into a state of self-defensiveness.

The social engagement system is an open state in which we are able to connect with other people and engage in shared attention and collaborative activity. When we are in this state, we automatically use patterns of vocalization, facial expressions, and gestures that promote the activation of the social engagement system in the communication partner. In short, when therapists or parents are in their social engagement system rather than a defensive state, they send messages of safety into the brains of mistrusting children, the "right" messages for helping the child shift states, moving from defensiveness into openness.

The social engagement system is the neural system behind a therapist's or caregiver's ability to promote the interstate travel children need to make to move from core mistrust to trust. This state of mind and body is conducive to brain growth and increased neural integration—a state conducive to dyadic attunement with a social partner in which both partners are open, curious, and energized by the relationship. To get into and stay in the social engagement system, we first have to feel safe. More specifically, our brain's neuroceptive system has to detect social signs of safety in another person before the social engagement system can be activated. In effect, the child's amygdala has to give the green light, the safety signal, before the child can engage openly with an adult.

Competing with the social engagement system are two defensive systems. The more primitive and evolutionarily older of the two is the dorsal vagal system—a parasympathetic (or automatic) system that supports the relaxation response and digestive processes but is also involved in the immobilization-in-fear system that we share with other animals. This is the system that enables us to shut down awareness, sensory processing, and pain when there is no escape via fight or flight, when the only option is to be present without feeling present. This deep parasympathetic state is typically mixed with the other defense system, which is the sympathetic, up-regulating system, creating mixed and often rapidly alternating states of parasympathetic dissociation and sympathetic rage. The sympathetic system supports the active defensive behaviors of fight and flight.

The timing of exposure to traumatic experiences has much to do with which defense system—the parasympathetic "hiding" system or the sympathetic "fight/flight" system—predominates in the defensive operations a child develops. The earlier in life unmanageable stress is encountered, the more likely the child has to resort to the freeze-in-fear immobilization option. Opioids released into this circuit help the child to shut down feelings and sensory processing, a chemical reaction that lays the foundation for chronic dissociation while protecting the child (in the original context of poor care) from being overwhelmed by the pain of neglect and abuse.

This down-regulation process also triggers a bodily shrinking reaction, a process of literally getting small to avoid being too visible by taking up too much space. This physical and emotional shrinkage is the hiding response that becomes habitual when the child experiences threats from the presence of other people. This hiding response involves not only hiding from the other but also hiding from oneself. In other words, the hiding response reduces self-awareness and the processing of all kinds of sensory cues both from without and from within. Whichever defense system the child employs, the parasympathetic or the sympathetic, both suppress the development of the social engagement system, making it difficult for the child to learn to feel safe in a more trustworthy environment later in life.

Interstate Travel: Co-Regulating the Child's States to Facilitate Up-Shifting to Social Engagement

Developmental trauma is lodged in the defensive systems of the child's brain, the systems the child has to use to process the frightening experiences with caregivers. This means that memories of trauma, which come from preverbal experiences early in life, are likely stored in a state-specific manner. If the child froze and used the primitive vagal system at the time of the traumatic experiences, the memories of these experiences are likely to be stored in this part of the nervous system, reemerging when the child reenters this parasympathetic state. This is why relaxation exercises can trigger anxiety in traumatized children (and adults). Likewise, memories of protest, of using the sympathetic fight and flight system, are stored more in the sympathetic defense system. When these memories are triggered, the child is likely to become angry and aggressive or to run away, displaying "blind rage" or "blind flight."

Using the three-state polyvagal model of the nervous system, we can think of trauma-focused therapy as a way for the therapist and, with coaching, caregivers to use their social engagement system to co-regulate the child's states and help the child shift from the defensive nervous system to the social engagement system. Since the social engagement system is only accessible when the child experiences sufficient safety in the presence of an adult, the adult has to be adept at sending safety messages into the child's midbrain defense system to help the child's brain make the desired shift from a defensive to an open state. It is only when the child is helped to access the social engagement system that new learning can occur in response to new experiences with caregivers and the therapist. This is why it's so helpful to understand the three-part model and how treatment can promote the state-shifting process.

Awakening the Higher Regions of the Child's Brain Interpersonally: Prosody, Facial Expressions, and Good Touch

When children have to dedicate their brain development to being good at rapidly detecting threats in other people's behavior, they hyperfocus on the auditory and visual signs of threat, the sounds of anger and the appearance of angry faces. There is a tradeoff here between listening to the sounds of safety and listening to the sounds of danger. Angry vocalizations use different, lower frequencies of sound than happy vocalizations. So when the child has to attend to danger over safety, the brain filters out the higher-pitched sounds of safety in order to pay exquisite attention to the least indications of anger in the voices of adults. This leads to many "false alarms," as the child detects anger in a parent's neutral tone or in subtle shifts from happy tones to serious tones. In order to help children recover from this "safety blindness," therapists and caregivers have to maximize their use of positive prosody—that is, keeping their vocalizations (and accompanying facial expressions and gestures) in the range of "sociality" and approachability, making the sounds of safety.

Certain patterns of vocalization combined with certain facial expressions can promote a shift in a listener's brain from the lower regions of the brain that process threats to the higher regions that process positive social information (Porges and Lewis 2010). For example, the sounds of a lullaby combined with expressive movements of the muscles surrounding the eye region of the singer can activate the social engagement system in the "receiver." When therapists and caregivers are in their social engagement system as they interact with a defensive child, they automatically use the prosody and facial expressions that are conducive to activating the social engagement system in the child. The better the adults are at staying in their "smart vagal" social engagement system, the better they can be at promoting the shift from defensiveness to social engagement in the child, a major goal of attachment-focused therapy.

When adults use the relational power of the social engagement system, using the vocal patterns and facial expressions inherent to sociality, they help the child access the social engagement system and bring the dyad into a shared, synchronous state of engagement. With this dyadic engagement in play, a therapist and a parent can have a much more positive influence on the child's thinking, emotions, and actions. When there is dyadic attunement within the social engagement system, the child is open to the adult's influence. In this shared state of sociality, the child's brain can process information about safety and become more aware of the presence of a trustworthy adult who is different from adults who failed to be trustworthy partners earlier in the child's life.

Attachment-focused treatment depends on the relational power of the adults to influence the brains of mistrusting children—to use relational processes to promote the necessary state shifting in the child's brain from the midbrain defense system to the social engagement system. It is this activation of the ventral "smart" vagal circuit that provides the neural support for social engagement. This is why it is so important to work with caregivers to help them learn to access their social engagement system and stay in this open state as long as possible, both when interacting with their child and when thinking about their children when they are not with them.

The social engagement system is conducive to reflection about relationships. This open state supports reflective functioning and the use of the default mode network—the brain circuit dedicated to mentalization, introspection, and "mindsight." We cannot access this system and use it productively when we are in a defensive state; this is only possible when we feel safe enough to go inside our mind, taking our attention off our external environment, to ponder, to wonder, to imagine, thinking deeply about ourselves and our loved ones.

"Cingulation": Using Prosody to Awaken the Call-and-Response System in the Parent-Child Dyad

A key part of the brain that needs to be activated in treatment is the anterior cingulate cortex, or ACC. The ACC is key to subjective experiences of emotion—to the process of "feeling and dealing" as opposed to dissociating, numbing feelings, and disengaging. The ACC is the brain region we use to generate and respond to sounds of distress. This region is especially sensitive to prosody—the emotional tone of voice that parents and children use to attune to one another and to signal the need for comfort, as well as to make the sounds of joy when experiencing the rewarding

nature of a good relationship. The ACC is a key part of the attachment system because this region, in connection with another brain region called the anterior insula
(or AI), forms a brain circuit associated with empathy and caring feelings, including
love. The ACC and AI are also rich in opioid receptors and are key regions involved
in the dissociative process when opioids are released to numb the pain of neglect
and abuse. The ACC-AI circuit has to be reawakened in the process of treatment so
that the child can learn to feel the attachment-related emotions of separation pain
and joy of connection—emotions that get blocked when the child has to suppress
attachment needs in favor of self-defensiveness.

Caregivers and therapists need to awaken the child's ACC-AI circuit, especially
with their voices, by making the sounds that are inherent safety messages. These are
the sounds that parents make when they are delighted by their babies or when they
are responding with empathy and compassion to their child's distress. This is called

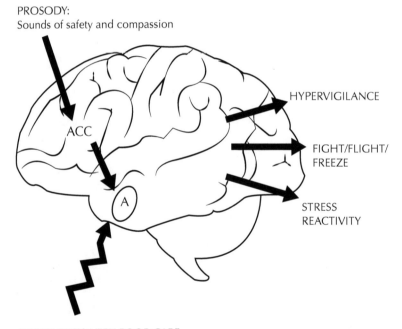

A : amygdala
ACC: Anterior cinglulate cortex

**Figure 3.5. Prosody and the ACC-Amygdala Circuit: Calming the Midbrain
Defense System Interpersonally**

"cingulation," the use of the voice to awaken the child's brain from the disengaged, dissociative state engendered by overuse of the opioid system.

Surprising the Child's Defensive Brain: Positive Prediction Errors to Awaken the Child's Higher Functions

Good care in the form of consistently empathic, compassionate responses to the child's defensiveness have the effect of surprising the child's brain, "violating" the negative expectations that are inherent to chronic mistrust. Neuroscientists call this surprise effect "error messaging" (Pourtois et al. 2010). When the surprise is an unexpectedly positive response, this generates a Positive Prediction Error, an electrical pattern in the child's ACC that has the effect of grabbing the child's attention, interrupting the child's automatic defensiveness, and generating curiosity, a state of therapeutic bewilderment, or novelty. Creating this kind of positive novelty is an essential component of treatment in brain terms, necessary for countering the unconcious operations of the child's defense system.

Comfort and Joy: Restoring the Child's Capacity to Experience the Pain and Pleasure of Good Connections

Children exposed to very poor care early in life have to suppress social emotions— both the emotions associated with the pain of separation that drive the need for comfort and protection and the feelings of pleasure that children are "wired" to experience when it is safe to interact with caregivers. Treatment has to help the child recover the capacity to experience both kinds of social emotions. The child needs the co-regulation of adults to safely recover the sadness and pain that got blocked, while also being helped to recover the potential for playfulness and for experiencing the intensely positive emotions that are part of securely bonded relationships.

Up the Brain: Regulation, Reversal, Reflection, Reappraisal

When the therapist, using her social engagement system, provides the social buffering of the child's defense system—and helps caregivers learn to do the same—the child can start to access the higher brain regions that promote the four Rs of change: regulation, reversal, reflection, reappraisal (Baylin and Hughes 2016). Neuroscience shows that secure relationships enable the use of the prefrontal regions of the brain that support emotion regulation, reversal learning, self-reflection, and the reappraisal of core beliefs about self and other. These functions emerge as the prefrontal cortex activates from the bottom to the top.

As mentioned above, activation of the anterior cingulate cortex (ACC) helps promote emotion regulation because the ACC can modulate the amygdala and other arousal-inducing regions of the brain. When the lowest region of the prefrontal cortex (PFC), the orbitol region, is activated, the child can engage in what neuroscientists call reversal learning—the process of learning from changing environmental contingencies to change behavior adaptively. Then, when the middle region of the PFC, the MPFC, comes on line, this region supports reflective functioning, "mindsight," and mentalization—the functions needed to understand and think about self-other relationships more deeply than is possible while the brain remains in survival mode.

Finally the topmost part of the PFC can be accessed, the dorsolateral PFC, or DLPFC, to support the process of generating new beliefs, revising old beliefs in light of new experiences and information, and creating new narratives, positive stories about self and others—which is known as the process of reappraisal. Family Attachment Therapy, discussed in chapter 13, is a model of treatment that focuses specifically on reappraisal, or creating new narratives. These processes become possible for the child when there is a social buffering "other" to help quiet the midbrain defense system and open up the higher regions of the brain for learning, reprocessing, and adaptive changes.

CAREGIVER WORK: HELPING CAREGIVERS BECOME TRUSTBUILDERS

Since a major goal of attachment-focused treatment is to strengthen the bond between the child and a caregiver, treatment needs to involve the caregivers in the process of learning to be "social buffers" for the child. Interventions need to help caregivers get in the "right mind" to stay open and engaged with children who are defensive. This can be very challenging for any parent and is especially challenging for adults who have unresolved issues stemming from their own childhood experiences.

Engaging in trust-building processes and trauma-focused work, which are components of the models highlighted in the coming chapters, can help caregivers provide the enriched care these children need. Each model outlined in this book describes essential ways of working with parents. Often therapy needs to address "blocked care" (Hughes and Baylin 2012)—the process in which the stress of parenting suppresses the parent's ability to sustain loving feelings and compassion for a mistrusting child. Treatment needs to help parents with blocked care reopen their hearts and minds, similar to the process of reawakening the potential for social engagement in children with chronic mistrust.

TOWARD A BRAIN-BASED INTEGRATIVE MODEL OF ATTACHMENT-FOCUSED TREATMENT

Using the rich window of fast-expanding knowledge about the brain, we are moving toward integrated models of treatment that combine processes in a mindful, intentional way, based on knowledge of how these processes facilitate neural integration and recovery from chronic defensiveness. Toward this end, the treatment approaches described in this book can be seen as highlighting different pathways into the traumatized brain to promote the brain-shifting, state-changing movement that can help maltreated children shift the trajectory of their development. It is through this lens of seeking pathways into the traumatized brain that the range of models included in the coming chapters can be seen as effective tools in fostering trust-based relationships between children and their families.

BIBLIOGRAPHY

Baylin, Jonathan, and Daniel A. Hughes. 2016. *The Neurobiology of Attachment-Focused Therapy: Enhancing Connection and Trust in the Treatment of Children and Adolescents.* New York: W. W. Norton.

De Bellis, Michael D. 2001. "Developmental Traumatology: The Psychophysiological Development of Maltreated Children and Its Implications for Research, Treatment, and Policy." *Development and Psychopathology* 13: 539–64.

Dozier, Mary, Elizabeth Meade, and Kristin Bernard. 2014. "Attachment and Biobehavioral Catch-Up: An Intervention for Parents at Risk of Maltreating Their Infants and Toddlers." In *Evidence-Based Approaches for the Treatment of Maltreated Children*, edited by S. Timmer and A. Urquiza, 43–60. New York: Springer.

Eisenberger, Naomi I., Sarah L. Master, Tristen K. Inagaki, Shelley E. Taylor, David Shirinyan, Matthew D. Lieberman, and Bruce D. Naliboff. 2011. "Attachment Figures Activate a Safety Signal-Related Neural Region and Reduce Pain Experience." *Proceedings of the National Academy of Sciences* 108: 11721–26.

Fisher, Sebern F. 2014. *Neurofeedback in the Treatment of Developmental Trauma: Calming the Fear-Driven Brain.* New York: W. W. Norton.

Hughes, Daniel A., and Jonathan Baylin, 2012. *Brain-Based Parenting: The Neuroscience of Caregiving for Healthy Attachment.* New York: W. W. Norton.

Lanius, Ulrich F. 2014. "Attachment, Neuropeptides, and Autonomic Regulation: A Vagal Shift Hypothesis." In *Neurobiology and Treatment of Traumatic Dissociation*, edited by U. F. Lanius, S. L. Paulsen, and F. M. Corrigan, 105–30. New York: Springer.

Liddell, Belinda J., Kerri J. Brown, Andrew H. Kemp, Matthew J. Barton, Pritha Das, Anthony Peduto, Evian Gordon, and Leanne M. Williams. 2005. "A Direct Brainstem-Amygdala-Cortical 'Alarm' System for Subliminal Signals of Fear." *NeuroImage* 24: 235–43.

Lieberman, Matthew D. 2013. *Social: Why Our Brains Are Wired to Connect.* New York: Crown.

Porges, Stephen W. 2011. *The Polyvagal Theory: Neurophysiological Foundations of Emotions, Attachment, Communication, and Self-Regulation.* New York: W. W. Norton.

Porges, Stephen W., and Gregory F. Lewis. 2010. "The Polyvagal Hypothesis: Common Mechanisms Mediating Autonomic Regulation, Vocalizations and Listening." In *Handbook of Mammalian Vocalization: An Integrative Neuroscience Approach*, edited by S. M. Brudzynski, 255–64. New York: Elsevier.

Pourtois, Gilles, Roland Vocat, Karim N'diaye, Laurent Spinelli, Margitta Seeck, and Patrik Vuilleumier. 2010. "Errors Recruit Both Cognitive and Emotional Monitoring Systems: Simultaneous Intracranial Recordings in the Dorsal Anterior Cingulate Gyrus and Amygdala Combined with fMRI." *Neuropsychologia* 48: 1144–59.

Stern, Daniel N. 2000. *The Interpersonal World of the Infant: A View from Psychoanalysis and Developmental Psychology*. New York: Basic Books.

Teicher, Martin H., Susan L. Andersen, Ann Polcari, Carl M. Anderson, Carryl P. Navalta, and Dennis M. Kim. 2003. "The Neurobiological Consequences of Early Stress and Childhood Maltreatment." *Neuroscience Biobehavioral Review* 27 (1–2): 33–44.

Tottenham, Nim, Mor Shapiro, Eva H. Telzer, and Kathryn L. Humphreys. 2012. "Amygdala Response to Mother." *Developmental Science* 15: 307–19. doi:10.1111/j1467.2011.01128.x.

van der Kolk, Bessel A. 2014. *The Body Keeps the Score: Brain, Mind, and Body in the Healing of Trauma*. New York: Viking.

II

ATTACHMENT-BASED CLINICAL MODELS

4

Infant/Child-Parent Psychotherapy

A Model of "Being With" Young Children and Their Families in Trouble

Michael Trout

If we wonder often, the gift of knowledge will come.

—Native American proverb

Peter is blind. Among the many behaviors in his repertoire that agitate his mother and inhibit closeness between them is his clawing at and biting her. Mother and child are part of a research and education program designed to help young children manage some of the many challenges to optimal development created by the fact that they cannot see. The year is about 1960; the place is New Orleans. The "teacher" is a child psychoanalyst, of all things. As she got to know Peter, she was taken aback when he "seized me and clawed me" (Fraiberg 1977, 33). She responded to these painful assaults by moving away, maintaining contact only with her voice. He would then appear lost, his affect would flatten, and he would begin swaying and rocking. Mother watched the sequence, which was most familiar to her.

Guided by her psychoanalytic understanding of the child's hunger for a reliable object, and her imagination about what it might be like to try to retain an object that cannot be seen—and, therefore, not held in the mind—Fraiberg said to Peter, as he was biting and clawing at her, "You don't have to be afraid. I won't go away." Peter released his "death grip" at once (33). It was a startling moment. Mother found herself suddenly looking anew at a behavior "she had always interpreted as aggressive and now began to understand . . . as a kind of inarticulate terror" (33).

Later in the session, when Peter exhibited the awful and familiar clawing and biting behavior directly with his mother, the home visitor said to Peter once again, "You don't have to be afraid. Mother will not go away" (Fraiberg 1977, 33). As before, Peter stopped. Mom was flabbergasted, not only at the strange connection that had been made but also by how close to him she began to feel after this simple interpretation. Behavior changed; attachment got a boost. It was "like magic," the mother said. An intervention was born.

This is how infant-parent psychotherapy (and its outgrowth, child-parent psychotherapy) began, really: with the in vivo discovery that there may be things happening in homes that are poorly understood by the family, and by most who try to help them. Some are driven by the unconscious of the parent or of the child. Making them conscious, noticing what is happening in light of the whole history of the child and the parent, can cause barriers to attachment to collapse. Both parent and child behaviors can change (Charon 2006; Cornett 2014).

This chapter will offer a framework for a unique model of investigating and treating early childhood disorders. The chapter will not constitute a primer on methodology, primarily because there is much more than methodology at play in infant-parent psychotherapy/child-parent psychotherapy (IPP/CPP). Not only must we be expert observers and able to impart complex information to struggling parents, but we must also be able to make a connection with them. We can't help parents and young children get closer to each other while we hold them at arm's length.

Since the first article that proposed something vaguely resembling a "model" of intervention with infants and their families was published (Fraiberg, Adelson, and Shapiro 1975), the core ideas began to be used in interventions with slightly older children and their families. Today, CPP is accepted as a multidimensional, evidence-based model of assessment and treatment for children from birth to six years of age (Baradon 2005; Lieberman and Van Horn 2008; Lieberman, Ippen, and Marans 2009; Shirilla and Weatherston 2002). Increasingly, it is thought of as the model of choice for "reducing symptoms of posttraumatic stress and enhancing security of attachment, social-emotional functioning, and cognitive achievement" (Reyes and Lieberman 2012, 20) in "young children who have been exposed to loss, separation, and other disruptions to attachment, as well as interpersonal violence and multiple traumatic events" (Moore and Osofsky 2014, 9).

At its heart, however, CPP is much more than a method of assessment and intervention. It is a way of "being with" families as they try to tell their story, as they try to discover what is actually the matter. CPP calls us to "be there" with families who are struggling, to surprise both parents and young children with our *presence*, to witness the unfolding of a dyad's narrative, and to slowly reflect on that narrative. In the process, we find that parents may discover new meaning in the behavior of their child, and important meaning in their own history. The therapist is more learner than teacher. The CPP clinician is intent on seeing what is just below the surface, and gently bringing it to light. Behavior is of critical importance, but not as *a thing to be fixed*. Behavior guides us to the story.

I knew rather little about adoption reversal when I met a most remarkable family who had experienced one. The parents were well educated, energetic, and thoughtful. After years of struggling with infertility, they now had a delightful ten-month-old adopted son named Adam. They said that all was well with this child except for one thing: he seemed to avoid eye contact with them. Was this a sign that there was something wrong with him? They wanted me to assess him.

Mom decided to mention a second issue troubling her once I arrived at their home: She thought she did not have "the right feelings" for her son. It didn't make sense to her, after all the planning and waiting. "I don't exactly know what the right feelings are, but I'm pretty sure I don't have them. I don't feel attached to this child. I care for him deeply, but sometimes I just can't seem to make a connection with him."

They spoke of their failed attempts to get pregnant, the unsuccessful medical interventions, and their decision to adopt. They had met a pregnant adolescent who chose them to be the adoptive parents of her child. Mother acknowledged that she made quite a personal bond with this teen mom, whom she found to be artistic and creative, much like herself. Dad painted "John Stanley" in a big sweep across one of the painted rainbows in the baby's room over the crib. Their new baby had a name.

The doctor set a date for the induction that he deemed medically necessary. The day came and went. There was no call, despite the fact that they had been invited to be present for the delivery. The family contacted the caseworker from the adoption agency the very next day. The caseworker tracked down the birth mother, who acknowledged that the baby had been born. She had changed her mind; there would be no adoption.

The almost-mother and almost-father went out to a movie that night and then went away for a couple days of retreat. Mom said they didn't know what to do with themselves. Later, in private, she recalled that Dad was angry and agitated, and she was in "some sort of strange mourning" while they were away.

It was later that same week when the caseworker from the adoption agency called with a consolation prize. She made no inquiry about the family's experience of loss. Her intervention was to offer a replacement. The parents gleefully agreed, eager to put the indelicacies of the preceding days behind them.

By the middle of the next week, they had Adam. Adam became the baby who would not look at them, and about whom his mother would say, "I don't have the right feelings."

There is often great wisdom tucked into parent observations, so in CPP we watch, we don't contradict, and we search for the wisdom. I was not greatly surprised to notice that Adam actually made a great deal of eye contact during the time I spent at their home.

There was, however, one curious interactive anomaly: he would turn his head distinctly aside, nearly ninety degrees, each time he was passed from one parent to the other.

I kept quiet about my observation while beginning to inquire about the "other child." Father was annoyed with all this talk and kept repeating how unfair it was that he had lost the money he had given to the birth mom.

Mom's sadness was more obvious, although she was at a loss to explain what she felt. She thought she should be grateful for the child they *did* get. I asked about their experiences in talking with each other and with other family members and supporters. It turned out that not a single word had been spoken about the matter since the day the caseworker confirmed that John Stanley would not be their baby. As we pondered all of this unknown sorrow and carefully tucked-away grief, Mom said about Adam, "I'm afraid he will look at me and will see that I'm thinking about John Stanley."

And she began to weep. Had we stumbled across the reason for Adam's reputed avoidance of eye contact? Did Mom not *want* her new baby to look into her eyes and notice the secret that lay there, lurking?

We began to ponder, together, Adam's curious gaze aversion when in transition from one person to another. What had been Adam's experience with looking at people while being passed from one to the other? Had he once looked as he was passed from his birth mother, only to then look back to find she was gone? Had he later also looked away from the foster mother with whom he spent about ten days, and the same thing happened again?

I proposed the possibility that Adam was pretty smart. His earliest transitions were, in his narrative, permanent. They signified loss. Maybe Adam had learned to avert his gaze during transitions for very good reasons.

It was startling to Mom that Adam might have some sadness about his own losses. It occurred to her that the three members of her family had something in common. Mom looked at her son differently than she ever had before. She was no longer afraid that he would discover that some of her heart was still connected to John Stanley. And she felt empathy for the little boy who had experienced considerable losses in his own short lifetime.

Mom later told me that Adam's peculiar interactive trait was never seen again after that day. His eye contact was perfect. It persisted, right through transitions. He stopped craning his neck to avoid seeing evidence of yet another loss. The rest of his development was just fine.

In infant-parent and child-parent psychotherapy, we are sometimes gifted with an opportunity to uncover a simple barrier to attachment. When we do, behavior change usually follows. We don't have to correct, to teach, or even to explain. It never ceases to impress me that parents are often quite capable of fixing things, on their own, once supported and engaged in looking for the ghosts. Sometimes our job is principally to "be there": to witness, to notice, to wonder about, to support.

THE CORE COMPONENTS OF CPP

What goes on in CPP? And when it works—when attachment improves, when abuse ceases, when development gets on track, when parental attitudes change, when challenging child behaviors morph into something manageable—what *makes* it work?

The successful CPP clinician must know a great deal, of course: about prenatal, perinatal, infant, toddler, and early childhood development; about how children and grownups create narratives; about how people of all ages do defenses; about the nature of memory, and resistance, and repetition, and adaptation; about the meaning of each developmental stage to the child and to the parent who supports it or resists it. The clinician must know her *own* story and be able to manage the affects of those with whom she works without falling into a pit of despair, or a spin of fixing, or detachment. A great deal must be known about the neurodevelopmental research that undergirds all of the above, and about the ways people go about grieving, and coping.

And abundant practical skills are required: being quiet; paying attention; synthesizing data, but not too soon; remembering details; noticing patterns; being organized enough to always be on time and to do what you say you will do. It helps to know how to engage people (both parents and children) who are understandably wary or suspicious about our presence and our intentions.

But, at its soul, I find that CPP works when these three core components are present:

1. The clinician has the capacity to *wonder.*
2. The clinician has the capacity to *follow.*
3. The clinician has the capacity to *hold.*

Wondering

Sarah was six, and mute. That's what the referral said: no one had ever heard her speak. While she had been assessed over and over, no one knew the reason why she didn't talk. And while she had received a great many services, nothing had ever changed.

Her developmental test results suggested a pervasive delay, giving rise to the theory that she had some sort of syndrome that would account not only for the total absence of speech but also for her other developmental delays.

I found it odd that the question had not been asked in all these years: Why, *really,* does Sarah not speak? Services seemed to have been oriented toward *getting her to talk,* not understanding why she didn't. Had we ever wondered, "Sweetheart, what is it? Why don't you talk? Can you tell us about it?"

And so she did. That often happens, when *wondering* is going on.

On the way upstairs to my office, Sarah pulled her mother into the bathroom, where she fetched two paper towels from the dispenser, folded them neatly into two-inch squares, and wetted them. Then she was ready to meet the big, bearded man with his funny, unasked question.

Sarah and her mom sat together on my couch. As I prepared to do my tests, Sarah began wiping her mouth with those squares of paper toweling—back and forth, ever so slowly, while never once taking her eyes off me. What was she doing? Was she wetting her lips? Was she cleaning her mouth?

Was she answering my question, already, just minutes into the examination?

I moved a few feet away and beckoned Sarah to me, so we could try some gross motor tests. She stood (next to the couch and close to her mom) but did not move any closer to me. Mother prompted her but used the strangest language to do so: "What's the matter, Sarah? Why won't you go be with the man?"

Sarah almost immediately answered her mom. She did it by pointing at her throat while making the most grotesque but plaintive sound: "Aaahhh! Aaahhh!" It was loud—a primitive, agonizing vocalization. I can't get it out of my head all these years later.

I had to stop the exam. I asked to be alone with her mom for a minute. I wanted to let Sarah know I had heard her, but I didn't know how. I didn't even know if I was right about what I thought I "heard."

As I was closing the door after situating Sarah in the other room, Mom began: "I know what you're thinking. But let me tell you this: He did not do it. He couldn't have done that."

I pretended not to know to whom she was referring, lest I contaminate whatever she was going to tell me. "Who are we talking about?"

She replied with anger: "You know who we're talking about. And I'm telling you he could *not* have done it. He knows how it feels." As tears began to come (how long she must have been sitting on this thing-that-I-know-but-can't-possibly-stand-to-know), she explained that her husband's father was still molesting his son when she met him, at age thirteen. Anyone who had had such an experience could never repeat it with his own child, she asserted.

I explained that I would have to make a hotline call, and I did, while she waited. That afternoon, the father was picked up by local police, at his job, and questioned. He made no defense whatsoever, unless you consider this a defense: "What's the big deal? She was just a baby. I only did it for a year or so, starting when she was about one. And then I quit. Anyway, I never stuck it in her *down there.*"

Indeed, he probably had not. Sarah had, at least from my perspective, been abundantly clear about that. It was her mouth that had become the problem. Stuff went in it over which she had no control. That orifice had to be managed better. And so she did. She stopped making sounds out of it.

This is not the story of a grand discovery after which everybody feels better. Dad went to prison, of course. Mom lost her husband; Sarah lost her daddy. There was much upset, and no small amount of sorrow. Sarah did begin to speak, but, of course, it took some years to make up what she had lost.

No, this is a story about *wondering*: about keeping the mind empty of preconceptions; about being "brilliantly stupid" (Koloroutis and Trout 2012, p. 100); about having humility in the face of the data; about looking at every situation as if it were brand new and novel (Langer 1997). When a CPP clinician is full of *wonder*, he is unimpressed with diagnoses that are put forth as if they capture the whole story. When a CPP clinician is full of *wonder*, she is determined to keep looking, to ask the broader questions, to never forget about context. Siegel (2007) suggests that such a posture invokes a state of "mindful learning," which is characterized by "intelligent ignorance, flexible thinking, the avoidance of premature cognitive commitments, and creative uncertainty" (234).

When we *wonder*, we set aside our hunger to know the answer. We make few presumptions. We become dogged scientists, searching everywhere for data. This is why a CPP assessment often turns up novel interpretations of behavior, novel ideas about what might be going on, and surprising possibilities about what to do next.

When we *wonder*, we demonstrate to the child and the parent our utter *presence*, our preoccupation with what is being said or acted out in the moment (all of which we are slowly fitting into the context of the family's story and the original referral problems).

We just can't stop being curious, and the family knows it. It makes us coconspirators with them in the search for meaning. It is key to the efficacy of CPP.

Following

I once met a foster mom who was a master at *following*. She could look inside a damaged child and know just what to do. She could do this not because she had a bag of tricks or because she ascribed to a particular parenting model. Instead, she had this uncanny capacity to watch a child in her care for a little while and soon *know* something that would tell her what to do next. She would come up with these sweet, straight-at-the-core-of-things responses that staggered me with the accuracy of their aim, the grandness of their simplicity. In other words, she knew how to *follow*.

Chelsea was four and had been in this magical mom's care for just a few weeks when I was asked to make a home visit and see if I could offer some recommendations to the child welfare agency about the best future for her.

She was in foster care in the first place for one of those reasons that is commonplace in child welfare but, I'm afraid, never did become commonplace for me. In a fit of overwhelming exhaustion and rage, her birth mother had bashed her baby brother's head against the wooden arm of a sofa, killing him. Chelsea watched. She was three or so. Mom then ran to the neighbor's home to call 911 and tell them that her awful three-year-old daughter, full of jealousy, had smashed her baby brother's head in a door jamb.

It didn't take the authorities long to figure out that the mother's story was bogus, and it didn't take Mom long to then drop this terrible condemnation of Chelsea. Chelsea would never see her mother again.

Chelsea, demonstrating expected traits of PTSD, stopped talking. She resisted all human touch. She avoided eye contact. No one could tell for certain if she was mourning the loss of her mother, mourning the loss of her baby brother, reacting to the apparent ease with which her mother tried to put it all on her, or reacting to what she saw. Maybe it was a combination of these. She pulled herself into a ball and was going to let *no one* in.

She had been this way for weeks, the foster mother told me. It didn't seem a surprise to this mom. As far as she was concerned, it was entirely reasonable that a little girl would act this way after what she had just gone through. She wasn't embarrassed by the little girl's refusal to look at me or talk to me or even leave her post on the staircase to enter the room where we were meeting.

We decided to go outside, where Chelsea, her foster mom knew, would be more comfortable. And that's where I was afforded a chance to see this little thing they did together. It was almost like a play, produced and directed entirely by Chelsea. (Can you imagine the import of that all by itself: that Chelsea could feel in *charge* of something?)

I watched this child climb aboard her trike and head directly for the street. Expecting Mom to run ahead to prevent this seemingly self-endangering act, instead I watched her calmly observe and then begin *following*, in both the physical and the clinical sense of the word. When she got to where Chelsea was sitting on her trike in the middle of the street, she affected a slightly higher pitch in her voice and said, "Oh no, my dear. In this house little girls are not allowed to be hurt or to hurt themselves. In this house, little girls get protected by their mommies." And then she guided this precious, tortured child back to the yard.

By the time Mom got back to where I was standing and watching (a bit slack-jawed, as I recall), Chelsea had quietly turned the trike around. She was going to do it again! There wasn't the slightest edge of impatience or "Didn't I already tell you? Why can't you *learn?*" tone in the mom's voice. She had a message to impart—one she had learned by watching her charge and *following* what she saw inside her—and it didn't seem to matter much how many times Chelsea evoked the message by riding into the street. Mom seemed to believe that the repetition of the message was what was important. Chelsea wasn't being asked to "get over it." Chelsea wasn't being asked to change her mind (quite yet) about her impulse to harm herself. Nothing was being asked of Chelsea at all, except that she allow herself to receive the one thing on the planet she needed most: loving care.

I never forgot Chelsea or the astounding foster mom who knew exactly what to do with a child who, without this mom's mindsight, may well have permanently tightened that ball into which she had curled herself. This foster mom saw right inside a girl who had visited a very bad place, and she responded to what she saw. She *followed.*

When CPP works, it is often because the clinician knows how to *follow.* This is not possible when the clinician is preoccupied with a clinical agenda, is working only to meet clinical "goals," or is busy entering responses on a laptop. One has to *look* (in the broadest sense of that word) if one is to have a chance at *following.* Following requires attention. Following is impossible without *presence*, without a commitment to conscious, full-body listening.

To be *followed* by another is an enormous compliment. Yet, for many parents and children, it may be unsettling. Careful listening may feel unfamiliar, uncomfortably intimate, even intrusive. What then? We *follow* those feelings and those responses, too! We back away (usually metaphorically, but sometimes literally) in response to certain cues, and we move closer in response to others, and we may even talk about what we're doing, as a way to demonstrate that we're right there, ready to *follow.*

In other words, we do sort of what a good mother does: she *sees* her children, and she reflects back her children's expressions of themselves. What a joy for the child to be seen, followed, and reflected so lovingly; it is so for parents as well. The clinician adopting this way of *being with* parents and children by *following* is key to the success of CPP.

Holding

I learned some things about *holding* from Rudie's family. They came to me when he was four. They explained that they had adopted him at age two, but it didn't take long for them to catch on to why a couple of earlier adoptive placements had not worked out. Rudie was gorgeous, funny, and utterly draining. He never stopped talking, moving, climbing.

His parents offered the usual litany of intervention efforts, drugs, diets, and strategies that had been suggested and tried. They offered their despair. In the course of the customary CPP evaluation, I asked what they thought propelled him. We all had a laugh at the imagery of his being jet-propelled up and down walls, at which point I asked whether they ever imagined his having *business to do*. Was he looking for something? Was he running *to* something or *from* something, or did they think his running was random, meaningless?

I was surprised at the sensitivity of their response and their willingness to pause. Truthfully, they didn't *want* to expend yet more energy on thinking about it; they just wanted him to *stop*. But the questions seemed to evoke a slightly altered view of him, at least for a moment. Perhaps he wasn't merely trying to drive them batty. Perhaps he was *after* something. Perhaps the thing that had been missed before was the possibility that his behavior had meaning.

Dad proposed, out of the blue, "I wonder if he's looking for his story." We were all a little spellbound by the idea. We sat in silence for several moments, taking it in.

We reviewed Rudie's story together—or the fragments of it we knew. He had been taken from his methamphetamine-using mother at birth. Drugs were in his system, they knew, but medical experts dismissed the role such prenatal drug exposure played in his current activity level four years later. Medically, that made sense.

We took note that we knew pathetically little about his life after removal, except that it was full of disappointments all around. He had been in several foster homes, two of which were pre-adoptive. From Rudie's perspective, this much was clear: No one could *hold* him. He pretended it didn't matter, of course; he would just run faster, break another toy, kick someone, run through the house while yelling, or pee in the laundry basket.

And so these parents decided that Rudie might feel *held* a little better if he knew what had happened to everybody, and to him. They started putting together a story for him, but they wanted me to be there as they told him each part. (Was it my job to *hold* the parents?)

When the day came for the first storytelling, I asked Rudie to lie with his head on one parent's lap and his feet on the other. I covered him with a weighted blanket. The parents, of course, thought I was delirious when I proposed this. He couldn't sit still long enough to tie his shoes! How could I expect him to quietly lie down on his parents' laps? I saw their point. Yet he *did* lie down, and he *did* stay there, and he *did* let me cover him with that blanket. That's how much I think he wanted to be there, in just this position, being *held*, to hear what they were going to say about the life he had lived. This is the story they told.

"We know that the place where you grew up, for the first nine months of your life, inside your mom, was a confusing place. It may have gotten loud sometimes. We think your mom didn't know too much about resting, even though she needed it, and you needed it.

"She was putting things in herself that made her mind race, and made her body race, and may have even made *you* race. You were too young to race. We think she needed someone to take care of her, maybe to cook for her, so she could feel calm and could put better things in her tummy. We wish we had been there, because we know a lot about cooking, and it would have been nice to help her, and to help you. We would have come to the house and said to your mom, 'Oh, sweet momma. You won't need to put this stuff in your body anymore, because we're going to come here every day and make scrumptious stuff for you to eat. It will smell good, and look good, and it will help you.'

"We would probably have held her hand while we were telling her all of this. And in that way, we would have sort of been holding your hand, too.

"We would also have given her lots of love, to help take her mind off drugs. And we would have fed her every day, even if we had to *actually* feed her, like with a spoon!"

There was a pause in the story. Rudie was very quiet. I suspect these parents didn't quite know what to do with a child so quiet. Rudie broke the silence with a soft-spoken question: "Did the bad stuff she put inside her get inside *my* tummy?"

Dad was choking back tears by now. Rudie went on to ask if the bad stuff made his birth mom's tummy hurt. Then he said that *his* tummy sort of hurt, and he brought his hand to his abdomen, under the blanket. He asked if the bad stuff had stayed in him.

And then the zinger: "Is that what makes me feel frazzled?"

These parents already knew about the speed, of course; indeed, they had probably wondered about its role in his inaccessibility and his lunacy-making and placement-busting behavior many times. But something seemed to come together for them in this moment. I think they were surprised to hear how much empathy for Rudie's first mother had come out of their own mouths. They imagined him inside that chaotic, lonely, desperate, loud uterus. Their hearts went out to him. They began to wonder if, in his case, "hyperactivity" was just a word that stood as a place-holder for "Bugs are in me. I can't think straight. I-need-you-but-don't-you-dare-come-near-me-'cause-I-don't-trust-you-since-you-can-change-in-a-heartbeat-into-someone-who-doesn't-see-me." So trying to tell Rudie his story turned out to open *them* up to that very story. They *held* him, in those storytelling moments, in more ways than one. And now they knew how to *hold* him, when he felt "frazzled."

Later, after mentioning how long his state of calm lasted after they left my office, his parents said the thing that really changed was not that Rudie "got cured" but that they knew more about what to do. They had tools. They could interrupt a new episode of outrageous behavior by merely asking if he was starting to feel "frazzled." This question would stop him in his tracks. It seemed to imply to him that his parents really "knew" him. And it always reminded him of their ability to *hold* him. Sometimes he would smile at whoever just asked him that magical question. Always, he would take a break from wherever he was heading.

Parents can't hold, of course, unless they have been held. Sometimes that becomes our job. Further, it becomes up to us to figure out just how to do it and when. I hope Rudie's parents felt *held*.

Holding is the thing that happens when you've done your work of *wondering* and *following* so thoughtfully, so openly, that the family comes to believe you're paying attention, that you will show respect, that you will take awfully good care of what they've said to you and shown you.

Holding is devotion. Holding is remembering a small detail shared by the parent—or shown in the behavior of a child—and bringing it up weeks later. *Holding* happens—and the parent or child feels it when the CPP therapist registers the gravity of what the parent has said or the child has shown. *Holding* is seen, and felt by the family, when the rare gift of *presence* is offered, when the family knows they have our attention.

CONCLUSION

Those who practice child-parent psychotherapy are not business-as-usual clinicians. We are asked to wander into homes where we are often unwelcome, to sit with people who have been knocked around by life and who feel they have been knocked around by the child welfare system or the laundry list of specialists to whom they have already been sent. If we are going to be the ones who crack the code of the disorder for which the child and/or the parent were referred, if we are going to be the ones who are actually let in to know all the stories about how the family got to where they are, we had better have something different to offer.

We don't offer just another new strategy, or a new diagnostic nomenclature that clears everything up, or a clever technique. We do offer a strange mixture of profound understanding about how children develop, from long before they're born, and how that development is affected by their lived and perceived experience, stirred together with a way of thinking about how parents get made, why they make the decisions they do, and why they think about parenting and attachment and loss the way they do. We add a capacity to observe, to invoke endless scientific curiosity about what we see in behavior and interactions, and what we think we "see" in the mental processes of babies and young children and the grownups who care for them.

We find "ports of entry"—a way to begin, a reason to be there, an opportunity to engage—through acts of being fully present, ready to attune, and waiting for guidance. Maybe it will be the behavior of the child in the moment or in recent history. Maybe it will be a representation by the child, in play, about what he has seen or perceived. Maybe it will be an offhand comment by Mom. It is at moments like these that the work really begins.

Sometimes we can scarcely believe our good fortune, that the parent or the child—or the two of them, in unconscious conspiracy—have created the agenda, pointed to something important. The mom insists that everything is fine in the family, except for the aggressive behavior of her five-year-old toward his toddler sister. She politely answers the clinician's inquiries about the birth of the little sister, whereupon the five-year-old (who appears to be paying no attention at all to this "adult talk" as he plays on the floor) blurts out, "Yeah. You went away for forty days." Mom giggles uncomfortably and demands, "What are you talking about? When did I ever go away?" And the boy responds, without ever looking up from his toys, "When Katie was born. You went away for forty days. I didn't know what to do." Mom's "going away"—likely a depression at the time of Katie's arrival—is revealed. The boy remembers, and he told, and now it's out there. His aggression toward Katie now looks a little different than it did moments before.

We offer developmental guidance, while assuring that we aren't too disappointed when the family rejects our wisdom and proceeds to do what they've always done. We ponder this rejection, wondering what it is about the parent's representation of their own experience that creates such fear of knowing the child differently, of trying something new, of seeing the child's "problem" in a new light, or simply of being more empathic. Then we try a new door, or a new way of transmitting the guidance, always alert to the emergence of new meaning.

At its heart, CPP is a way of "being with" mothers and fathers and babies and young children who are in trouble. We enter not with a bag of toys, but with ourselves: our presence, our attunement, our willingness to wonder, to follow, and to hold. We draw on what knowledge, skills, and practices we need to forward the work. Sometimes silence results. Sometimes action results. But always we are there, fully there, ready to *be with*.

BIBLIOGRAPHY

Baradon, Tessa. 2005. *The Practice of Psychoanalytic Parent-Infant Psychotherapy: Claiming the Baby*. New York: Routledge.

Charon, Rita. 2006. *Narrative Medicine: Honoring the Stories of Illness*. New York: Oxford University Press.

Cornett, Stacey. 2014. *Home-Based Services in Infant and Early Childhood Mental Health*. Kingston, NJ: Civic Research Institute.

Fraiberg, Selma. 1977. *Insights from the Blind: Comparative Studies of Blind and Sighted Infants*. New York: Basic Books.

Fraiberg, Selma, Edna Adelson, and Vivian Shapiro. 1975. "Ghosts in the Nursery: A Psychoanalytic Approach to the Problems of Impaired Infant-Mother Relationships." *Journal of the American Academy of Child Psychiatry* 14 (3): 387–421.

Hughes, Daniel. 2006. *Building the Bonds of Attachment: Awakening Love in Deeply Troubled Children.* Lanham, MD: Rowman and Littlefield.

Koloroutis, Mary, and Michael Trout. 2012. *See Me as a Person: Creating Therapeutic Relationships with Patients and Their Families.* Minneapolis, MN: Creative Health Care Management.

Langer, Eric. 1997. *The Power of Mindful Learning.* Cambridge, MA: Da Capo Press.

Lieberman, Alicia, and Patricia Van Horn. 2005. *Don't Hit My Mommy! A Manual for Child-Parent Psychotherapy with Young Witnesses of Family Violence.* Washington, DC: Zero to Three.

———. 2008. *Psychotherapy with Infants and Young Children: Repairing the Effects of Stress and Trauma on Early Attachment.* New York: Guilford Press.

Lieberman, Alicia, Chandra Ghosh Ippen, and Steven Marans. 2009. "Psychodynamic Treatment for Child Trauma." In *Effective Treatments for PTSD: Practice Guidelines from the International Society for Traumatic Stress Studies,* edited by Edna Foa, Terence Keane, Matthew Friedman, and Judith Cohen, 370–87. Second edition. New York: Guilford Press.

Moore, Michelle, and Joy Osofsky. 2014. "Benefits of Child-Parent Psychotherapy for Recovery from Traumatic Loss." *Zero to Three* 34 (6): 9–13.

Reyes, Vilma, and Alicia Lieberman. 2012. "Child-Parent Psychotherapy and Traumatic Exposure to Violence." *Zero to Three* 32 (6): 20–25.

Shirilla, Joan, and Deborah Weatherston. 2002. *Case Studies in Infant Mental Health: Risk, Resiliency and Relationships.* Washington, DC: Zero to Three.

Siegel, Daniel. 2007. *The Mindful Brain: Reflection and Attunement in the Cultivation of Well-Being.* New York: W. W. Norton.

5

Embedded Relational Mindfulness in Child and Adolescent Treatment

A Sensorimotor Psychotherapy Perspective

Pat Ogden and Bonnie Mark-Goldstein

When our body is not at peace, it is hard for our mind to be at peace.

—Thich Nhat Hanh

Andy wants to hit something . . . or someone. The sensation takes over his body, rules his actions, and transpires in a millisecond, 0-to-60 rage. Part of him knows "I'm going to regret this." But he can't stop. Later that day, he tells himself he'll to do it differently next time. Then . . . next time comes, and nothing changes. Andy, age twelve, struggles with the impulses, sensations, feelings that overtake him in interpersonal interactions. He recalls saying to himself, "I'm not going to be like my dad." Yet when he comes to therapy, his first words are "I can't help myself."

This chapter offers a unique foundation for treating children such as Andy, addressing both the verbal and the nonverbal legacies of trauma and attachment disorders prioritizing the body's innate intelligence. While many therapeutic interventions depend almost entirely upon verbal narrative, through the lens of Sensorimotor Psychotherapy, a bottom-up approach targets the body, which plays a crucial role in regulating behavioral, emotional, and mental states. Collaborative therapeutic interventions include mindfully witnessing and supporting the sensations and impulses that arise during Andy's therapy, along with deepening awareness into the progression—both the child's awareness and the therapist's noting of these experiences as they arise. Through this approach, physiological and somatic regulatory capacities can be enhanced.

The effects of Andy's traumatic childhood as a victim of physical abuse and witness to domestic violence provide the framework to illustrate a Sensorimotor Psychotherapy approach. We will introduce Embedded Relational Mindfulness, one of the foundational elements of Andy's treatment that helps him become more mindful, present, aware, and conscious, noticing what is happening within himself and between self and other (therapist and group). Collaborative Embedded Relational Mindfulness intervention teaches the child to observe, become curious, make connections, deepen awareness, and develop trust that what emerges from within during this therapeutic journey holds wisdom and healing power.

Children often have difficulty accurately interpreting their life experiences and interactions with others, and this erroneous meaning making can lead to dysregulation, confusion, and maladaptive behaviors. Examining unresolved past and present conflicts and interpretations helps children understand how the meanings they make can lead to a life filled with unintended choices and possibly unsatisfying relationships.

Psychodynamic therapy and other insight-oriented modalities focus primarily on how meaning making, especially unconscious meaning making, manifests in a child's present-day life through decisions, behaviors, thoughts, and dreams. Yet these insight-oriented modalities are limited, especially with our younger clients, who do not have an extensive verbal capacity to self-reflect or describe their experience. Additionally, it is the implicit processes that elude language—the memories, feelings, images, movements, and body sensations—that contribute most strongly to cognitive distortions, maladaptive behaviors, and dysregulated emotions.

Early attachment dynamics are the beginning templates for children's developing cognition, affect array, regulatory ability, and physical patterns. How children make sense of early life experiences that either are not remembered consciously or cannot be represented verbally, along with genetics and epigenetics, has an overarching impact on the developing child and adolescent. The unconscious meanings and emotions elicited in early attachment are visibly reflected in posture, physiology, facial expressions, eye gaze, gesture, and other body movement, and they powerfully underlie the verbal narrative in therapy. Without conscious intent, these implicit processes persist and our younger clients often feel at the mercy of confusing and sometimes overwhelming effects.

Relying on the "talking cure" can be problematic in psychotherapy with children and adolescents, as difficulties developing a coherent verbal narrative may be challenging, with memories less clear, communications problematic, and engagement with the therapist more tenuous. Sometimes memories or details of childhood trauma are difficult to access and events cannot be reflected upon and thus elude revision. Memories may be distorted, based on input of others. They may be dissociated—split off from conscious awareness—as we see with some trauma survivors who "remember" only isolated affective, sensory, or motor aspects of their experience. Moreover, attempting to describe the processes that precipitate implicit "remembering" can lead to failure and frustration, resulting in clinical impasses, relational failure, and feelings of inadequacy, on the part of both the therapist and the client.

As an alternative to an exclusive focus on insight and verbal language, therapists can capitalize on the language of the body. This rich nonverbal vocabulary exposes a "lifetime of joys, sorrows, and challenges, revealed in patterns of tension, movement, gesture, sorrows, and challenges" (Ogden and Fisher 2015, 25). Sensorimotor Psychotherapy offers a unique lens through which we can help our younger clients and their families uncover, explore, and develop awareness of this somatic reflection of cumulative life experience and implicit processes. Differentiated from most psychotherapy models, where the verbal narrative serves as the entry point into the therapeutic process, Sensorimotor Psychotherapy prioritizes the somatic narrative—the story of the body—and the implicit processes this story reflects and sustains. By "working 'beneath the words,' it elucidates ways the body contributes to the challenges of the individual . . . including aspects that may not be apparent through the lens of more traditional psychotherapies" (Mark-Goldstein and Ogden 2013, 123). Sensorimotor Psychotherapy looks at how the body holds onto memories and experiences, uncovering ways the body gives access to unspoken, painful, or hidden occurrences that cannot be known or illuminated by "insight" therapy alone.

In addition to the focus on the body's expression, building mindful awareness of the moment-by-moment *experience* of implicit patterns over trying to construct a cohesive narrative, engaging in conversation, or "talking about" can help children and adolescents discover and change the underlying determinants of well-being (Kurtz 1990; Ogden and Minton 2000; Ogden, Minton, and Pain 2006; Ogden and Fisher 2015). Current research has repeatedly validated the effectiveness of mindfulness practices for reducing symptoms of depression, anxiety, pain, and trauma in our younger clients, while also improving their ability to tolerate emotions, however unpleasant, thus changing children's experience of themselves and their ability to self-regulate. In Sensorimotor Psychotherapy, the use of mindfulness is foundational to exploring and changing implicit processes.

This chapter illustrates Sensorimotor Psychotherapy's "Embedded Relational Mindfulness" to highlight the wisdom of the body and the impact of primary attachment relationships in the treatment of child and adolescent clients. Emphasizing a therapeutic alliance and collaborative development of treatment goals, the method blends theory and technique from cognitive and psychodynamic therapies and mindfulness practices, incorporating both verbal and nonverbal communication. Movement interventions that promote empowerment and competency are introduced, and interventions are adjusted according to particular needs that arise during the session.

Building on the principles of Sensorimotor Psychotherapy and Embedded Relational Mindfulness, this chapter describes a set of skills for using mindfulness to amplify the therapeutic process between therapist and client and delineates interventions from Sensorimotor Psychotherapy (Ogden, Minton, and Pain 2006; Ogden 2014) that address the in-the-moment experience of implicit processes.

EMBEDDED RELATIONAL MINDFULNESS

Conventional mindfulness is typically characterized as a nonverbal, internal endeavor, usually taught as a solitary, silent activity, although often practiced in group settings. Sometimes mindfulness practices are described as "concentration practices" because they promote focusing attention upon particular elements of either internal experience (such as a mantra, breath, or body sensation) or the external environment (e.g., sound, music, or candle flame). Williams and colleagues depict mindfulness as "the awareness that emerges through paying attention on purpose, in the present moment, and non-judgmentally to things as they are," a perspective that takes into account internal experience as well as "those aspects of life that we most take for granted or ignore" (Williams et al. 2007, 47). Mindfulness practices often encourage openness and unrestricted receptivity to whatever arises.

Building on these perspectives, Ron Kurtz (2004) described mindfulness as being "fully present to our [internal] experience, whatever it is: our thoughts, images, memories, breath, body sensations, the sounds and smells and tastes, moods and feelings and the quality of our whole experience as well as of the various parts. Mindfulness is not our notions about our experience, but even noticing the notions" (2004, 39).

Drawing on the work of Kurtz, in Sensorimotor Psychotherapy mindfulness is not practiced as a solitary activity, nor is it taught through structured exercises. Instead, it is integrated with and embedded within what transpires moment to moment between therapist and client through the cocreated relationship. Therapists encourage clients to observe internal experience in the present moment and verbally share what they observe as their experience is occurring. Thus, Embedded Relational Mindfulness encompasses several critical elements: the therapist observes the visible elements of clients' here-and-now experience, directs children to become aware of their present-moment experience, and asks them, when possible, to verbally report to the therapist what they notice.

To work with mindfulness, it is essential to pay attention to five "building blocks" of present-moment internal experience—cognition, emotion, five-sense perception, movement, and body sensation (cf. Ogden, Minton, and Pain 2006; Ogden 2014). These building blocks are elaborated in figure 5.1.

In Sensorimotor Psychotherapy, the focus of therapy is not only on the verbal narrative but also on the present-moment building blocks that illuminate implicit effects of trauma and attachment failure as well as those that reflect self-regulatory resources, positive affect, competency, and mastery. Together, therapist and child or adolescent become mindful of the building blocks, collaboratively identifying them (Ogden et al. 2006; Ogden 2009; Ogden, Goldstein, and Fisher 2012).

Introducing mindfulness to our younger clients is facilitated by evoking their curiosity. Kurtz suggests that mindfulness is "motivated by curiosity" (Kurtz 1990, 111). The therapist helps children cultivate attitudes of curiosity and develop "the skill of seeing [the] internal world, and . . . shapes it toward integrative functioning" (Siegel 2010, 223).

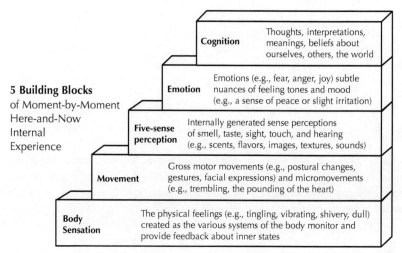

5 Building Blocks
of Moment-by-Moment
Here-and-Now
Internal
Experience

Cognition — Thoughts, interpretations, meanings, beliefs about ourselves, others, the world

Emotion — Emotions (e.g., fear, anger, joy) subtle nuances of feeling tones and mood (e.g., a sense of peace or slight irritation)

Five-sense perception — Internally generated sense perceptions of smell, taste, sight, touch, and hearing (e.g., scents, flavors, images, textures, sounds)

Movement — Gross motor movements (e.g., postural changes, gestures, facial expressions) and micromovements (e.g., trembling, the pounding of the heart)

Body Sensation — The physical feelings (e.g., tingling, vibrating, shivery, dull) created as the various systems of the body monitor and provide feedback about inner states

Figure 5.1. The Five Building Blocks of Present-Moment Experience (figure design by Anne Westcott)

DIRECTED MINDFULNESS

Unrestricted mindfulness toward any and all of the five building blocks may be disturbing and overwhelming to children, often proving problematic, as judgment, self-criticism, and further dysregulation may arise. To help prevent this, the Sensorimotor Psychotherapy approach employs mindfulness in a very specific way, termed "directed mindfulness," which entails carefully and firmly directing the patient's mindful attention toward one or more of the five building blocks considered important to therapeutic goals (Ogden 2007; 2009; 2014). Ogden and Fisher (2015) state, "Critical to [the therapeutic] process is the therapist's purposeful influence on clients to attend to specific elements of their internal experience. Instead of allowing clients' attention to drift randomly toward whatever emotions, memories, thoughts, movements or sensations they might be drawn to, therapists purposefully use 'directed mindfulness' to guide the patient's awareness toward particular elements of internal experience" (42).

Children can be triggered by reminders of past trauma or attachment failures such as intrusive images, smells, sounds, disturbing body sensations, or movements. Andy, age twelve, a victim of physical abuse and witness to domestic violence (described in detail later in the chapter), stated, "I know I'm not a bad person, but my anger takes over, running through my body, and I feel myself shaking with rage." Directed mindfulness was used to advantage when Andy's overwhelming anger emerged during the session. His therapist directed his mindful attention to the sensation in his legs, in order to support a sense of grounding in the present moment. Fostering Andy's awareness of this somatic resource enhanced his ability to self-regulate and provided a tool he could use in subsequent bouts of rage.

THERAPEUTIC SKILLS THAT FOSTER EMBEDDED RELATIONAL MINDFULNESS IN CHILD TREATMENT

To explore our clients' present-moment experience, Sensorimotor Psychotherapy employs a set of specific therapeutic skills (Kurtz 1990; Ogden, Minton, and Pain 2006). These skills are as follows:

Track

Close observation of the fluctuation of the five building blocks is one of several foundational skills of Embedded Relational Mindfulness. Tracking entails noticing the child's unfolding experience of body sensations, movements, five-sense perceptions, emotions, and thoughts in response to particular stimuli, such as a description of past trauma or current difficulty, or to a particular intervention. The clinician is watchful for changes in sensation (like blushing), internally generated perceptions (verbal description of images, smells, tastes, sounds), shifts in movement (facial expression, posture, or gesture), emerging emotions (tearfulness or a change in the child's prosody), or beliefs and cognitive distortions that emerge as children describe their experience. The relationship among the building blocks is noticed. For example, the thought "I'm a terrible person" may be expressed as a child reports the image of his father's angry face arising when he thinks of a time when he accidently offended his dad. At the same time, feelings of sadness and hopelessness may be reflected in the child's slumped-over body and sad facial expression.

Contact Statement

The second skill of Embedded Relational Mindfulness is for the therapist to name what has been noticed through a "contact statement." Since the building blocks often occur outside of awareness, these present-moment experiences are often unnoticed by the child until the therapist brings attention to them. Examples of contact statements are "As you see your father's angry face, your posture seems to slump" or "You seem to feel helpless right now." Contact statements should convey empathic understanding of the child's experience (Kurtz 1990; Ogden et al. 2006). Thus it is not only the words therapists say but also the nonverbal body language, affect, and prosody that communicate understanding, and therefore promote a sense of safety and foster engagement.

Contact statements that communicate that the therapist understands the child's narrative ("That must have been so hard for you"), used across all therapies, are critical to convey that the therapist is following the details of the child's story. But to evoke mindfulness, the therapist must also provide contact statements reflecting present moment *experience*. Only reflecting the narrative suggests that the verbal story, rather than present-moment experience, is of greatest import, fueling continued conversation; however, contacting present experience—essential in Sensorimotor Psychotherapy—teaches the child mindfulness—to pay attention to the here-and-how fluctuation of the five building blocks.

Frame

Highlighting here-and-now experience paves the way to define or "frame" the focus of mindful attention. The therapist and our younger clients collaborate to determine what to explore, which establishes a certain direction for the session in general—whether to start by exploring the present-moment experience, or instead explore resources such as relaxation, a sense of joy, a "positive" cognition, or a peaceful image.

For example, as the child discusses an image or memory, the therapist may track and contact shifts that arise ("It seems you tighten your shoulders when you talk about this memory"). Suggestions such as "Let's find out more about that slump in your posture" become the frame. If the child nods or agrees, his or her posture then becomes the focus of mindful attention.

Mindfulness Questions

Mindfulness questions are asked only after the therapist tracks, contacts, and frames collaboratively with the child or adolescent. For example, if tension in the arms is contacted and framed, mindfulness questions might be "As you sense that tension, can you tell if it is pulling up, or in, or forward? Is it the same in both of your arms and hands?" Alternatively, thoughts can provide abundant opportunities for mindfulness questions. For example, if the thought "I know I'm not my father, and I can control my anger and I'm not going to hurt anyone" arises, the induction to mindfulness might be "Stay with that thought . . . 'I know that I'm not going to hurt anyone; I can control my anger'—what emotions or body changes do you notice?"

Experiments

Therapeutic experiments are conducted to make discoveries about the client's internal organization of experience. For example, a therapist might say, "Repeat the words 'I can control my anger' in your mind, and let's notice what happens—what images, body sensation, or emotions come up by themselves?" This fosters awareness of the spontaneous emergence of the building blocks in response to a particular stimulus (e.g., the thought "I can control my anger"). Any one of the building blocks can be used as an experiment ("What happens when you make that movement? When you see the image of your father's angry face? When you feel sad?"). The phrase "What happens when . . . ?" is used to set up the experiment and instructs the client to observe the effect of the experiment on body and mind: how he or she organizes internally in response to the experiment. Therapeutic experiments stimulate curiosity by inviting exploration and discovery without investment in a specific outcome, an attitude that renders "right" and "wrong" irrelevant because whatever the client experiences is grist for the therapeutic mill.

CASE EXAMPLE: ANDY

In this section we will illustrate Embedded Relational Mindfulness skills in the treatment of twelve-year-old Andy, a victim of physical abuse and witness to domestic abuse. Sensorimotor Psychotherapy follows a phase-oriented treatment approach, identified by Janet (1898) as having three phases: symptom reduction and stabilization, treatment of traumatic memory, and personality integration and rehabilitation, all of which will be briefly illustrated. Andy gets angry in ways that are similar to his father, and currently his escalating anger is overwhelming to him and results in a cascade of disruptive, dysregulated behaviors.

Andy's unbridled anger was hurtful with his friends, his teachers, his basketball coach, and his mother and repeatedly landed him in the principal's office at school, after which he was referred to therapy. He said he wanted to control what he called "the monster in the box."

The first essential step in helping Andy become mindful was to track and contact his present-moment experience. To do this, the clinician might point out, "You seem to be feeling upset right now as you talk about it. It looks like you've stopped breathing," and "You're getting more tense, huh?" These statements naturally bring the child's attention to his here-and-now experience of the building blocks.

After tracking and contacting present experience, the therapist suggested a frame for their first session by saying, "Let's explore this part of you that gets so angry—what you call 'the monster in the box,'" with the intention of helping Andy learn self-regulating skills that would meet the goal of stabilization for phase-one treatment. Andy agreed, saying that ever since one of his dad's rageful evenings he'd been working hard to keep "the monster in the box." He told his mother, "I'm not going to ever be like Dad."

Andy's therapist turned this statement into an experiment, asking him to repeat the words and see whether his body or feelings were affected. This experiment brought tears, which Andy wiped away saying, in an angry voice, that he had not been able to stop himself from being like his dad.

More contact statements with present-moment building blocks, such as "You're in a lot of pain," "You sound a bit angry," and "Your body seems to be curling up," helped Andy become mindful of both his emotions and his body. He seemed to visibly grow smaller, curled up even more, hunched his shoulders, and balled his fists tightly. The thread of meaning making was heard in Andy's words ("I am a monster") and his prosody (said in a self-deprecating but angry manner). Tracking and making contact statements with specific elements of Andy's present experience ("You feel bad about yourself, huh?") eventually led to deeper meaning as Andy said, "I am a bad person like my father." A few minutes later, his therapist tracked and contacted that Andy's legs were shaking ("I notice your legs are shaking"), which helped Andy identify that he was feeling very angry. Collaboratively refining the frame ("Let's focus on how his anger lives in your body") was followed by directed mindfulness questions: "What happens when you sense that feeling in your legs? Can you describe that shaking? Do you feel it equally in both legs?"

As Andy turned his attention to his legs, his therapist tracked that the shaking increased and his agitation escalated. Realizing that this was an opportunity to teach Andy a body-based skill, or somatic resource, to regulate his anger, she refined the frame further by gently redirecting Andy to an experiment ("Let's find out what happens when you press your feet into the floor"). Andy sat up taller as he followed her suggestion. After a few minutes of pushing his feet into the floor, he said that he felt his anger washing away, with an accompanying hand gesture of waving and the sound of swooshing. This taught Andy a somatic resource to help him regulate his anger, and his therapist encouraged him to practice pushing his feet into the floor at home, with and without shoes, and discover which he liked better. Andy liked without shoes best, and he was able to utilize this resource to help him control his anger.

Initially, Andy was not interested in addressing the memories of his father's ranting, raving, violent behavior. Yet, as trust developed with his therapist, he shared a forgotten incident, which enabled phase-two treatment of resolving traumatic memory. He recalled a time that he reached out for help, dialing 911 and then quickly hanging up (unaware that if one dials 911, the response team will trace the call and visit the caller). Andy remembered his father's submissive behavior toward the police, but he also recalled the violent rage, depicted in his eyes, as they bore down on Andy in the presence of the police. He remembered feeling both terrified and empowered by his calling 911—even though he had hung up moments after dialing.

As he remembered this incident, his therapist tracked that his posture shifted: he sat up tall, head held high. He was unaware of these shifts in posture until she named, or contacted, them by saying, "As you remember this incident you seem to straighten up." Andy became curious and sat up even taller. His therapist, capitalizing on this opportunity to use his aligned posture to mitigate Andy's self-deprecating meaning making, turned this action into an experiment ("Notice what happens when you sit tall—what happens in your body, or how do your emotions or thoughts change?"). Andy reported feeling strong, a calm yet powerful feeling, generated from his own shifts in posture. With a little smile, he said tentatively that he felt good about himself.

Later in therapy, as phase-two treatment continued, Andy recalled a particularly difficult evening when he had watched his dad hit his mother and storm out of their home. Tracking and contacting Andy's hands growing tense and his fists curling into a ball evoked his curiosity about this physical response that he was unaware of prior to his therapist pointing it out. Therapist and client agreed that this tension would be the frame for the session. Using directed mindfulness questions targeted toward the frame ("What happens when you sense this tension? Is the tension in both arms

or hands equally? How is it pulling?") helped to shift the focus from the conversation about his father's violence and the upsetting memories that felt overwhelming to
specific here-and-now manifestations of his body's response during his recollections.

Directing Andy to sense, or become mindful of, the tension that was emerging
from within his body, all on its own, led to his fists tightening and untightening,
and he said, "I wanted to kill him" (his father). Recognizing the tension as indicative
of an instinctive defensive response (to fight), accompanied by anger, provided an
opportunity to mindfully explore Andy's physical impulses. Redirecting his attention
exclusively to his body, his therapist said, "Take your time; just sense your body."
Gentle suggestions such as "Let's put the image of your father aside for now and just
follow what your body wants to do" allowed Andy to become aware of the physical
impulses of wanting to hit out. As his therapist held a pillow so that Andy could
slowly execute a pushing motion, she asked him to describe how it felt, and he said,
"This feels good!"

Directing mindful attention to his body led to his rediscovery of powerful yet
regulated feelings and action, and the memory of prior times when he was able to
defend himself and protect his mother. It was important that Andy experience his
anger as regulated and powerful, rather than dysregulated and troublesome, as it had
been in his current interactions. In turn, his anger diminished, the meaning that
he had made about himself (that he was a "monster") dissipated, and his mother
reported that there was a marked improvement in behavior at home. Over time, his
teachers also reported dramatic reduction in interpersonal conflicts, as he seemed
better able to control his anger.

Phase-three treatment goals include increasing capacity for relationships with others and resolving attachment issues. Mindful exploration of relational tendencies can
be fostered with younger children through inviting them to explore the therapeutic
relationship itself. This can include the incorporation of proximity-seeking actions
(Ogden 2014).

Andy's therapist encouraged him to notice what happened inside his body when
he explored the proximity-seeking action of reaching out toward her. Note that Andy
was originally reluctant to come to therapy, initially refusing to get out of the car and
ranting and raging to his mother that he didn't want to talk to another person that
"she made him see." Andy had had a series of other therapeutic experiences, including one mandated by Child Protective Services following a physical altercation and
raging exchange between his parents.

The movement of reaching seemed to make him feel uncomfortable, and his
therapist suggested that instead of reaching toward her with his arm, he select one
of the beanie babies (small stuffed animals) and pass it to her. As Andy reached out,
a self-protective part seemed to emerge, and his action was inhibited (he started to
reach out with the beanie baby, and then abruptly stopped and looked away). He
reported that he didn't want to do the exercise.

Exploring actions that are alternatives to habitual action can bring forward parts
of the patient that are "inhospitable and even adversarial, sequestered from one

another as islands of 'truth,' each functioning as an insulated version of reality" (Bromberg 2010, 21). In Sensorimotor Psychotherapy, one aim is to illuminate these habitual actions, bringing them into awareness and tapping into the roots of familiar but problematic thoughts, feelings, and behaviors in order to support more adaptive actions in relationship.

Repeating the exercise, Andy seemed more hesitant as he started reaching out, abruptly stopping, ending the exercise, turning away, and sitting down. He avoided eye contact and his body appeared to be shrinking. His therapist, contacting these elements of his experience, then said, "Maybe I pushed you to do something that you didn't want to do." He nodded, but continued to avoid eye contact. His therapist then apologized for asking him to do something that he didn't want to do in the session and acknowledged the part of him that may be angry about it or that wanted to get up and leave. Andy smiled a bit, saying, "Yeah," but in that utterance there was a sigh of relief, as if had he discovered a new part of himself—the part that was learning self-regulation—as he didn't storm out.

Subsequently, he and his therapist were able to continue playing with possibilities of reaching out by first passing a smooth river rock selected from a basket of rocks back and forth, and then reaching out, hand extended, to his therapist. At one point he said he never had anyone to turn to for help with his dad, and he seemed sad. But he became more comfortable with the action (which acquired the meaning of reaching for help) and spontaneously maintained eye contact with his therapist. His posture gradually grew elongated, tall, and seemed to be empowering, and his therapist wondered out loud if this aligned posture could be translated into words. Andy said, "Usually, when I get angry, it's all a big mess." Eventually he recognized that he could get angry at his therapist or at others without the accompanying dysregulation or cascade of feelings that came out unbridled.

Through mindful exploration such as these described in phase-three therapy, Andy began to learn that it was possible to regulate his anger and stay in relationship, and that seeking connection, support, comfort, and help could be safe and nourishing.

CONCLUSION

Using Embedded Relational Mindfulness to foster present-moment awareness in a relational context is fundamental to collaborative therapy with our younger clients, prioritizing mindfulness over conversation. Using mindfulness of old implicit processing can then create new experiences. This helps change old patterns, as "the brain changes physically in response to experience, and new mental skills can be acquired with intentional effort with focused awareness and concentration" (Siegel 2010, 84).

The case study of Andy describes the skills of Embedded Relational Mindfulness and collaboration, foundational in addressing the procedural tendencies of body and mind that emerge spontaneously. As new ways of regulating and organizing experience were embodied, new opportunities emerged between therapist and client, between client and his mother, and with his schoolmates. While we were not aiming for Andy to never again get upset, as interpersonal emotional conflicts are inevitable for children of all ages, learning better ways to recognize, regulate, and channel his anger toward adaptive behavior became our collaborative goals.

Sensorimotor Psychotherapy (Ogden, Minton and Pain 2006; Ogden and Fisher 2015), conceptualizes Embedded Relational Mindfulness as an overarching approach that provide tools for working with our younger clients. Utilizing Embedded Relational Mindfulness invites curiosity and opens doors for entertaining new, more constructive possibilities. Moreover, since the consciousness of one overlaps with the consciousness of another, when the client's here-and-now experience changes toward more expansion, it activates a resonance of the same in the other. Therefore, the therapist is also changed in these moments of Embedded Relational Mindfulness.

BIBLIOGRAPHY

Bromberg, P. M. 2010. "Minding the Dissociative Gap." *Contemporary Psychoanalysis* 46 (1): 19–31.

Janet, P. 1898. *Neuroses et idées fixe.* Paris: Felix Alcan.

Kurtz, R. 1990. *Body-Centered Psychotherapy: The Hakomi Method.* Mendocino, CA: LifeRhythm.

———. 2004. *Level 1 Handbook for the Refined Hakomi Method.* Retrieved January 4, 2012, from http://hakomi.com/.

Mark-Goldstein, B., and P. Ogden. 2013. "Sensorimotor Psychotherapy as a Foundation of Group Therapy with Younger Clients." In *The Interpersonal Neurobiology of Group Psychotherapy and Group Process*, edited by S. P. Gantt and B. Badenoch, 123–45. London: Karnac Books.

Ogden, P. 2007. "Beyond Words: A Clinical Map for Using Mindfulness of the Body and the Organization of Experience in Trauma Treatment." Paper presented at Mindfulness and Psychotherapy Conference, Los Angeles, CA: UCLA/Lifespan Learning Institute.

———. 2009. "Emotion, Mindfulness and Movement: Expanding the Regulatory Boundaries of the Window of Tolerance." In *The Healing Power of Emotion: Perspectives from Affective Neuroscience and Clinical Practice*, edited by D. Fosha, D. Siegel, and M. Solomon. New York: W. W. Norton.

———. 2014. "Embedded Relational Mindfulness: A Sensorimotor Psychotherapy Perspective on the Treatment of Trauma." In *Mindfulness-Oriented Interventions for Trauma: Integrating Contemplative Practices*, edited by V. Folette, J. Briere, D. Rozelle, J. Hopper, and D. Rome, 227–39. New York: Guilford Press.

Ogden, P., and J. Fisher. 2015 *Sensorimotor Psychotherapy: Interventions for Trauma and Attachment.* New York: W. W. Norton.

Ogden, P., B. Goldstein, and J. Fisher. 2012. "Brain-to-Brain, Body-to-Body: A Sensorimotor Psychotherapy Approach for the Treatment of Children and Adolescents." In *Current Perspectives and Applications in Neurobiology: Working with Young Persons Who Are Victims and Perpetrators of Sexual Abuse*, edited by R. Longo, D. Prescott, J. Bergman, and K. Creeden, 229–55. London: Karnac Books.

Ogden, P., and K. Minton. 2000. "Sensorimotor Psychotherapy: One Method for Processing Traumatic Memory." *Traumatology* 6: 1–20.

Ogden, P., K. Minton, and C. Pain. 2006. *Trauma and the Body: A Sensorimotor Approach to Psychotherapy.* New York: W. W. Norton.

Siegel, D. 2010. *The Mindful Therapist: A Clinician's Guide to Mindsight and Neural Integration.* New York: W. W. Norton.

Williams, M., J. Teasdale, Z. Segal, and J. Kabat-Zinn. 2007. *The Mindful Way through Depression: Freeing Yourself from Chronic Unhappiness.* New York: Guilford Press.

6

Delight in Me

Repair of Developmental Trauma and the Birth of the Self

Kenny E. Miller

There is no such thing as a baby . . . there is a baby and someone.

—D. W. Winnicott

The first part of my initial session with the Jackson family was done. I had just met with the grandfather of twin thirteen-year-old boys from a small rural community outside Tucson. The social history and current struggles of his grandsons were recorded, and I walked the sixty-two-year-old railroad mechanic turned second-time-around father back to the waiting room. This history included having the boys literally dropped off at his doorstep when they were five, and their substance-abusing mother, his daughter, could no longer even attempt to care for them.

"Come on back, you guys. Do you like to build things with Legos?" I said to both Joshua and Jamie as they entered my office. "Oh, yeah, I'm very good at building," said Josh. "Take a look at the different trays and choose the ones that seem best to you," I responded. Now the Legos in my office are intentionally offered in open trays and baskets, and they range from the two-inch, "chunk-style" Legos for preschool children all the way up to the "how do they mold plastic in such tiny pieces?" Legos, which are designed for the young teenage crowd. Without hesitation, both Joshua and Jamie went straight to the two-inch "chunk-style" Legos, brought the basket containing them to the floor, and then sat together and began building a structure. They talked easily and happily to each other about it. The discrepancy between their chronological age and the intended age of the toys that they had chosen was dramatic. They showed great pleasure in their building.

As I reflected on this and numerous experiences in my work as a mental health consultant for Early Head Start Programs, an underlying truth began to emerge, and it was a truth that seemed to offer a hidden power. Despite a catastrophic environment of early care giving, the bodies of these young teens had perfectly preserved the availability of the original fuel of child development: shared pleasure and sensory joy. As is often the case for caregivers, their grandparents had become very frustrated with their inability to make a difference. My mechanic-grandfather had expressed enormous concern at the apparent destructiveness of his grandsons: when given age-appropriate toys, they would often promptly be destroyed within days, if not hours, of reaching the boys' hands. The unmet developmental needs of these boys were sabotaging the efforts of important people, preventing them from offering support that could make a critical difference. I could not help but imagine the potential for change if this fit between need and environment could be fine-tuned.

A VIEW FROM OBJECT RELATIONS

This chapter seeks to offer an object relations perspective on attachment and developmental trauma disorders in children. Object relations theory provides a unique lens for understanding the often confounding behaviors of these children, as well as a template to organize intervention and treatment. The work offered here, due to limitation of space, focuses only on understanding the child through this lens, and on several of the interventions that target the first, the second, and the third to fifth years of life. The work shared here is taken from the author's comprehensive therapeutic model, which I have created and named Developmental Attachment-Based Psychotherapy (DABP©). The full model also includes an understanding of caregivers and parents through a similar attachment-based lens, and it offers specific interventions to support them in their work with the child.

This work focuses the lens through which we understand the origins of developmental trauma, and it defines these origins from the perspective known as object relations, a psychological theory we will learn more about. It concentrates initially on the release, in real time, of the child's inborn, instinctual, and deeply wired-in drive to make a connection, to attach. We have, until now, not understood this drive in the context of children with developmental trauma. We have lacked the keys to unlock the missed components of normal child development with this special population, and we have often been predominantly focused on the "lock" that trauma presents to new relationships. Another model with roots in object relations theory and also featured in this volume is that of Theraplay (Jernberg and Booth 1999), whose founders are grounded in the very same theory.

In the opening vignette we begin to see with both Joshua and Jamie the possibility of "shared sensory joy," a first-year-of-life experience for children. In a safe and structured environment, with an attuned and available caregiver, the long locked-away capacity of the body to respond with pleasure and delight to a missed developmental experience is observed. It is possibly being experienced for the very first time, the age of the client notwithstanding.

OBJECT RELATIONS: GETTING THE SAFETY INSIDE

Object relations theory, coming out of the psychoanalytic tradition, was the first comprehensive way of understanding the psychological journey of the early years of life, which all human beings pass through on the road to attempting to become a whole human being. A comprehensive road map for this journey was first provided by the theorist and researcher Margaret Mahler in the groundbreaking 1975 work, *The Psychological Birth of the Human Infant* (Mahler, Pine, and Bergman 1975). With this work, Mahler gave us the six stages of the birth of human identity and the self. The goal for the completion of this journey (which we can now understand is a lifelong project!) is a person fully capable of "autonomy within relatedness," as described by the researchers and clinicians with the Circle of Security project (Powell et al. 2014). These two poles define the human condition in both our attachment and our exploratory drives: deep belonging and embedded-ness with others, as well as sovereignty and the ability to pursue one's own unique agenda and gifts toward life.

Object relations theory, for all its helpfulness in navigating the earliest years of our emotional life, is often not an easy nut to crack when it comes to a clear understanding of what these theorists are talking about. For our purposes, I want to offer you the five-minute course in object relations theory. I will save you the hours I spent in graduate school, locked in the library, trying to understand what the heck these folks were talking about! Object relations can be most helpfully understood in the words of therapist, trainer, author, and adoptive mother Holly van Gulden: "What starts outside goes inside" (van Gulden and Sutton 2013).

Object relations theory says that the skills, the capacities, and the tools we need to grow in this life start outside of ourselves, and we put them inside of ourselves, and we do it through relationship. So in the beginning of life a parent is involved in doing for the child, and offering to the child, all the important skills we want children to have, such as calming and soothing, control of impulses, the experience of empathy, feeling treasured and valued, and the experience of being recognized as separate with feelings and needs of their own. When these skills are consistently available and offered to the child, throughout hundreds of such interactions in the first years of life, the child puts inside himself a mental image and representation of the parent. Out of these early interactions with caregivers we form our own identity. By the time the child reaches the age of four to five years, those things that the parent offered to them and did for them are now firmly locked inside the child and reliably available for the child to do *for herself.* What starts outside goes inside.

When we consider this journey of getting these early relationship skills inside the child, it is the sensory-based connection to the parent that offers the safety, comfort, and warmth that is most important. This connection itself provides fuel and energy for the child's development. It is this safety, comfort, and warmth, beginning with all of the sensory experiences of the caregiver, that becomes stored in the child's body in increasing amounts and stages. In the beginning of life, it is important to remember that we are all body. It is only through the portal of the five senses that children first come to know their caregiver, the world, and themselves. There are no higher cognitive buffers or interpretive skills; it is raw sensory data from which early learning about self and other are made.

STAGES FOR THE "SAFETY INSIDE"

We can see the stages in normal child development by which this sensory-based safety, comfort, and warmth become available to children and *are in fact the fuel and source for their growth.* These early stages offer important parallels for understanding the emotional world of self and other (caregiver) of the older children with whom we are concerned. From the very earliest hours of their life, as the work of T. Berry Brazelton (2005) has shown, children, when presented with two distinct speaking voices, will gradually turn and orient to the voice of the biological mother. From the womb there is a stored sensory connection and recognition of the mother.

By the age of seven months, as the child begins to push away from the body of the parent and crawl to explore the world, that child has enough "safety" stored inside to be on his own for several minutes before "checking back" and turning to locate the parent. It can be a couple of minutes before he needs a real-time sensory connection of seeing the parent. Upon getting this visual connection, "Life is good, let's get back to it, I can resume exploration!" For just another couple of minutes—and then: check back. If a child of seven months turns to locate the parent visually and the parent is not to be found, it's development endgame (for now): Pull the plug on that exploration, stop and cry to bring the parent, and reestablish connection.

I am reminded of my work with an eight-year-old girl who was adopted out of the domestic child welfare system at the age of four, following multiple placements and an early history that could only be called catastrophic. This child's struggles were intense at the beginning of her treatment. Indeed, she tried to crawl onto my lap in the very first session and showed little to no selective attachment. I knew that we had made substantial progress, however, when the child would be found right outside the bathroom door whenever the mother went in to use it. Her mom would indeed "disappear" behind the door. The child's constant presence just outside the door, even going so far as to knock and talk to attempt to engage her mother, initially drove her mother crazy and felt very intrusive. I was able to share with the mom that this behavior on the girl's part was clear evidence that she was now losing her sense of connection when the mom "disappeared" into the bathroom. This behavior was something that never happened in the beginning of our work together, and it was a clear marker of growth and success. Object relations theory in action: out of sight is out of *existence* in the beginning of life.

I have come to understand that perhaps the strongest challenge to teaching and truly internalizing this model is a good one, in that, thankfully, most of our own (but not all) early histories have given us a reasonable strength of object constancy. This makes wrapping our mind around the concept of not having these early skills a challenge. It is implicit for us, and by design we are supposed to take these skills for granted. Like the operating system of a computer, they are out of sight and in the background, but powerfully executing important behavioral decisions where our relationships are concerned.

Now let's go a little farther down the developmental road and imagine another ten months of interactions with the caregiver that continue to store safety, comfort, and warmth inside the body of our now seventeen-month-old toddler. Our toddler now reaches a huge milestone of development: There is enough safety, comfort, and warmth internalized that an object, a symbol, a stand-in for the real-time sensory connection of the parent becomes available for the child to accomplish the feeling of safety. And now we find the constant companion of the toddler: the blankie! The blankie, whose soft cloth rubbed against the face of our toddler, is now able to evoke the stored sensory-based memory of the parent's safety, comfort, and warmth. And the child can now take the blankie, roam all over the house, and stay away from the parent for many minutes of independent exploration before returning to refuel. Look how the child's world has expanded in this new stage! A concrete object is now available as a stand-in, a "portable parent" that can accomplish what at seven months only immediate, real-time sensory connection to the parent could accomplish. At seven months of age, there is no stand-in that will work; it has to be the parent in the flesh to offer the sensory connection. The use of a "transitional object" to evoke the safety of the connection to a caregiver is a powerful therapeutic intervention for the older child, as we will see.

The last marker on the road to the milestone of "object constancy," or having the sensory-based connection of safety, comfort, and warmth of the caregiver now locked inside, is found predominantly in the fourth and fifth year of life, which we call "partnered learning" and also "perspective taking." At this age there is enough of an emerging sense of self-as-separate-yet-connected to truly have a collaboration of plans and agendas between parent and child. As the child, I now have enough of my own distinct identity available to allow a beginning consideration of my parent as separate with feelings and needs of her own. As an egocentric toddler, I could not do that. It was all about me, all the time! As a toddler, I might be coaxed to comply, but I am not capable of true shared planning and collaboration where the agenda of each partner is considered and a plan decided upon.

THE HALLMARK OF OBJECT CONSTANCY

By the age of five years (or so) the child has consolidated inside him- or herself what I refer to as a "container" of safety. This is the milestone that we refer to as object constancy (Mahler, Pine, and Bergman 1975), and it is the defining psychological hallmark of development from this perspective. For it is at this point, and not before, that the child will have reliably available those capacities that our own experience wants to assume that human beings possess—skills such as empathy, conscience, ownership of wrongdoing, self-soothing and regulation, the respect of boundaries for other's belongings, and so on.

The metaphor of "container" is particularly helpful for understanding what is in fact an incredibly complex and in many ways still mysterious phenomenon: the cocreation of a unique and separate identity for the child out of the parent-and-child interactions. "Good enough" (Winnicott 1964) parents provide "containment" for the child's emotions in the first years of life. This containment gives boundaries and limits and organizes those emotions. As children grow and increasingly internalize this containment, they become able to separate feelings from self, and the beginning of the all-important "reflective space" is created.

Children who are victims of developmental trauma have been left alone in the earliest years of their life, often by intimate caregivers, and/or they may have been hurt by those same or other caregivers. What has confounded those of us who aim to help them is often this: the body of the child keeps growing, the mind and intelligence often keep growing, yet the internal working model of self and other needs a relationship, an attuned relationship that is "bigger, stronger, kind and wise" in the words of John Bowlby (1988) to grow. When this relationship is never outside, or outside in very limited and intermittent forms, then it is impossible to grow those capacities, and the "container of safety," inside.

SYMPTOMS VIEWED AS MISSING DEVELOPMENTAL SKILLS

Having access to the developmental understanding that an object relations perspective provides, we can make direct sense of the confounding, disruptive, and often disturbing behaviors that are common "symptoms" of developmental trauma disorders in children. These symptoms can now become, in fact, clear markers of what developmental skills the child is missing, and pointers to where on the continuum of attachment the child has experienced deficits that now need strengthening.

It was training with Holly van Gulden, the author and clinician mentioned earlier, that provided two life-changing moments for me and my own attachment journey to wholeness as a person and clinician. The first of these was her creation of the phrase "What starts outside goes inside" in reference to understanding the frequently impenetrable object relations theory! The second of these moments came in listening to Holly express the concept that virtually all of the behaviors that have characterized reactive attachment disorder in older children are *normal behaviors under the age of four*, which young children use to cope with situations of stress and frustration. These behaviors of early childhood are a direct expression of where the child is on Mahler's continuum for separation-individuation between self and caregiver. And so it is for our older children with attachment disorders, often left alone in the earliest years of life with quite overwhelming experiences.

To make this understanding come alive, I would like to look at three of the most challenging behaviors found in children with attachment difficulties and understand them through this developmental lens. We will begin with lying. For the older child with attachment difficulties, this lying is done with depth, with a complete charismatic conviction, and is often the only time the child will gaze directly into the eyes of the caregiver/parent! We have come to call it "crazy lying" because such is the intensity and conviction of the child that parents often doubt themselves, questioning their own sense of reality, often wondering, "Am I going crazy? I thought I saw him take that food!"

Let's travel now in our imagination to the home of a well-attached, developmentally intact, treasured, and adored three-year-old child, whom the mother finds in the kitchen of the home. In the kitchen the mother discovers her precious darling with her hand in a jar of cookies, as well as the presence of cookie crumbs strung from mouth to clothing to floor. Confronting the child, the mother will say, "Darling, what are you doing eating those cookies?" At which time the three-year-old child will turn, stare directly into the eyes of her mom, and say with complete belief and passion, "What cookies? I'm not eating cookies. Mr. Alligator ate these cookies, I'm sorry you missed him, he said to say hello, but it wasn't me!" And the three-year-old child engages in this normal developmental "lying" because she is not sure the anger her mother feels toward her for breaking a rule will turn out well for her!

A mother's anger toward her three-year-old child threatens at a minimum the loss of connection to the mother, and that has survival implications for a child this young. So the child gives reality a spin to hold on to her own safety in the world, to stay connected to the parent. She believes it with all her heart, she needs to believe it with all her heart, and she puts everything into making the mother believe it, because her survival depends on it from within the limited container of safety she has at this point on her journey. At five years old it will be easier to admit, and at seven years old it may become reliable, depending upon the strength and security of the attachment. We wouldn't normally think of a three-year-old as "choosing" to lie, because we have instinctive empathy for their emotional vulnerability. Yet, when confronted with a ten-year-old child who has been saddled with a history of multiple placements, and a history of very limited "safety outside themselves," we often conclude that her lying is a "manipulative" choice on her part. This extremely common "negative attribution" on the part of caregivers often serves to seriously erode the reservoir of good feelings toward the child.

Our second symptom is an often complete lack of empathy, minimal conscience, as well as the intentional hurting of others. These are the behaviors that raise our deepest concern and fear, both for and sometimes of the child. Consider this normal boundary negotiation for an eighteen-month-old child: If you take my toy, I hurt you! Swiftly, immediately, and often with the full force of my being! "You bet I hit him, he deserved it, he took my toy" would be the child's response. So what can appear to the world as sociopathic behavior in an older child of ten or twelve years of age chronologically can be understood through our object relations lens as having the safety inside—the emotional sense of self and other available under stress—of a much younger child. Especially under the stressor of having something taken away or the anger of not getting something that is desired. From the inside out, what coping skills do these children have available when under stress? It is the self and object representation that organizes the emotional response to the caregiver and to the child's peers. The challenge becomes the perceived capacities an older child would and should have available, if not for a history of developmental trauma.

The third behavior to understand through our developmental lens is the equally pervasive and equally disruptive behavior of stealing. Stealing relates directly again to the child's point of development on the separation-individuation continuum, as described by Mahler (Mahler, Pine, and Bergman 1975). The boundary of yours-versus-mine, which plays out in the practical and real worlds, comes directly out of the sense of a separateness and identity for self and other in the psychological world. Before the ages of four to six years, this boundary is very fluid; the self of parent and of child is not yet distinct in the child's mind. The language we use in therapy to express the younger part's perspective is "I see it, I want it, I take it, mine!" and that is the thought process of the young child. There is an older, age-appropriate part also inside the child that knows things that a child of this chronological age knows about the world, rules, and so on. It is the younger part, however, that carries the day under the "stressor" of seeing something desirable. The older part at that moment is not "on line" and is nowhere in consciousness to be found.

The behavior of stealing can be used to illustrate a larger difficulty with holding to this view of understanding these behaviors across the whole range of symptoms. There may be times, many times in fact, when these children can behave in age-appropriate ways and nail it in terms of caregivers' expectations. This has contributed strongly to the conclusion that when they are not responding to the world with age-appropriate skills, they are *choosing* not to, that their behavior is a choice. And this view leads straight to the word that so often accompanies descriptions of their behavior: manipulative! From an object relations perspective, if I am feeling safe and connected to my caregiver, I am calm, regulated, and able to act from my neocortex, where my age-appropriate knowledge of the world is stored. Under stress, when challenged, I lose that connection of safety, drop down through the midbrain, and end up in brainstem/fight-or-flight. *It is from this place of loss of safety and fight or flight that the coping skills of birth to four in older children are found.*

It is important to remember that in early childhood this sensory-based connection of safety to the caregiver can be an actual moment-to-moment affair, by virtue of the limited container of safety available. We can now say with certainty that children with catastrophic early histories, by definition, are not "choosing" the things they do. The word "manipulative" implies too much volition, as if there were truly another alternative they could use and don't. From a developmental perspective, if the capacity is available and on line at the time, then the child is going to use it; it's what is there. Only a child with good object constancy, with the "reflective space" that comes with this milestone, has a "choice" that is truly available and able to be considered.

GROWING JOSHUA'S SKILLS: THE RAILROAD MECHANIC (GRANDPA) BECOMES AN ANCHOR OF SAFETY

It is the continuing ability of the child's body to awaken to unmet developmental needs, despite chronological age and trauma history, that becomes the cornerstone for leveraging change. We can make available for these children the same sensory-based connections of safety, comfort, and warmth that they missed and that become, as it is for normal child development, the fuel for their growth. Understanding from our object relation's perspective the child's available relationship skills, we can offer parenting that goes around the defensive structures that age-appropriate parenting inevitably evokes.

Over years of trying, testing, and teaching these ideas, I have come to a formulation that simplifies the model into interventions that target the first year of life, those that focus on the second year, and those focused around the third to fifth years of life. Our model assumes, and practice has proved, that it is possible to "drop down" into the larger pool of unmet needs from each of these stages in the child's development and use interventions that target a particular stage, depending upon the challenge and stressor that is activated for the child.

Let's dive into the work that was tried for Joshua and see how this played itself out. We will call the grandfather Joseph, who, for all the gruff, masculine, and hard-working demeanor that he carried outwardly, was inwardly like a big, sweet teddy bear! He would often come to sessions with his hands in that "never really clean" state that working with grease and oil will produce. He worked hard physically for a living; however, he had an extremely soft and sensitive heart where his grandsons were concerned.

THE FIRST YEAR OF LIFE

We are going to concentrate for limitations of space on the relationship between Grandpa and Joshua. For Joshua, the work began in teaching his grandfather about "pleasure instead of praise." In this model of support, as it is in growing attachment with infants, it is the seemingly small things, many times each day, happening over and over, where the relationship is built and strengthened. It is reflexive for us to praise children when they get something right. Praise for a child who has a conviction of worthlessness at the core of their being presents some problems—three specifically. For one, it is easily defended against. Quite simply, they don't believe it's possible. Second, the credibility of the caregiver, whom we want to match outside with inside, goes down. Third, and the real kicker: now from outside the child comes a belief of goodness, while inside lives the belief of worthlessness. We are all wired to create congruence between what's inside and what's outside. Heaping praise on a child with developmental trauma will often have the effect of the child then acting out at the level of negative behavior that matches the level of praise. A whopping dose of praise will get you a whopping level of acting out! This serves to get the inside and outside balanced again. "I'll show you what's really true about me," to put words to the unconsciously driven behaviors.

I taught the grandfather to use an "I statement" of his delight in Josh's behavior, instead of praise: "I just love the way you got right onto your homework"; "I was delighted when you made the bus on time for school today." With "I statements" of the grandfather's delight, there is nothing for Josh to do but take that pleasure straight inside; no defenses get activated as they do for praise. "Someone enjoys me in the world, shared joy, first year of life!" I taught Grandpa to notice Joshua's affect when he did this, watch for the light in his eyes to see it work. Multiple times a day there is the opportunity to offer this connection of pleasure to the child. It is seemingly a small thing, but it is inwardly transforming of the relationship and self.

Both hide and seek and "the lumps game" would regularly light up Joshua's face with delight. The lumps game is often done first thing in the morning, the child hiding under the bedcovers. Josh's grandpa would ask, "What's that lump on the bed, did I leave my laundry on the bed?" Poke, poke, giggle, and giggle. "No, it's too hard to be just laundry" and several other ideas would be offered before Grandpa pulled back the sheet and exclaimed, "It's Joshua under that sheet!" Finishing an office session with a game of hide and seek was extremely popular, and scheduled at the end of the day when office mates have gone home and left their empty offices for hiding!

One of the most helpful first-year interventions for Joshua was the "bridge of relationship" for negotiating transitions. This technique dramatically reduces the oppositional behaviors commonly found around times of transition; behaviors that come straight out of the birth-to-four playbook of self and other. Consider a normal two-and-a-half-year-old child, sitting and watching TV about fifteen feet from the parent. Do you say, "Turn off the TV and come to dinner, honey"? You will surely have a meltdown if you persist with that expectation! Rather, we come up beside the child, offering proximity. Next we touch them on the shoulder, offering further connection, and then we turn off the TV. With this level of connection, the child gets happily up to come with us, the bridge of relationship carrying them across the transition. There is, in this simple interaction, great wisdom for our work!

Both morning and evening routines for Joshua were transformed and oppositional behavior reduced by teaching Grandpa the components of the "bridge of relationship." These are proximity, touch, and language, or PTL for short. First, offer proximity. Come preferably beside, and not in front of Joshua. Second, touch Joshua on the shoulder and then say, "It's time for *us* to get ready for bed," or "*We* need to get ready for school." Proximity of physical closeness, touch, and language that offers connection and a shared identity instead of a separate self will dramatically change the child's ability to respond with compliance. In his recent work on the polyvagal theory, Stephen Porges (2011) teaches us the power of body position, body language, and tone of voice to either access the child's social engagement system (and thus decrease the threat) or activate a fight, flight, or freeze response. It is an often completely hidden freeze response that is frequently mistaken for oppositional behavior in these children.

THE SECOND YEAR OF LIFE

There are three main interventions used to teach relationship skills from the second year of life. These are the "limit sandwich" of interactive repair; "parts work," which targets constancy of self and caregiver; and the use of transitional objects to evoke the connection of safety when the child must be away from the caregiver. Of these three, interactive repair has the most opportunity for use, and the most far-reaching impact.

Interactive repair for Grandpa and Joshua worked like this: Whenever Joshua does something wrong, has a meltdown, or there is an angry exchange, the connection of safety to Grandpa is broken. One of the things Joshua struggled with was taking things from his brother's room. For Grandpa, the key was to intervene in the middle of the disturbance between the two boys only to break it up and end the confrontation, not to discuss "consequences" or resolve the issue in a final way.

When Joshua is calm and his state of mind more peaceful, then age-appropriate parts are on line and available to take in the repair with Grandpa. The repair consists of the "limit sandwich" that Grandpa will offer him. The sandwich begins with a statement of valuing the child. Some form of pleasure in the child is the deepest version of this. Something good they have done, some quality appreciated; it doesn't matter what, but it must express Josh's value to Grandpa. Concrete details and not abstract qualities are preferred! Let's use the following as an example: "Josh, I saw the grade that you brought home on your math test, and I was so proud of you." This statement of value and pleasure is followed by the word "and" and *never* "but." "*And* I want to talk to you about the plane you took from Jamie's room last night. In this family we do not take things that don't belong to us without asking; it's not respectful of Jamie to do so." This offers Joshua the limit we want him to learn. The statement of limit is then followed by another statement of value: "And I can't wait to see what you're cooking for dinner tonight; I really enjoyed those eggs you made."

The "limit sandwich" of value + limit + value accomplishes something transformative for Joshua. For children with a first-year-of-life experience that put no delight, treasuring, and value inside, the break in the relationship with the caregiver clears the decks; it takes them all the way back to a condition of worthlessness, of absolute loss of the value in their existence. From this position of being overwhelmed, it is impossible to hold on to anything that comes after. This is what makes consequences so ineffective for these children, when not delivered with a mind to first restoring the child's value and worth to the caregiver. Delivering an affirmation of pleasure, delight, and value (first year of life) makes possible the taking in of the limit (second year of life). And it is indeed not just words but also the affect to match, which the parent will need to project with body language, tone of voice, and body position playing an important role in minimizing the child's defenses.

So Joshua, though he had spent the previous eight years in the safe and structured environment of the grandfather's home, had in fact not been offered attachment-based parenting that he needed to "take inside" and grow himself. As a result, he presented with the profound challenges of developmental trauma, and the severe social-emotional delays that often present in this disorder.

Parts work and transitional objects (van Gulden and Sutton 2013) are the last interventions that we will look at for Joshua. Like many children with developmental trauma, Joshua was seldom able to do well at both home and school at the same time. It was one or the other; take your pick! Joshua struggled at school, as is typically the case, when he was "between the lines" of his daily structure. On the playground, in line for lunch, wherever there was "transitional space" that was not structured, he would struggle. To help Joshua with this, we used a transitional object to connect him to his grandpa when he was away at school. The first form this took was a set of dog tags that we had made especially for Joshua, and that he could wear around his neck while he was at school. These dog tags used a special process to etch into the metal a picture of Joshua and his grandpa, side by side, with big smiles on their faces.

The second form of transitional object we used for school was actually a daily phone call, scheduled and set up with the counselor at school, for Joshua to talk to and hear the voice of his grandpa. This was scheduled for the time of day that Joshua would typically begin to struggle. These two interventions made a huge difference for Joshua in reducing his acting out behaviors at school. It is the sensory-based connection to the parent that gives the child the needed fuel when the container of safety is being strengthened. It is one of the deepest and most efficient ways to change behaviors, again, from the inside out.

Parts work was used to help Joshua with the behavior of stealing. As discussed in the section on symptoms, both an age-appropriate part of self and a younger part of self are identified for the child. At thirteen years of age, Joshua could reference the behavior of younger children, and in fact he had some younger cousins who were often around the house and who were known to occasionally take things from his room without permission! The trick for Joshua was in identifying correctly the age of his younger part.

Joshua wasn't buying the concept until I upped the age of his "younger part" to five years of age. Once he could own this younger part, we could work at teaching him, could draw posters depicting the younger and older parts of self with the language used by each: "I see it, I want it, I take it, mine!" for the younger. And the older part adds to this: "I ask for it, maybe I get it, maybe I don't." Grandpa could also reference these posters in a teaching mode. Grandpa could use interactive repair as well. Once he stopped being punished for this behavior—and who would punish a four-year-old for something normal?—then Joshua was quickly able to at least begin taking responsibility for having taken things. The shift to a relationship-focused teaching mode takes time, but changes are then truly lasting from the inside out, leveraged by the child's desire for the parent's approval and connection.

A TURNAROUND FOR JOSHUA

Over a twelve-month period, the work with Joshua and his grandfather effected significant change. At home and at school his behaviors dramatically improved, his relationship with Grandpa deepened greatly. A serious blow occurred for Joshua when his grandfather had a heart attack, nearly taking his only anchor of safety in the world! The grandfather survived, however, and the last I heard Joshua had graduated high school successfully and was holding down a job in their small town.

WHERE CAN WE GO FROM HERE?

Object relations theory makes clear much of what has been confounding about developmental trauma disorders in children. It shines a welcome light onto the inner experience of the child's self and caregiver. The continued availability of the traumatized body for shared sensory joy is tremendous! When caregiver intervention matches the inner structure of self and other the wired-in capacity for growth can be released. This understanding could shift the responses of the clinical and parenting world in significant ways concerning these children.

Understanding object relations also paradoxically sheds light on what is perhaps the biggest barrier to a shift in our understanding of these children: our own unconscious experience of these "skills" of early childhood, now stored in the "operating system" of our own implicit memory. *We project onto children what is true for us*: that *they* have an anchor of "safety-in-relationship" stored inside of them; that *they* are in fact separate and autonomous; that *they* can stop and think about their behaviors; we project those things that are true for us onto the older latency and teenage children with developmental trauma, when in fact those capacities are often not there at all, yet. They are waiting to be grown! Let us make the unconscious conscious, in the words of Carl Jung, a famous psychiatrist (1989), and strive for a more experience-near interpretation of their needs and of the interventions to support them.

BIBLIOGRAPHY

Bowlby, John. 1988. *A Secure Base: Parent-Child Attachment and Healthy Human Development.* London: Basic Books.

Brazelton, T. Berry. 2005. *The First Years Last Forever*. DVD. Directed by Rob Reiner. US: Parents Action for Children.

Jernberg, Ann M., and Phyllis B. Booth. 1999. *Theraplay*. Second edition. San Francisco: Jossey-Bass.

Jung, Carl. 1989. *Memories, Dreams, Reflections*. New York: Vintage.

Mahler, Margaret S., Fred Pine, and Anni Bergman. 1975. *The Psychological Birth of the Human Infant: Symbiosis and Individuation*. New York: Basic Books.

Porges, Stephen. 2011. *The Polyvagal Theory: Neurophysiological Foundations of Emotion, Attachment, Communication and Self-Regulation*. New York: W. W. Norton.

Powell, Bert, Glen Cooper, Kent Hoffman, and Bob Marvin. 2014. *The Circle of Security Intervention*. New York: Guilford Press.

Van Gulden, Holly, and Ann Sutton. 2013. *And You Are Still You: Developing and Maintaining a Stable Sense of Self*. Raleigh, NC: Lulu Publishing Services (Internet).

Winnicott, D. W. 1964. *The Child, the Family, and the Outside World*. London: Penguin.

7

Theraplay

Creating Felt Safety, Emotional Connection, and Social Joy in Relationships

Sandra Lindaman, Phyllis Booth, and Gloria M. Cockerill

She must come to see herself, reflected in the therapist's eyes, the image of herself both as lovable and fun to be with.

—Phyllis Booth, cocreator of Theraplay

Anna was placed in foster care at birth. By two months of age, she had endured multiple changes in placement and a hospitalization. At ten months of age, Anna was transported by adoption workers from her birth country to her adoptive parents, Jeff and Cindy. The sights and sounds of her world changed dramatically, adding to the transitions and adjustments she would have to make. Her early physical growth and cognitive development were normal. As a toddler, Anna had difficulty with the transition to day care; she became more demanding and sensitive to sensory and environmental stimuli. Her difficulties worsened after placement in a preschool that encouraged free choice and exploration. Anna's parents sought help from an occupational therapist, which took the form of verbal direction to "turn her motor down," with limited positive effects.

At the age of eight, Anna was very active, craved high levels of sensory input, and was easily overwhelmed and dysregulated by her experiences. She was highly anxious when alone and sought frequent reassurance. She slept poorly. She sucked her thumb vigorously, and she sometimes soothed herself by masturbating. Jeff and Cindy described her as "clingy and whiny" and stated that they avoided any action that might trigger a tantrum. Anna engaged in a great deal of imaginary play with her mother but dictated all aspects of the play. Her mother felt that they could only engage if they took imaginary roles and that she did not have a "real" relationship with her daughter. Overall, Anna had been successful in school, reading several levels above her grade. In the months prior to Theraplay treatment, Anna spoke more about being adopted; her dysregulation, controlling behaviors, and separation anxiety escalated; and her academic progress began to decline.

As therapists planning treatment for Anna's relational trauma and its impact on her adoptive family, we asked ourselves: What is the underlying meaning of Anna's difficult behaviors and how can we best help the family? Could we help her parents become confident guides and sources of comfort so that Anna does not have to rely on her own strategies for survival and soothing? How can we help Anna and her parents experience a relationship that is present-focused, interpersonal, joyful, and genuine? Theraplay's responses to these questions will be addressed in this chapter.

DESCRIPTION OF THERAPLAY

Theraplay is modeled on the moment-to-moment early interaction between parent and child: face to face, back and forth, up and down regulating, caring and soothing, smiling and laughing, rhythm and rhyme. When this process goes well, it is characterized by parent availability, responsiveness, and sensitivity, with resulting arousal regulation, parent-child synchrony, attunement, repair of mis-attunements, co-regulation, and moments of meeting. Within this warm and responsive relationship, the baby feels safe, experiences shared joy, and gains a positive view of himself and what he can expect from others. He also learns, at a visceral and emotional level, the rules of interaction and basic problem solving. The shared experience of synchrony, attunement, co-regulation, and joy expands the parent's emotional development as well. This positive early interaction develops the child's emotional circuitry and is the foundation for the development of a secure relationship for both parties.

Unfortunately, this natural process may be interrupted by many factors, including parent or child developmental disability, mental illness, physical illness, toxic stress, physical separation, natural disasters, war, death, and family violence. In addition to these factors, considerations regarding the impact of transracial and transcultural adoption must be considered for both the child and the parents. Parents may have little preparation, resources, knowledge, or positive experience to bring to the role of parent. The outcome for the child of negative early interactions is elevated fear and stress levels, dysregulation, lack of trust, a negative view of self, and insecure or disorganized attachment.

In order to help such families, Theraplay re-creates the direct, here-and-now, interactive caring and playful experiences that can lead to healthy social-emotional development for both child and parents. Theraplay treatment sessions consist of therapist-guided sequences of interpersonal play and care that are typical of (in the case of young child clients) or reminiscent of (in the case of older clients) the positive interaction that we describe above. In order to capitalize on the parent-child bond and parental strengths, parents are full participants in Theraplay sessions. This makes it possible also to address the parents' needs. Bowlby supports our clinical application of attachment theory and the use of the healthy parent-child model when he says, "The pattern of interaction adopted by the mother of a secure infant provides an excellent model for the pattern of therapeutic intervention" (Bowlby 1988, 126).

The goal of Theraplay is to create felt safety, a more positive internal working model for parent and child, and a more secure attachment.

HOW THERAPLAY BEGAN

Theraplay was developed by Ann Jernberg, clinical director of psychological services for Head Start Programs in Chicago. She created a program designed to meet the needs of children identified as having behavioral and emotional difficulties. Mental health workers went into the Head Start settings to spend time with individual children. They were asked to engage each child assigned to them in the same way parents interact with their young children: sensitively, spontaneously, face to face, with no need for toys, simply inviting the child to join them in joyful, interactive play. In weekly supervisory sessions these young mental health workers were helped to reflect on their own, and the child's, experience in order to be more attuned to each child's needs. Together the group came up with new activities that could be used to engage and delight the children as well as to calm and comfort them. They saw the children two or three times a week and averaged about fifteen sessions per child. *And it worked*: sad, withdrawn children became livelier and more outgoing; angry, aggressive, acting-out children calmed down and were able to engage with others in a friendly, cooperative way.

From the beginning, Theraplay focused on interpersonal engagement, play and joy, touch and the body, and arousal regulation. Researchers and clinicians in the fields of affect regulation (Schore 1994); interpersonal neurobiology (Siegel 1999); the emotional circuitry of the brain, including PLAY circuits (Panksepp 1998; Panksepp and Biven 2012); and polyvagal theory, arousal regulation, and the Social Engagement System (Porges 2011; 2015) have enriched the practice by identifying key elements of early interaction and how it affects the developing brain of the child. A greater understanding of the mechanisms and impact of early trauma (Schore 2003; van der Kolk 1994; Perry 2006) helps fine-tune our approach to meet the individual needs of each child and parent. The third edition of the Theraplay text incorporates the above discoveries and is the current manual for best practice in Theraplay training, supervision, and certification (Booth and Jernberg 2010).

THERAPLAY DIMENSIONS

In order to make use of the parent-infant model in our work with families we find it helpful to think of the myriad ways of interacting as falling into four dimensions: structure, engagement, nurture, and challenge. Being aware of the value and effect of a particular dimension or kind of interaction helps the Theraplay therapist choose activities that meet the child's and parents' needs at any one moment: organizing, energizing, creating safety, calming, or challenging to try something new. We use the

Marschak Interaction Method (MIM), a structured, clinical observation of parent-child interaction, to determine which dimensions we need to focus on for a particular child and parent (Booth, Christensen, and Lindaman 2011).

Structure

The therapist is responsible for creating a good, well-regulated, interactive experience for the parent and child. His or her actions create environmental regulation via organization and clear boundaries and expectations, and relational regulation through pacing, choice of activity, and level of arousal (Hart and Bentzen 2014). This guidance and regulation creates predictability, safety, and co-regulated interaction. Examples include making a stack of hands at slow, medium, and fast speeds; blowing a cotton ball to the other person's hands; or popping bubbles with the body part that the adult names.

Engagement

The therapist uses her or his own social engagement of in-the-moment, contingent, warm facial expressions, prosodic voice, and welcoming gestures and head movements to stimulate the parent and child's social engagement and promote a calm physiological state or neuroception of safety (Porges 2011). The therapist also engages the parent and child in attachment-enhancing experiences of attunement, synchrony, repair of mis-attunements, co-regulation, moments of meeting, and intersubjectivity. Examples include face-to-face baby games with physical contact and lilting rhythmic words. Older children enjoy simple interactions that draw the participants toward each other, such as creating a handshake together or decorating each other with feathers.

Nurture

The therapist sets up several gentle, caring, and soothing activities per session, often involving touch. He/she also looks for opportunities to express appreciation and concern and to take care of the parent and child. These caring activities are down regulating and stress reducing. Examples include taking care of hurts with a cotton ball or dot of lotion, singing a special song to the child, and feeding a snack at the end of the session.

Challenge

The therapist supports the child's growth by joining with the child in playful, physical activities that extend the levels of high and low arousal and encourage the child to try new things. When the parent and child work together to complete challenging play activities, they both feel more competent and confident. Examples include blowing a soap bubble back and forth as many times as possible before it pops, jumping off a stack of pillows into the parent's arms, or karate chopping a paper streamer when the parent gives a signal.

Sequencing the Dimensions

Using the dimensions as a guide, the therapist organizes the interaction between parent and child to create maximum connection and co-regulation. A typical thirty- to forty-five-minute session contains eight to ten activities focused on the dimensions most beneficial to the particular child. It will include the following: an entrance activity, a checkup, four to six goal-directed activities, feeding, a song, and a final activity that facilitates the exit from the Theraplay session. The entrance activity signals that the experience will be pleasant and interesting. The checkup allows for a moment of connectedness; the therapist notices the child, assessing and attuning to the child's state in the same way new parents take notice of their infant: counting her fingers, noticing her responses. Goal-directed activities focus on the dimensions that the dyad/family would benefit most from, related to the identified treatment goals. The Theraplay therapist is thoughtful in preparing and planning, ensuring that the treatment sequence flows from a low energy level, building to an optimal level of arousal that may extend the child's window of affective tolerance, and back toward a relaxed state before leaving. The nurturing activities at the end of the session allow for the return to this calmer state, preparing parent and child for the transition home.

WORKING WITH PARENTS IN THERAPLAY

When a parent and child who previously were distressed or in conflict are able to share an experience of pleasure and emotional connection, they learn a new meaning of togetherness. This new way of being together contributes to the child's emotional growth and allows the parent to develop new or expanded internal representations of the child, the self, and the relationship. In addition to interacting directly with their child in sessions, the parents verbally process their experiences in sessions with the therapist where they review video clips of sessions and discuss their own experience. Parents generally report that their participation in Theraplay is positive and rewarding. In some parent-child dyads, the parent may experience pleasurable parent-child interactions for the first time in their life or with this particular child. Some parents may find parts of the experience uncomfortable, as it challenges the parent's past experiences, feelings, and beliefs. At these times, the therapist plans more reflection, support, and individual parent therapy, depending on how severe a barrier to change and health is posed by the parent's discomfort.

THERAPLAY WITH ANNA AND HER PARENTS

Jeff and Cindy long struggled to manage their daughter's behaviors. They wondered what had happened to their "happy baby" who used to sing all the time and could be playful. Because they had adopted her at such a young age, they dismissed the notion that her behaviors might be related to attachment issues or relational trauma. In the five months leading up to their seeking Theraplay treatment, Anna's dysregulation, controlling and "bossy" behaviors, and separation anxiety escalated. This worsening followed an incident in which Anna misbehaved and, as a consequence, her parents removed a beloved toy. They described Anna as having a "breakdown" about this punishment. She began refusing to go to school and her academic progress declined. She seldom slept through the night. Throughout the summer break, Anna avoided activities that previously brought her joy.

Anna also talked more about being adopted and spoke of a desire to meet her birth parents. Shortly afterward the parents attended a talk about adoption and attachment. As they reflected on recent events and their daughter's experiences and behaviors, they began to think of Anna's difficult behaviors not as oppositional but as signs of distress and attachment insecurity. Jeff and Cindy realized they needed additional help and sought treatment at the Theraplay Institute as their first level of intervention.

During the intake process, Cindy described her own childhood as "focused on independence," noting that her parents were not very available and that she cared for herself as soon as she was able. She maintained a distant relationship with her parents via occasional phone calls. Cindy recognized that she did not have a positive "role model" for parenting Anna. She found it hard to be playful, experienced a low tolerance for her daughter's emotional outbursts, and did not feel close to Anna. Their days together were focused on tasks of daily living with little enjoyment.

Jeff's upbringing was quite different. He described his large family as close knit and interactive. His childhood was spent playing with and being cared for by his mother and older siblings. He felt this was good preparation for playful interactions with his daughter.

In the following description of the Theraplay process, we begin by describing our observations during the MIM parent-child interaction assessment. We briefly summarize our clinical hypotheses about the observations and then present a discussion of treatment that relates to each dimension.

Structure

Throughout the MIM, Anna was controlling, highly sensitive to stimuli, and easily dysregulated. Her parents avoided any action that might trigger a tantrum. In the activity "adult and child each take one squeaky animal and make the two animals play together," Cindy tentatively offered a series of options to Anna. As the questions continued, Anna began to wiggle; her movements sped up and became increasingly physical. She hit and bounced her pig on her mother's pig and challenged Mom to keep up with her. Suddenly Anna declared that it was time to move on to the next activity.

Her mother's questions and lack of clear guidance seemed to make Anna anxious. Anna's resulting dysregulated, controlling behavior signaled her need for a caregiver who could provide predictability, consistency, and organization to help her manage the new situation. We hypothesized that Anna's early multiple changes in caregivers, coupled with her parents' uncertainty about how to provide the needed sense of safety, had left Anna feeling that she must provide this for herself. In their efforts to avoid angry outbursts, Anna's parents asked questions and gave choices instead of proceeding with the confidence that would have led to a sense of safety for Anna.

During the first Theraplay session, the therapist, Grace, took the initiative and clearly let Anna know how the activity would go. Anna's parents watched until Grace signaled for one of them to take a turn. For instance:

> Grace took Anna's hand and guided her to a large pillow just outside the therapy room. "Anna, I am going to hold your hands and have you stand on this pillow. When I say 1, 2, 3, Go! I will help you jump to the next pillow. Ready, 1. 2. 3. Go! Wow! What an amazing jumper your girl is, Mom. Mom, take Anna's hands. Anna, when Mom says 1, 2, 3, Go! she will help you jump to the next pillow."

Throughout the sessions, Grace guided Anna through many clearly structured activities—for example, hand-clapping games, crawling to her parents through a tunnel in various ways, and making a stack of their hands. She gave clear directions and cues that allowed Anna to know just when an activity would begin and end, thus preparing her for the transition to the next activity. Through these structured Theraplay activities, Anna's parents learned how to become more effective and confident leaders. This new stance allowed Anna to relax and feel comfortable and confident in her parents' ability to set clear expectations for her. In the parent review session following the first parent-child session, Cindy reflected, "It was structured. I knew what my role was and Anna knew what her role was. There was no struggle for control or who's making what up. It felt much more relaxed, easy to do, and a lot less stressful."

Engagement

Anna's anxiety, high energy, and impulsive behavior made it hard for her parents to attune to her frequent changes in affect and demonstrate that they understood her. During the MIM activity "adult and child put hats on each other," both Cindy and Jeff became focused on making sure that everyone followed the rule to "put hats on each other." Anna happily joined each parent in selecting a hat for the other parent. She repeatedly pointed to a hat that was her favorite. When they didn't respond to her signal, she grabbed it and put it on herself. When Cindy reminded her that they were supposed to pick a hat for her, Anna grabbed the hat off her own head and plopped it back in the bin, saying in a whining voice, "Oh, but I really like this one." She lowered her head and turned away from her parents. Cindy, clearly hoping to engage her again, placed another hat on Anna's head, saying, "This is pretty; you will be as pretty as a peacock!" Jeff chimed in, "It's beautiful!" But Anna continued to pout and look down, slowly pulling the hat from her head and laying it in her lap. Focusing on the task at hand, neither parent was able to recognize or acknowledge Anna's experience of sadness and disappointment.

As treatment progressed, Cindy and Jeff began to respond openly, warmly, and positively to all of Anna's feeling states. As a result, Anna appeared more comfortable; she was able to accept their efforts to make a connection, and she showed that she wanted to prolong the connection.

> Anna sat gazing intently at her father' as Grace guided him to hold Anna's foot and attend to the special spot on her toe. She then asked Jeff to touch each of Anna's toes firmly (to avoid tickling) and say what food each little piggy likes to eat—choosing Anna's favorite foods. As Grace spoke, Anna took her other foot and gently placed it close to her father's hands, silently indicating her wish that he complete the activity for all ten toes. Grace nodded and smiled at Jeff. Jeff began, "This little piggy likes ice cream," and Anna smiled, gazing in wonder at her father. With each little piggy, her smile grew, her eyes brightened, and she maintained eye contact with her father as he looked from each toe to her bright eyes.

Jeff was able to engage Anna in this variation of the Little Piggy game using firm, gentle touch; eye contact accompanied by a big smile; and an enticing, yet even, tone of voice. These components and his positive response to Anna's facial expressions activated both his and Anna's social engagement system, creating a shared sense of calm and inner safety. With a little prompt from Grace, Dad understood that Anna's placing her other foot by his hands was a signal for more and not an attempt to control the activity. This awareness allowed him to attend to her other foot without misunderstanding her cue.

Theraplay creates opportunities for parents and children to engage in playful, attuned, synchronous ways, sharing moments of delight while at the same time accepting and responding to negative feelings. As they reviewed a section of a videotaped session with Grace, Jeff and Cindy could see that Anna was able to stay focused on the interaction when Grace approached her confidently using a melodic tone of voice and warm facial expressions. They soon found that when they approached her in a similar way, Anna was able to sustain this focus with them. They also recognized that if they validated her feelings of uncertainty or disappointment—for example, "You're not sure about this activity"—she was able to try an activity with them rather than fall apart.

Anna's sense of felt safety increased through sessions, and the pure joy and delight she shared with her parents helped Anna feel seen and accepted in the moment. Anna's attempts to engage in pretend play in sessions and at home decreased over time. A sign of Anna's more relaxed state came at the end of the very first Theraplay session: Anna began to sing as she left the office. That evening she allowed her mother to guide a game for the two of them, and for the first time ever Anna was able to put herself back to sleep in the middle of the night without assistance from one of her parents.

Nurture

During the MIM, Anna and her parents seemed comfortable being physically close. Anna frequently sat in her parents' laps, sought affection, and responded positively to moments of closeness. However, the parents reported it was more typical that when they tried to provide calm forms of care and nurture, Anna would abruptly move on to something else or refuse to accept their comfort. Disappointed, they often retreated from their efforts rather than persevering. In the MIM task "Apply lotion to one another," Anna allowed her father to apply a little lotion but soon asked him to tickle her. This turned the potentially calming activity into an exciting game.

Jeff and Cindy welcomed every sign that Anna wanted to be close to them. When closeness became too much for Anna and she asked for tickling, they complied, not recognizing the negative impact that the vigorous tickling had on Anna: she gasped for air, was unable to settle, and frequently hit or kicked them. While Anna's parents could see the dysregulating effect of the tickling as they watched a video clip of it, they were puzzled about how to change their approach. They were afraid that if they denied her requests for tickles, she would feel rejected. Grace's plan for sessions was to provide the high level of sensory input that Anna needed to help regulate her agitated body, as well as to provide calming, nurturing experiences that she could accept. Once it was clear what would help Anna, Grace guided Cindy and Jeff to lead such activities.

The beginning and ending moments of a Theraplay session are times when parents can nurture their child. The child accepts, or in some cases learns to accept, his/her parents' soothing efforts, allowing them to provide down-regulating experiences. Being noticed, as in a "checkup" activity, allowed Anna to feel seen and accepted by her parents for the wonder that she is, thus supporting the development of her self-worth. During the checkup, Grace counted Anna's special freckles, checked her strong muscles, and measured her happy smile. She put lotion on her arms and legs using deep pressure. She sang a special song all about Anna. At the end of each session Anna's parents fed her a snack. Early in treatment, Anna showed her pleasure at having her special freckles pointed out by pointing out new ones for them to count.

> Anna's mother sat facing her and took her legs in her lap. She began applying lotion in slow, rhythmic motions, using just the amount of pressure that felt relaxing for Anna. As she did this, Anna turned to Grace, "We did special spots this morning! Mom found two more on my chest." She smiled as her mother and Grace recounted how many they had found throughout previous sessions. Anna then pulled her pant leg up to her knees as a sign that she was ready for more lotion on her legs.

By the end of treatment, Anna had shifted her requests for tickles to requests for counting her special freckles or having lotion firmly rubbed on her arms and legs. This deep pressure met some of her sensory needs. Other sensory needs were met through structured activities that involved jumping and swinging. Her parents were surprised that she abandoned the tickling so quickly and relieved to have new skills that helped them feel closer to their little girl.

Challenge

During the MIM there were several opportunities to assess the level of the parents' expectations as well as Anna's response to challenge: "Adult takes one set of blocks, builds a structure, and encourages child to build the same structure"; "Adult makes a quick drawing and asks child to copy it"; and "Adult teaches the child something the child doesn't know." Cindy's and Jeff's expectations were well tuned to her abilities, and Anna appeared to enjoy accomplishing the tasks. When Anna had some difficulty following Cindy's instructions about how to do cartwheels, Cindy quickly recognized the problem and broke the task down into smaller steps so that Anna could succeed. They both delighted in her accomplishment.

Cindy and Jeff reported that they were less successful in "real life," where they relied heavily on verbal redirection, which Anna was unable to follow. Since Anna appears older than her chronological age, both verbally and physically, her parents' and teachers' expectations were often higher than what she was capable of achieving, especially when she was anxious and unsettled.

In Theraplay, challenge activities are designed so that parent and child can work together toward the outcome, thus building the child's confidence in being able to take developmentally appropriate risks with a parent's support. In order to provide Anna with an opportunity to experience success in a physically demanding activity, Grace checked to see how many pillows Anna could balance on her feet before she kicked them across the room.

> Anna lay with her head on a pillow and her feet up in the air. Cindy and Grace took two pillows and stacked them on the flat part of her feet, adjusting the pillows as needed to make sure that Anna could balance the weight. Cindy counted, "1, 2, 3!" and Anna kicked the pillows off, propelling them across the room. "Wow!" Cindy said, and Anna smiled. When Anna successfully tossed three pillows, Cindy exclaimed, "She can definitely do three pillows!" With a proud smile on her face, Anna returned to the starting position for the next round with four pillows.

Cindy made sure the pillows were stable and provided physical and verbal cues to ensure that Anna could experience success with these activities. Anna reveled in her mother's positive reaction to her success, her smile reflecting her sense of pride. Now confident in her ability to participate, Anna returned to try again, ready to take the additional risk.

GENERALIZING THE MODEL TO HOME AND SCHOOL

Initially, the idea of bringing the Theraplay model home seemed daunting for Cindy and Jeff. How could they create within their own busy home the supportive environment that was created in the treatment setting? How could they find the time in their hectic daily lives to engage with their daughter? Cindy, in particular, worried about "thinking fast enough on her feet" to be playful and responsive to Anna. She said that she "had never received this kind of parenting." She craved it for herself, and wanted to provide it for Anna, but was uncertain that she could implement it at home. Grace provided additional support during parent feedback sessions, e-mail correspondence, and phone calls. In addition, Grace consulted with Anna's OT therapist and with school personnel to ensure that Anna and her family would have the support of her teachers and school administrators for a smooth transition to a new school year.

PARENTS' ASSESSMENT OF TREATMENT PROCESS

Comments about the Parent-Child Interaction Assessment (MIM)

It was very important to see what was happening, as it adds a whole new dimension to understanding what we do as parents and how Anna responds as the child. You see it in a whole new way that you can't see it when you're "in it."

Comments about Theraplay Sessions

This was a very big piece to the trauma puzzle for us. Our daughter responded so well to the physical activities and you could watch her day by day building the trust and the closeness. Our daughter has bloomed again, not through talking about it, but through moving her body with us in ways that she feels safe.

Comments about Parent-Only Sessions

That was also an important piece for us, as it helped answer questions and explain what we needed to change and how to do it. It was also comforting to have someone to talk to that understood exactly what we were going through as a family.

Ongoing Process

Anna's mother reported that this success continued in their home, at school, and in social situations. Within weeks of starting treatment, Anna had a play date at her home for two playmates. Anna engaged her friends confidently, teaching them a game and allowing them each to take a turn in the lead. In the past, the focus of a play date would have been a pretend play situation in which Anna dominated the decision making, melting down when her friends chose to not cooperate.

The prognosis for Anna is good. Theraplay helped Anna's parents understand and accept a wider range of her emotions, understand and meet her sensory needs, and guide her with confidence. Anna responded with more relaxed and regulated behavior. Together they experienced moments of meeting that led to a more trusting, joyful, and genuine relationship. Additionally, the co-regulation, attunement, and nurture of Theraplay set a foundation for the work that lies ahead for Anna to process her early trauma.

SUMMARY

When parents interact with their baby in safe, attuned, regulated ways, the baby's emotional circuitry can develop in a healthy, regulated manner. The young child who has experienced attachment insecurity and complex trauma has had deprivations at the sensing and feeling levels of development. These sensing and feeling areas must be addressed before secure development can proceed.

Theraplay stimulates deep areas of the emotional brain of the child and parent through establishing security and order (structure), activating the social engagement system and attachment experiences of synchrony, attunement, and intersubjectivity (engagement), soothing and caring (nurture), and encouraging growth and development with the parent's help (challenge), while delighting and having fun (play). In addition to having new, positive parent-child experiences that shift the inner working models of both parties in a positive direction, parents are helped to reflect on the Theraplay experience.

BIBLIOGRAPHY

Booth, Phyllis B., and Ann M. Jernberg. 2010. *Theraplay: Helping Parents and Children Build Better Relationships through Attachment-Based Play*. San Francisco: Jossey-Bass.

Booth, P., G. Christensen, and S. Lindaman. 2011. *Marschak Interaction Method (MIM) Manual and Cards* (Revised). Evanston, IL: The Theraplay Institute. www.theraplay.org.

Bowlby, John. 1988. *A Secure Base. Parent-Child Attachment and Healthy Human Development*. New York: Basic Books.

Hart, Susan, and Marianne Bentzen, eds. 2014. *Through Windows of Opportunity*. London: Karnac.

Panksepp, Jaak. 1998. *Affective Neuroscience*. Oxford: Oxford University Press.

Panksepp, Jaak, and Lucy Biven. 2012. *The Archaeology of Mind*. New York: W. W. Norton.

Perry, Bruce D. 2006. "Applying Principles of Neurodevelopment to Clinical Work with Maltreated and Traumatized Children: The Neurosequential Model of Therapeutics." In *Working with Traumatized Youth in Child Welfare*, edited by N. B. Webb. New York: Guilford Press.

Porges, Stephen W. 2011. *The Polyvagal Theory*. New York: W. W. Norton.

———. 2015. "Making the World Safe for Our Children: Down-Regulating Defence and Up-Regulating Social Engagement to 'Optimise' the Human Experience." *Children Australia* 40: 114–23. doi:10.1017/cha.2015.12.

Schore, Allan N. 1994. *Affect Regulation and Origin of the Self*. Hillsdale, NJ: Erlbaum.

———. 2003. "Early Relational Trauma, Disorganized Attachment, and the Development of a Predisposition to Violence." In *Healing Trauma: Attachment, Mind, Body, and Brain,* edited by Daniel Siegel and Marion Solomon, 106–7. New York: W. W. Norton.

Siegel, Daniel J. 1999. *The Developing Mind*. New York: Guilford Press.

van der Kolk, Bessel A. 1994. "The Body Keeps the Score." *Harvard Review of Psychiatry* 1 (5): 253–65.

8

Group Theraplay

Evangeline Munns

> Group play therapy creates a way of "being in, being for, and being with" clients of all ages.
>
> —Clark Moustakas, *Relationship Play Therapy*

The power of groups to enable individual members to make significant changes behaviorally, emotionally, and socially is often amazing. Why does this happen? Is it because we have an innate need to connect with others and in a group that facilitates this connection in a safe, positive way, people feel accepted, their defenses diminish, and they become freer in their actions, emotions, and thoughts? Is this atmosphere created by an attuned leader? This certainly seems to happen often in Theraplay groups, whether it is in a group of peers, parent-child dyads, or multiple families. Part of the format of a Theraplay group includes the leader making a personal recognition and acceptance of each group member at the beginning of each group session, which helps to create an atmosphere of warmth and welcome for each member. This will be described more fully later in this chapter.

The following is an example of a parent-child Theraplay group: a group of fathers and their sons gather once a week for forty-five minutes with an underlying quest to feel more attached with each other. The fathers have voiced this in their own words as one of their goals: "I want to be closer to my son." Another main goal was "I want my son to be more cooperative and obedient."

This father-son group started with children sitting with a space between themselves and their fathers. It ended up with the boys leaning into the fathers sides or sometimes in their laps. Spontaneous hugs became increasingly familiar. The boys became more cooperative and spent less time resisting and more time just enjoying the interactions with their fathers and the group. Toward the end of this twelve-week group, comments were heard such as "This is the most precious time in the week for me and my son." The children insisted on coming even when they were sick. There was almost 100 percent attendance each week (in spite of bad weather). The members did not want the group to end. This group will be described more fully later in this chapter.

THEORY

First of all, what is Theraplay? As noted in chapter 7, Theraplay is a short-term, structured, nonverbal model of play therapy where parents first observe and then are actively engaged with their child under the guidance of a therapist. It is based on attachment theory, with the belief that our first attachment with our chief caregiver forms a template for later relationships throughout a person's life (Bowlby 1988). Theraplay goes back to this earliest relationship and tries to replicate normal parent-child interactions that foster attachment (Booth and Jernberg 2010; Munns 2009). Troubled children often have an emotional age that is much younger than their chronological age. Theraplay meets them at their emotional age. This means that at the beginning of treatment, activities are chosen that one might do with a younger child. As treatment progresses, activities are included that match the child's chronological age. This principle holds true in group Theraplay as well, where activities are first geared for the emotional age of the children. This is especially true in parent-child groups.

GOALS

The primary goals of Theraplay, whether it is in the family or group format, are to increase the healthy attachment between parents and their child; to increase the trust, acceptance, and self-esteem of each family member; to feel valued and cared for; to be more attuned to each other; and to promote self-confidence and self-regulation. Another main goal is for everyone to enjoy each other, to feel connected, and to have fun. This is evidenced by the joyous laughter that is often heard in Theraplay sessions.

SUBJECTS

Family or group Theraplay is suitable for clients across the age span: infants, preschoolers, latency aged, adolescents, adults, and the elderly (Munns 2005; 2008; Buckwalter and Finlay 2009; Kim 2011). It has been used successfully for a wide range of emotional, behavioral, and social problems such as acting out; dysregulated, behavior-disordered children; ADHD; withdrawn, depressed children; mutism; those on the autism spectrum; and those with attachment and/or relationship difficulties, such as those found with step-, foster, and adoptive children (Munns 2000). Theraplay has been used successfully with sexually and/or physically abused children and with those who have experienced trauma. It is important, however, to modify Theraplay with the latter, so that physical touching by the therapist and others is done in an attuned, sensitive manner. Nothing is ever forced, and the child is not coaxed.

Although there is generally a lot of physical contact in Theraplay, the pacing of such contact is carefully calibrated to the reactions of the child. For example, in group Theraplay, if a child does not want any powdering or lotioning of their "hurts" or does not want to be fed, then the therapist offers the activity but accepts the child's refusal, recognizing the child's discomfort. For example, the therapist may say, "That makes you uncomfortable. You don't want any lotion today. That's okay," and goes on to the next child. However, over time, most often when the abused child sees that other children accept the lotion and there are no harmful outcomes, he or she will start accepting the nurturing touch of having "hurts" cared for. An example of this was a six-year-old girl called "Sally," who had been suspected of having been sexually abused. (An investigation did not confirm this.) Sally in group Theraplay continued to refuse the "taking care of hurts" activity. She was very interested, though, in watching how the other children were being nurtured. After a few sessions, the supervisor suggested that the group leader ask Sally if she would like to powder the hurts of the child sitting next to her. Sally was eager to do this. After two more sessions, Sally cheerfully accepted being powdered herself. The group had provided a safe environment for her to learn that touch could be positive and pleasurable. Abused children need to learn the positive aspects of appropriate touch. This view is shared by some of the leaders in the past and also in the present in the treatment of abused children: "Learning to touch in the safety of the therapeutic environment may be one of the most important components in therapy for victims" (Hindman 1991, 170; see also Ford 1993; James 1994; van der Kolk 2014).

DIMENSIONS OF THERAPLAY

Normal parent-child interactions can be categorized into four main dimensions: structure, engagement, nurture, and challenge. These dimensions guide all Theraplay activities, whether in family or group format.

Structure

All children need some structure in their lives, so their world becomes safe, secure, and predictable. Parents are normally in charge to provide direction and structure in their child's daily life—for example, regular times for sleeping, eating, and playing, as well as rules for safety. When these are not provided for the child, then his or her world can become chaotic and unsafe, even dangerous. In Theraplay, the therapist or parent is in charge, giving directions for the activities, following a clear agenda that is preplanned according to the child's needs, with a definite beginning and end—for example, an *entrance*, such as follow the leader; *a welcome song, checkup, taking care of hurts,* and *other Theraplay activities*; and then *feeding* and *a goodbye song* at the end. For children who need a lot of structure, many activities with very clear rules are included—for example, "Red light" (stop), "Green light" (Go), or "Mother May I." Structure is emphasized for children who are resistant, uncooperative, impulsive, dysregulated, overly controlling, behavior disordered, conduct disordered, and "parentified."

Engagement

Normally, parents engage with their children in many delightful ways that bring joy and laughter to both parent and child, such as the "peekaboo" games or "patty-cake" songs with very young children. With older children, a hand-clapping game may become more complex, such as "Miss Mary Mack." Engagement brings a sense of connection between people and helps a child to be clear about his/her body image. In Theraplay, the therapist engages the child as soon as he or she sees the child in the waiting room—for example, "Hi Billy, I have been so looking forward to seeing you again." In group Theraplay, all the children are individually welcomed at the beginning of the sessions with a welcome song with everyone holding hands: "Hello Jimmy, hello Lisa, hello Sandra, and so on. We're glad you came to play." Throughout the session, the therapist tries to keep all the children engaged by giving clear directions and choosing activities that have the children interacting with each other—for example, "hand stack" (two or more children face each other and build a rising stack of hands by placing the palms of their hands on top the other's hands, and then reversing coming down) or "cotton ball blow" (two or more children blow cotton balls to each other across a piece of paper or cloth). These activities help the children to build recognition, awareness, and an attunement with each other. Engagement activities are especially used with withdrawn, timid, depressed, or fearful children, including those on the autism spectrum.

Nurture

Nurture is the most important dimension, in this author's opinion. All children need to be nurtured: not only meeting their basic needs, such as food and shelter, but also caring for them in a loving, warm way, such as receiving physical affection, cradling and rocking, and soothing the child when distressed. Nurture gives the child a sense of being valued, important, and loved. When nurturing is done consistently in an attuned, empathic way, the child's "inner working model" (Bowlby 1988), or self-concept, becomes more positive and the attachment between caregiver and child grows.

In Theraplay, some nurturing activities, such as powdering or lotioning of hurts, feeding a snack, and so on, are included in every session, whether it is group or family Theraplay. For children who have missed out in receiving adequate nurturing in their early lives, activities are sometimes included such as being cradled and rocked in the adult's arms while drinking from a straw in a juice box or being fed a favorite snack while the adult sings a song about the child, such as "Twinkle twinkle little star, what a special girl you are." Dr. Rick Gaskill (2014), who practices neurosequential programming, states that in nurturing experiences, such as being rocked and fed, a process happens "where the child and therapist have become neurologically attuned through eye contact, face-to-face gaze, soft tones and gentle touch" (209).

As mentioned before, all children need nurturing, but especially children who have been neglected, deprived, abused, or traumatized. Nurturing often includes a lot of touch, and this can pose a challenge for nurturing a child who has been abused. The therapist has to be particularly sensitive to the child's cues, and if the child looks anxious or frightened, the therapist needs to reflect this feeling: "I can see this is making you uncomfortable. We will do something else." The therapist then proceeds to find another way of nurturing that child that is more acceptable. As an example, if the child refuses to have his or her "hurts" powdered, the therapist can suggest making powder handprints where the baby powder is lightly dusted on the child's hands and perhaps spread lightly by the adult over the child's palms and then pressed into a sheet of colored construction paper, leaving the imprint of a hand. Handprints from the adult and child can then be compared.

Nurturing is also stressed for dysregulated, acting-out, aggressive children, who often are in trouble with adults and who rarely get the love and affection they need. Parentified children, who have taken on the role of caring for others, often need to regain their childhood and be cared for themselves.

Challenge

Children usually enjoy challenging activities as long as they are within their mastery. From the beginning of a child's life, the parent challenges their little one to sit up, to take his or her first steps, and so on. If the developmental level of the child is appropriate for the task and the child succeeds, then his or her self-confidence and self-esteem blossom. Usually both parents and child are delighted with their child's newfound skills. Challenging activities help the child take age-appropriate risks and develop a sense of "I can do it." In Theraplay, challenging activities are geared to the child's ability so the child is assured of success. Activities requiring higher skill levels are gradually introduced, in pace with the child's capabilities.

Challenging activities are emphasized for children who have been overprotected and are timid, fearful, and lacking in self-esteem and for adolescents, who usually enjoy taking risks and meeting challenges. Sometimes challenging activities are also used as a means for tension release in aggressive children.

In Theraplay, the majority of activities are done in a playful way. There is a give-and-take manner in the activities, which take place in a lighthearted, playful atmosphere. Children often laugh uproariously in activities such as "squeaky body part," "pop cheeks," "pass a funny face," and others. It is important that we stimulate the "joy juice" in our brains (Panksepp 1993).

Playfulness is needed by all children, especially those who have had little happiness in their lives, such as deprived, neglected, and abused children; those who are depressed, withdrawn, and fearful; and those on the autism spectrum.

RESEARCH

The research showing significant results for the use of Theraplay has grown from case studies to simple designs comparing pre- and post-treatment scores and use of control groups, both nonrandomized and randomized with matched controls (Munns 2009). Theraplay has reached the status of "promising research evidence" by the California Evidence-Based Clearinghouse for Child Welfare.

Research with group Theraplay is encouraging. Ammen (2000) found increased empathy in high-risk teenage mothers; Hong (2004), higher self-esteem scores; Kim (2007; 2011), higher attachment scores and higher self-esteem scores in an elderly group, respectively; Kwon (2004), significantly higher emotional intelligence quotient; and Siu (2009; 2014), significantly higher self-esteem and significantly higher social awareness, motivation, and communication in disabled children with development problems, respectively.

A pilot study that has not been published yet (Tucker 2015) compared pre- and post-scores in a large group (n = 206) receiving a form of group Theraplay called "Sunshine Circles," designed for regular classrooms in schools that are teacher led. The findings of this study showed the Theraplay group, compared to the control group, improved significantly on anxious, hostile-aggressive, distracted, inattentive, and total behaviors and on fine motor skills, problem solving, and personal-social domains. Observer ratings of teacher-student interactions were also significantly more positive in the Theraplay group than in the control group. A much larger research project using Sunshine Circles is planned for the future. More research details can be found in Munns (2011), Meyer and Wardrop (2009), Lender and Lindaman (2007), and www.theraplay.org.

Related Brain Research

Some of the latest neuroscience research lends credibility to the tenets of Theraplay. Theraplay helps to stimulate the right hemisphere of the brain, which is the nonverbal part of our brains that processes sensory-motor perceptions and social emotional experiences and is the seat of our creativity. This is in keeping with Schore's emphasis on the importance of the right brain in the attachment process (Schore 2005; Schore and Schore 2008).

Theraplay also fits in well with Dr. Bruce Perry's neurosequential programming, which advocates starting treatment with the level of brain functioning of the client (which often differs from the chronological age) (Perry and Szalavitz 2006; Perry

2009). Dr. Perry believes that clients whose emotional and behavioral difficulties started early in life when the lower brain was maturing should begin with treatment geared to giving the kind of experiences that were missed but were needed to help organize that part of the brain. The lower brain is the first to develop in the first two years of life and governs our survival instincts of breathing, heart rate, core temperature, digestion, sexual urges, and the instinct of "fight, flight, or freeze" when danger is sensed. The lower brain also includes the cerebellum, which controls rhythm and movement (Levitin 2007). The next part of the brain to mature is the middle or "mammalian" or "emotional brain" (limbic system), which governs our emotions. A key part of the emotional brain is the amygdala—the "watchdog" of the brain. If the amygdala perceives danger in the environment, it triggers the lower brain into the fight, flight, or freeze response. Theraplay is geared to stimulating the lower brain with its inclusion of sensory motor activities and those requiring rhythm and movement, which are used extensively in helping dysregulated children. Theraplay also stimulates the emotional or middle brain by eliciting laughter and joy in many of its activities while also raising self-esteem and feelings of security. It is believed that the nurturing, soothing aspects of Theraplay may help to calm down an overactive amygdala.

Related Touch Research

There is a lot of physical contact in Theraplay activities. We live, however, in a touch-phobic world. For example, generally, therapists are not allowed to touch their clients. Teachers are not allowed to touch their pupils, even when the latter might be hurt and crying. In a growing number of schools, children are not allowed to touch their peers—not even a positive touch such as a hug. But children need touch to thrive (Ford 1993; Field 2000; Gerhardt 2004; Makela 2005; Nicholson and Parker 2009). The most advanced sensory system when infants are born is tactile. Affectionate touching, such as caressing, cuddling, and being held and rocked, releases hormones such as opioids and oxytocin that help the child to regulate emotions and affect the bonding between parent and child (Gerhardt 2004; Sunderland 2006). If children do not receive enough positive touch, they may turn to negative touch, such as shoving, pinching, or hitting. Some research suggests that countries having the least amount of positive touch among family members also have the highest rates of violence within (e.g., the United States) (Thayer 1998).

There are well-designed research studies using randomized control groups that indicate the significant, positive effects of touch (such as massage) on weight gain and sensory-motor development of premature babies; reduction of aggression in juvenile delinquents; and more focused concentration in ADHD children (Field 2000). Studies using "kangaroo care" (skin-to-skin touch) between parent and baby have shown significant positive results (Ludington-Hoe 1993; Sunderland 2006). Prominent clinicians such as Hindman (1991), James (1994), Perry and Szalavitz (2006), and van der Kolk (2014) advocate the use of positive, appropriate touch to help in the healing of traumatized clients.

ADDITIONAL ASPECTS OF GROUP THERAPLAY

The goals for group Theraplay are similar to those for family Theraplay, but in addition to raising self-esteem, trust, attachment, and self-regulation, there is an emphasis on social skills, such as increasing an awareness of each other and the needs of others; promoting a feeling of care and concern for each other; increasing the ability to take turns; and increasing the ability to relate to each other and to feel connected in an atmosphere of enjoyment, playfulness, and fun.

Group Theraplay sessions are usually held at least once a week for about forty-five minutes (twenty to thirty minutes for preschoolers), but preferably they should be held more often with very young children when the brain is developing so rapidly. The sessions are often held for at least three months, then evaluated and continued or stopped depending on results and circumstances (like long waiting lists).

It is important not only to have a consistent leader but also to have a coleader (and extra adult help if the group consists of a lot of behavior-disordered, aggressive children or those on the autism spectrum or if the children are very young). The average number of children in a group varies from four to eight for peer groups with troubled children, or twelve members for parent-child groups, but in regular classrooms with normal children the number can be much higher (for example, twenty-five to thirty children).

All the activities are preplanned and printed on an agenda that is pinned on a wall and is easily read by the leader. It is important to balance the activities with active versus calm ones, as well as those requiring physical closeness and others allowing the children to move freely. Sometimes problems are caused simply because the children have been sitting too long and they get restless or are allowed to move freely for too long, contributing to overexcitement and hyperarousal. The leaders also need to be sensitive to children who cannot tolerate intimacy for too long and to pace the timing of these activities to the cues of the children.

Groups have a structured format that is repeated for each session, which brings predictability and a sense of security for the children. The format is stable, but the activities within the format are usually changed from session to session. Each session is started by an entrance, such as "follow the leader" or "choo-choo train," where the leader walks from the doorway to the center of the room and everyone sits down forming a circle. The leader then sings a welcome song for each member—for example, "Hello Johnny, Hello Sally," and so on until everyone is welcomed. (With adolescent groups the leader may do a special handshake with each member instead of a welcome song.) The leader then repeats the three rules of Theraplay: "no hurts" (verbally or physically), "stick together" (everyone does the activities together), and "have fun."

This is followed by an "inventory," or "checkup," where the leader notices something positive about each child: for example, "Susan, I see you have brought your sparkly blue eyes." After the inventory, each child's hands are examined for any hurts such as scratches and bruises. Each "hurt" is taken care of by smoothing lotion or baby powder around the hurt or hurts. Then further activities take place that reflect the four Theraplay dimensions of structure, engagement, nurture, and challenge. Feeding each child a snack such as potato chips, pretzels, or pieces of fruit occurs toward the end of the session, followed by a goodbye song including everyone's name while holding hands (for example, "Goodbye Johnny, goodbye Sally. . . . We will see you again next week").

DIFFERENT GROUP FORMATS

The three main formats for groups in Theraplay are peer groups, parent-child groups, and multifamily groups.

Peer Groups

Group Theraplay with peers has been successfully used with a variety of ages: infants (Ammen 2000), toddlers (Munns 2008), preschool and kindergarten (Martin 2000), latency (Munns 2001), adolescents (Buckwalter and Finlay 2009; Gardner and Spickelmier 2009), elderly (Kim 2011), and populations such as handicapped and developmentally delayed (Azoulay 2000) and those on the autism spectrum (Bundy-Myrow 2000).

For example, successful peer groups are being held where Theraplay-based activities are used in an attachment-based curriculum at a children's center in Salt Lake City, Utah. Sandra Lindaman, who helped to organize these groups and acts as a consultant, reports that among the changes noted in the children are that they seem more engaged, calmer, more regulated, more cooperative, and happier. Teachers enjoy the children more, and their relationships are more positive. Teachers are using Theraplay tools throughout the day. A larger project is currently underway comparing treated (receiving Theraplay) and untreated children (controls). Very exciting results have also been found in some schools situated in northern Alberta in Canada (Munns and Arruda-Block 2014), where the school population is 91 percent aboriginal children. Group Theraplay has been used with "bullies" (some of the most aggressive children) so successfully that these formerly aggressive children are now seen as exceptionally sensitive to needs of their peers. As well, in a number of schools, group Theraplay is being conducted in all of the classrooms from kindergarten to grade 6 because of its positive effects and teacher requests for this therapy.

Parent-Child Groups

Parent-child groups can be very powerful, as both child and parents are experiencing Theraplay and its benefits. Parents usually support each other and delight in the interactions with their children. In one agency, therapists turned to forming parent-child groups partially out of necessity. The waiting list was extremely long and there was no extra funding to hire extra staff, so they turned to using parent-child groups and multifamily groups (Munns 2000) as a way of seeing more clients.

The first parent-child group formed at this agency was a mother-daughter Theraplay group for young mothers and their daughter toddlers. This had positive results, with mothers obviously enjoying their children more and increasing their acceptance of them. These two groups of mothers and children were expanded to include any gender and age. Next, they turned to forming a father-son group (note that children referred to children's mental health centers are usually in the ratio of four boys to one girl). This group was profoundly helpful to both the fathers and their sons and was described briefly at the beginning of this chapter. Here are more details regarding this group.

Father-Son Theraplay Group

Six father-son dyads with children ranging in age from five to thirteen years (ordinarily the age range is only two or three years apart) formed this group. The children included were diagnosed with ADHD, behavior disorders, oppositional defiant disorder, depression, Asperger's, and attachment disorder. One of the very aggressive boys was living in a residence for troubled children. Family and developmental histories were first taken of each child before the commencement of the group. Referral problems revealed three common characteristics of the children: low self-esteem, poor self-regulation, and antisocial behavior. Two of the fathers were stepfathers and one was suspected of alcoholism.

A meeting was held first with just the fathers where Theraplay was described and the expectations of the group were discussed: for example, meeting for two hours in the evening once a week over a twelve-week period. The first hour was to be devoted to Theraplay and the second hour for parent counseling while the boys were taken outside to play or do crafts and games with the co-therapists. As mentioned before, the fathers verbalized two goals: (1) wanting to be closer to their sons and (2) wanting their sons to be more obedient. This helped the therapists to determine that the dimensions of structure and nurture would be emphasized for this group. The format for the agendas for each session was typical of group Theraplay as described previously, with a few modifications. The leader and coleaders, all three males, demonstrated many of the activities first before asking the group to do them. This was particularly important for some of the nurturing activities. For example, one of the activities called for the child to sit in his father's lap with eyes closed while the father fed him different foods, some sweet and others sour or bitter. The father's task was to guess from the child's facial expression whether he liked the food. (The underlying goal of this activity was for the fathers to be more sensitive to their child's cues.) To demonstrate this, a co-therapist sat in the leader's lap (both mature males and fathers themselves). This demonstration was met with a lot of laughter from the group, and after that, no one hesitated to try the activity.

Example of a Group Agenda:

Entrance: "Choo-choo" train.

Welcome song.

Three rules: "No hurts, stick together, have fun."

Group mixer, "Hello, Thank You": Participants toss beanbags to each other while calling out a name first: for example, "Hello Jim." Jim catches the ball and says, "Thank you, Harry," and this continues until everyone has received and thrown the beanbag to someone else.

Inventory or checkup: Children sit in a circle facing outward while the fathers sit in front of their child. Each father notices two or three special positive things about his son that he expresses to his child.

Caring for hurts: Each father finds hurts on the hands of their child and puts powder or lotion around them.

Mirroring: Father and child face each other standing up. Father moves his arms slowly in any direction, and the child tries to mirror these movements by imitating them at the same time that the father moves. The child then takes a turn being the leader, and his father mirrors him.

"Simon Says": Everyone stands in a line while the leader calls out, "Simon says move your arms," or "clap your hands," and so on. Everyone does the action except when the leader omits saying "Simon says" first. In Theraplay, additions are inserted such as "Simon says say one nice thing you like about your neighbor" or "Simon says to give your neighbor a handshake or a hug."

Pass a funny face: The leader makes a funny face, and this is imitated and passed around by each person. Sometimes each person adds on an additional funny face that is passed around.

Cotton ball blow, fight and soothe: Two lines are formed with fathers and sons facing each other. They cup their hands from which they blow cotton balls to each other. This is followed by a mock fight where members can throw cotton balls at each other while calling out their names. Later, the fathers take a cotton ball and gently move it around their child's face, while commenting on their child's positive features.

Feeding: Fathers feed their sons popcorn, chips, fruit pieces, or some other snack directly into their child's mouth.

Goodbye song: While everyone holds hands, a song is sung including everyone's name (previously described).

Goodbye hug: Everyone places his arms on his neighbor's shoulders and gives a gentle squeeze.

After the Theraplay session, the children would leave with the co-therapists to have a snack and play games outside, do puzzles or crafts, and so on, while the fathers remained for the parent counseling session, where there was a debriefing and inquiries about home and school behavior were made and discussed. It was also very important to feed the fathers a snack (for example, coffee and cookies or pastries).

They needed to be nurtured too! (For descriptions of additional Theraplay activities, see Munns [2000; 2009] and Booth and Jernberg [2010].) Fathers were encouraged to practice the Theraplay activities of their choice at home.

Progress of Groups

This was a highly motivated group, with almost 100 percent attendance for each session, in spite of occasional foul weather or a child being sick—they still came! All of the groups ran for twelve sessions and were evaluated using pre- and post-measures, such as Achenbach's Child Behavior Checklist (Achenbach and Edelbrock 1983) and the Parenting Stress Index (short form). The results showed a significant drop in aggression scores and the externalizing factor and a gain in the parent-child interaction factor in the Parenting Stress Index. Verbalizations from the fathers confirmed the test findings: fathers felt closer to their children, children were more obedient and just more enjoyable to be with. Results were also verified by the therapists' observations of the group: there was a noticeable increase in spontaneous affection between the dyads, the children rarely resisted and were easily redirected, more fun and laughter was apparent, and a greater intimacy occurred during the nurturing activities.

An additional benefit that was not entirely expected was the friendships that developed within the group. All of the boys had previous difficulties with social skills and few, if any, friends. This changed within the group, as evidenced by the boys inviting each other to their birthday parties, for overnight stays, and for outings. One dyad lived on a farm, to which the whole group was invited for an afternoon. At the end of the twelve sessions, no one wanted to stop. (For further description of this group, see Sherman [2000].)

Multifamily Groups

The same agency's first multifamily groups consisted of two families each having two daughters. The therapists tried to match the socio-educational levels of the parents in selecting the families. This turned out to be not as important as simply "Did the parents like each other?" A key factor in matching families was the age of the children. In the first multifamily group all the girls were teenagers, which meant they could relate to each other's issues, laugh at the same jokes, and share mutual interests. In the counseling sessions immediately after the Theraplay sessions, parents could support and sympathize with each other as well as offer useful advice (Manery 2000; Sherman 2000; Rubin 2000; Finnell 2000).

CONCLUSION

Group Theraplay, whether it is with peers, parent-child, multifamily groups, or classrooms, has proved to be a powerful, cost-effective way of helping both children and adults. Children of all ages with a variety of problems who have been dysregulated, aggressive, resistant, anxious, withdrawn, neglected, abused, or traumatized have made significant positive changes through group Theraplay. Research studies (more are needed) have supported many of the clinical observations of children and adults increasing their self-esteem and becoming less aggressive and more cooperative and engaged. Parents (including adoptive, step-, and foster parents) have reported feeling closer to their children and appreciating them more. This has been echoed by teachers.

BIBLIOGRAPHY

Achenbach, Thomas M., and Craig S. Edelbrock. 1983. *Manual for the Child Behavior Checklist: And Revised Child Behavior Profile.* University of Vermont, Department of Psychiatry.

Ammen, Sue. 2000. "A Play-Based Teen Parenting Program to Facilitate Parent/Child Attachment." In *Short-Term Play Therapy for Children,* edited by H. Kaduson and C. Schaefer, 345–69. New York: Guilford Press.

Azoulay, Deborah. 2000. "Theraplay with Physically Handicapped and Developmentally Delayed Children." In *Theraplay: Innovations in Attachment Enhancing Play Therapy,* edited by E. Munns, 279–300. Northvale, NJ: Jason Aronson.

Booth, Phyllis B., and Ann M. Jernberg. 2010. *Theraplay: Helping Parents and Children Build Better Relationships through Attachment-Based Play.* Third edition. San Francisco: Jossey-Bass.

Bowlby, John. 1988. *A Secure Base: Parent-Child Attachment and Healthy Human Development.* New York: Basic Books.

Buckwalter, Karen Doyle, and Annette L. Finlay. 2009. "Theraplay: The Powerful Catalyst in Residential Treatment." In *Applications of Family and Group Theraplay,* edited by E. Munns, 81–93. Lanham, MD: Jason Aronson.

Bundy-Myrow, Susan. 2000. "Group Theraplay for Children with Autism and Pervasive Developmental Disorder." In *Theraplay: Innovations in Attachment Enhancing Play Therapy,* edited by E. Munns, 300–320. Northvale, NJ: Jason Aronson.

Field, Tiffany. 2000. *Touch Therapy.* New York: Churchill Livingstone.

Finnell, Norma. 2000. "Theraplay Innovations with Adoptive Families." In *Theraplay: Innovations in Attachment Enhancing Play Therapy,* edited by E. Munns, 235–56. Northvale, NJ: Jason Aronson.

Ford, Clyde W. 1993. *Compassionate Touch: The Role of Human Touch in Healing and Recovery.* New York: Simon & Schuster.

Gardner, Brijin, and Mary Spickelmier. 2009. "Working with Adolescents." In *Applications of Family and Group Theraplay,* edited by E. Munns, 249–64. Lanham, MD: Jason Aronson.

Gaskill, Rick. 2014. "Empathy." In *The Therapeutic Powers of Play,* edited by C. Schaefer and A. Drewes, 195–209. Second edition. Hoboken, NJ: Wiley.

Gerhardt, Sue. 2004. *Why Love Matters: How Affection Shapes a Baby's Brain.* New York: Brunner-Routledge.

Hindman, Jan. 1991. *The Mourning Breaks.* Oregon: Alexandria Associates.

Hong, J. 2004. *The Effects of a Family Resilience Promotion Program Applying Family Theraplay.* Seoul, South Korea: Sookmyung Women's University.

James, Beverly. 1994. *Handbook for the Treatment of Attachment-Trauma Problems in Children.* New York: Lexington Books.

Kim, Y. 2007. "Development and Evaluation of a Group Theraplay Program to Enhance Attachment of Infants." In *Research Supporting the Effectiveness of Theraplay and the Marschak*

Interaction Method, edited by D. Lender and S. Lindaman, 20–23. Chicago: Theraplay Institute.

———. 2011. "The Effect of Group Theraplay on Self-Esteem and Depression of the Elderly in a Day Care Center." *Korean Journal of Counselling* 12 (5): 1413–30.

Kwon, E. 2004. "The Effect of Group Theraplay on the Development of Preschoolers' Emotional Intelligence Quotient." In *Research Supporting the Effectiveness of Theraplay and the Marschak Interaction Method*, edited by D. Lender and S. Lindaman. Chicago: Theraplay Institute.

Lassenius-Panula, L., and J. Makela. 2007. "Effectiveness of Theraplay with Symptomatic Children Ages 2–6: Changes in Symptoms, Parent-Child Relationships, and Stress Hormone Levels of Children Referred for Psychiatric Care in Three University Hospitals in Finland." Paper presented at the Third International Theraplay Conference, Chicago, Illinois.

Lender, Dafna, and Sandra Lindaman. 2007. "Research Supporting the Effectiveness of Theraplay and Marschak Interaction Method." Paper presented at the Third International Theraplay Conference, Chicago, Illinois.

Levitin, Daniel J. 2007. *This Is Your Brain on Music.* New York: Plume.

Ludington-Hoe, Susan. 1993. *Kangaroo Care: The Best You Can Do to Help Your Pre-Term Infant.* New York: Bantam.

Makela, Jukka. 2005. "The Importance of Touch in the Development of Children." *Finnish Medical Journal* 60: 1543–49.

Manery, Glen. 2000. "Dual Family Theraplay with Withdrawn Children in a Cross-Cultural Context." In *Theraplay: Innovations in Attachment Enhancing Play Therapy*, edited by E. Munns, 151–94. Northvale, NJ: Jason Aronson.

Martin, Doris M. 2000. "Teacher-Led Theraplay in Early Childhood Classrooms." In *Theraplay: Innovations in Attachment Enhancing Play Therapy*, edited by E. Munns, 321–37. Northvale, NJ: Jason Aronson.

Meyer, Linda A., and James L. Wardrop. 2009. "Research on Theraplay Effectiveness." In *Applications of Family and Group Theraplay*, edited by E. Munns, 171–82. Lanham, MD: Jason Aronson.

Morgan, C. E. 1989. "Theraplay: An Evaluation of the Effect of Short-Term, Structured Play on Self-Confidence, Self-Esteem, Trust and Self-Control." Unpublished research, York Centre for Children, Youth and Families, Richmond Hill, Ontario, Canada.

Moustakas, Clark. 1997. *Relationship Play Therapy.* Northvale, NJ: Jason Aronson.

Munns, Evangeline, ed. 2000. *Theraplay: Innovations in Attachment Enhancing Play Therapy.* Northvale, NJ: Jason Aronson.

———. 2001. "Group Theraplay." In *Hand in Hand*, vol. 2, edited by B. Bedard Bidwell, 57–73. Burnstown, ON: General Store Publishing House.

———. 2005. "Theraplay with Adolescents." In *Play Therapy with Adolescents*, edited by L. Gallo-Lopez and C. Schaefer, 30–47. Lanham, MD: Jason Aronson.

———. 2008. "Theraplay with Zero- to Three-Year-Olds." In *Play Therapy for Very Young Children*, edited by C. Schaefer, S. Kelly-Zion, J. McCormick, and A. Odnogi, 157–70. New York: Jason Aronson.

———, ed. 2009. *Applications of Family and Group Theraplay.* Lanham, MD: Jason Aronson.

———. 2011. "Theraplay: Attachment Enhancing Play Therapy." In *Foundations of Play Therapy*, edited by C. Schaefer, 275–96. Second edition. Hoboken, NJ: Wiley.

Munns, Evangeline, and Maribela Arruda-Block. 2014. "Group Theraplay in Schools: Reducing Aggression from Bullying to Caretaking." Presentation at the APT International Conference, Houston, Texas, October 10.

Munns, E., D. Jensen, and L. Berger. 1997. "Theraplay and the Reduction of Aggression." Unpublished research, Blue Hills Child and Family Services, Aurora, Ontario.

Nicholson, Barbara, and Lysa Parker. 2009. *Attached at the Heart*. New York: Universe.

Panksepp, Jaak. 1993. "Rough and Tumble Play: A Fundamental Brain Process." In *Parents and Children Playing*, edited by K. B. MacDonald, 147–84. Albany: State University of New York Press.

Perry, Bruce D. 2009. "Examining Child Maltreatment through a Neurodevelopmental Lens: Clinical Applications of the Neurosequential Model of Therapeutics." *Journal of Loss and Trauma* 4 (4): 240–55.

Perry, Bruce Duncan, and Maia Szalavitz. 2006. *The Boy Who Was Raised as a Dog and Other Stories from a Child Psychiatrist's Notebook*. New York: Basic Books.

Ritterfeld, U. 1990. "Theraplay auf dem Prufsland: Bewertung des Therapieerfolgs am Beispiel sprachauffalliger Vorsehulkinder" (Putting Theraplay to the test: Evaluation of therapeutic outcome with language delayed preschool children). *Theraplay Journal* 2: 22–25.

Rubin, Phyllis B. 2000. "Multi-family Theraplay Groups with Homeless Mothers and Children." In *Theraplay: Innovations in Attachment Enhancing Play Therapy*, edited by E. Munns, 211–34. Northvale, NJ: Jason Aronson.

Rubin, Phyllis B., and Jeanine Tregay. 1989. *Play with Them: Theraplay Groups in the Classroom*. Springfield, IL: Charles C. Thomas.

Schore, Allan N. 2005. "Attachment, Affect and the Developing Right Brain: Linking Developmental Neuroscience to Pediatrics." *Pediatric Review* 26 (6): 204–17.

Schore, Judith R., and Allan N. Schore. 2008. "Modern Attachment Theory: The Central Role of Affect Regulation in Development and Treatment." *Clinical Social Work Journal* 36 (1): 9–20.

Sherman, Jamie. 2000. "Multi-Family Theraplay." In *Theraplay: Innovations in Attachment Enhancing Play Therapy*, edited by E. Munns, 195–210. Northvale, NJ: Jason Aronson.

Siu, Angela F. Y. 2009. "Theraplay in the Chinese World: An Intervention Program for Hong Kong Children with Internalizing Problems." *International Journal of Play Therapy* 18 (1): 1–12.

———. 2014. "Effectiveness of Group Theraplay on Enhancing Social Skills among Children with Developmental Disabilities." *International Journal of Play Therapy* 23 (4): 187–203.

Sunderland, Margot. 2006. *The Science of Parenting*. New York: Dorling Kindersley.

Thayer, T. 1998. "March Encounters." *Psychology Today* (March): 31–36.

Tucker, C. 2015. "Research Project Using Sunshine Circle (Group Theraplay) with Headstart Preschool Programs." Personal communication.

van der Kolk, Bessel. 2014. *The Body Keeps the Score*. New York: Viking.

Weir, Kyle N., Song Lee, Pablo Canosa, Nayantara Rodrigues, Michelle McWilliams, and Lisa Parker. 2013. "Whole Family Theraplay: Integrating Family Systems Theory and Theraplay to Treat Adoptive Families." *Adoption Quarterly* 16 (3–4): 175–200.

Wettig, Herbert H. G., A. Coleman, and Franz J. Geider. 2011. "Evaluating of Theraplay in Treating Shy, Socially Withdrawn Children." *International Journal of Play Therapy* 20 (1): 26–37.

Wettig, Herbert H. G., Ulrike Franke, and Bess Sirmon Fjordbak. 2006. "Evaluating the Effectiveness of Theraplay." In *Contemporary Play Therapy: Theory, Research, and Practice*, edited by C. Schaefer and H. Kaduson, 103–35. New York: Guilford Press.

9

Dyadic Developmental Psychotherapy

Dafna Lender and Vivien Norris

We must learn to regard people less in the light of what they do or omit to do, and more in the light of what they suffer.

—Dietrich Bonhoeffer, *Letters and Papers from Prison*

Katherine, fifteen years old, and her foster mother, Anne, are making an elaborate puzzle on a snowy Sunday afternoon. Anne offers to make hot chocolate. She gets up to get a spoon and notices the dishwasher hasn't been unloaded. Anne looks at Katherine and says, "Katherine, remember our deal that you would finish your chores before we started the puzzle?" Abruptly the atmosphere changes and is spoiled. Katherine leaps from her chair, runs to her room, and slams the door. Anne goes after her to reassure Katherine that they can do the chore together and get right back to the puzzle; however, when Anne opens her door, Katherine screams, "I hate you! Get out of here!" Anne, startled by the fierceness of Katherine's voice, closes the door and returns to the kitchen alone.

Although it is widely accepted that positive and sustained relationships are the key to good mental health and development, what do you do when faced with a child who does not know how to relate, who seems to actively work against forming a relationship with you, her parent? When you try to offer comfort or kindness, your child rejects or attacks you. When she only seems content if you do what she says, in response to an exacting and ever-changing prescription. Parents in this situation will frequently redouble their efforts to try and find a way through to this child whom they are trying to love, but over time they become exhausted, dispirited, and desperate. Who is this child? What has happened to make the fundamental human need to connect and be close to another person appear to work against them? And how can we help them?

121

Dyadic Developmental Psychotherapy (DDP) is an attachment-informed family therapy developed by clinical psychologist Dr. Daniel Hughes. The approach developed from his many years of experience working with fostered or adopted children whose families were severely struggling to form healthy attachments. DDP as a model has developed significantly over the past twenty years, integrating our expanding knowledge of neurobiology, and it is being used across many countries worldwide as both a framework for thinking about this group of families and a specialist therapy model. This chapter will describe the core components of DDP and then illustrate different aspects via examples from work with families.

To start from the beginning, how is it that an otherwise healthy infant, primed and ready to relate from birth (and even before), can grow into a toddler who bites when cuddled and runs away from his caregiver when distressed, or who stares into space, blank and lacking in life and curiosity? Infants are totally dependent on the adults caring for them to provide safety and nurture, to accurately interpret and meet their basic human needs. When infants or young children are faced with adult caregivers who are unresponsive, insensitive, highly unpredictable, or frightening over a sustained period of time, the impact on the child can be profound and debilitating. For young children, it is irrelevant what the motivation of the adult may be. If they are left cold, wet, and alone or startled as a result of fighting around them, then this is their lived experience, one of a world that is lonely and frightening. And over time this becomes embedded as a lens through which other people and experiences are interpreted. The term *developmental trauma* is useful as a way of describing the profound developmental impact of this kind of relational chronic trauma that occurs at the hands of their parents. The impact on the child's developing brain and a broad range of areas of development, social, emotional, physiological, and cognitive is now well recognized (van der Kolk 2005, 406).

DDP draws on theory around developing attachment and also, importantly, on the development of intersubjectivity (Hughes 2006; Trevarthen and Aitken 2001). It is not enough (though it is certainly essential) to have safe adults who provide the basics and are available when needed. In order to grow and be well, a person needs to feel connected, special, enjoyed, and worth being with and to have an experience of someone being alongside, sharing in life's experience. This is at the core of intersubjective experience. Intersubjectivity requires a level of attunement (reading and picking up on the cues of the other), joint attention (that the two people can find a way to mutually attend to something), and complementary intentions (that an idea can be shared—for example, one person points to something and the other joins to look). Challenges in these areas are often at the core of the difficulties these children are facing. They have few genuine intersubjective experiences to build on, and their survival responses resulting from the lack of safety in these early months prevent them from taking the risk of joining or relying on another person. It is safer to look away from rather than toward the other, in spite of a deep and yearning need to do the latter.

Within the DDP model, providing opportunities for intersubjective experiences between parents and their children is a key focus. The work is about the relationship, not the individuals. And the constant question is "What can we do in this moment to provide sufficient safety for this dyad to allow them to take the risk of becoming more connected?" How this often looks in practice is that the overall approach and demeanor of the therapist or parent is very open, with clear communication about the positive impact that the child is having on the adult. The aim is to create as much genuine connection as is possible, the content of what might be spoken about is secondary to the atmosphere of togetherness. The therapist attempts to communicate to the child (and entire family) that they are interested in the whole of the child, not just the problems. Sessions will often begin with a "connect and chat" type of warm informality, recognizing that this child may need reconnecting with at each new meeting.

A key tenet of the DDP model, to establish the kind of interpersonal communications that are most likely to generate genuine connection, is some combination of being *playful*, showing *acceptance*, and showing *curiosity* and *empathy*, described as adopting an attitude of PACE. There is often a sing-song melodic kind of quality to the tone of voice, with a high level of nonverbal communication of warmth and interest from the therapist. Within sessions the therapist may move between these different styles of interaction, attuning to the situation in the room. So, for instance, if a person becomes upset or is describing a difficult situation, the therapist may respond with acceptance and empathy to help deepen the emotional experience and connection (deepening the affect); if someone is stuck or in a repetitive and unhelpful pattern, such as lecturing or delivering a monologue, the therapist may become playful with gentle teasing or playful interruption to try and reengage in a reciprocal dialogue. If an issue is raised, the therapist may show deep curiosity and use a range of strategies to try and help the individual articulate more about what the experience is like.

The aim of the attitude of PACE is to help the child and parent have a deeper understanding of their own and the other's experience in a way that feels supportive and nonjudgmental. Moving seamlessly between these different attitudes often creates a feeling of informality and genuine interest and allows difficult themes to be introduced or woven into the narrative without a gloomy sense of "dealing with the hard stuff." The aim is to allow emotional states to be safely deepened (for the child or parent to have an affective experience and become close to their distress) and also to provide opportunities for some reflection on those experiences. This is referred to as an affective-reflective dialogue and is one of the ways the child begins to make sense of their experiences. There are a range of techniques for helping this process to unfold within a wider general attitude of PACE. First, the therapist often needs to lead the child into interaction rather than be solely child-led since in this situation the child will nearly always avoid delving into such painful experiences. This has been described as a follow-lead-follow approach. In reality the degree of following or leading will vary significantly depending on the child's situation and stage in the therapy process. High levels of sensitivity and attunement to what the child is showing (or not showing) are clearly present, but the therapist will make deliberate and often persistent attempts to lead the child into new intersubjective territory on the basis that without gentle challenge, little change will be made. The therapist will be particularly attentive to nonverbal cues of distress or disengagement and may bring their observation of this into the room, again as a means of making communication explicit and safe to be talked about. The focus remains on the relationships. For example, "You know when your mom came into your room to try to talk to you, you screamed, 'I hate you!' I wonder whether you felt like Mom was being mean to you on purpose by making you do your chore?"

Given that this approach is actively drawing the child into uncomfortable experiences (since intimacy and being connected are new), the therapist will be very attentive to when the child needs a break in intensity. At these moments turning to the adult and talking about the child and what they may have been experiencing may help to reduce the intensity of the shameful or overwhelming feelings. At other times the therapist may want to help deepen the emotional experience, particularly where children are cut off, flat, or consistently retreating from engaging with difficult material, using various means like diversion, jokes, or jumping around. "Talking for the child" has the impact of deepening intensity of affect—for instance, where the therapist sits alongside the child and talks as if he is the child: "But Mom, I don't like it when you go out; it makes me really scared, and then I don't know what to do." The child is able to listen in and engage with the emotive content of what is being said without being under pressure to identify and formulate words for what he may be feeling.

A core goal is to find ways of increasing the child's capacity to tolerate an intersubjective experience with another person, and in time to connect more deeply with his or her own internal experience and that of others so the child can begin to experience comfort and joy with a trusted adult. One of the barriers to this is that children who have experienced disrupted early relationships are highly sensitive to feeling shame, a debilitating and deeply unpleasant experience. This is best understood when comparing this child's early experiences to a "typical" infant/caregiver pattern.

Within an ordinary developmental pathway where a baby has a responsive and sensitive caregiver, the first year or so of life will be filled with multiple unconditional experiences of being cared for and attended to by a warm parent. The infant doesn't have to do anything in order to receive love and care and this repeated and attuned connection forms the foundation upon which later development builds. As they approach toddlerhood, a natural socialization process begins whereby children may do something, such as throw down a spoon or reach for a plug socket, and their parent intervenes by telling them to stop. Once the toddler realizes that the parent is disapproving (rather than it being a game), the child is filled with a negative experience of shame and becomes distressed. The parent quickly notices and moves to repair the relationship with their child, providing comfort and supporting the child to regain a sense of connection and safety. This dose of shame is short and repaired very quickly, and the parent-child pair returns to an equilibrium. Over many repeated similar experiences the young child will begin to understand and anticipate this process and in time develop an internalized sense of how to behave within the particular familial context. When they then knowingly move outside of what is "approved" behavior, they will feel apprehensive and guilty: "I knew I wasn't supposed to do that and I did it anyway." Through this natural shift from an experience of shame (a deep feeling about oneself being no good) to one of guilt (a feeling about one's behavior not being good) comes learning, as well as a growing ability to regulate to some extent one's behavior.

For a child who has missed the early experience of unconditional responsiveness and love from a parent, this shift does not occur as described. Instead, when things go wrong, even in very small ways, the child tips into an overwhelming sense of shame, feeling worthless and humiliated. The experience is "I am bad" rather than "I did something wrong." The child is likely to have experienced this kind of gut-wrenching distress many times in the early developmental years. If children feel deeply that they lack worth, that they are "bad" or something is wrong with them (a very typical state of affairs for children who have experienced chronic relational trauma), then to be shown affection and thoughtfulness or given a compliment can easily trigger this overwhelming sense of shame in the same way that being scolded or making a mistake would. Now that they are older and have more strategies at hand, they will understandably try to avoid this shame experience however they can. And when being close to another person, sharing experiences, showing pride, or simply being connected runs the risk of triggering this shame experience, children will be highly avoidant of these kinds of situations.

Within a caring relationship, whether that be familial, friendly, or therapeutic, this presents a persistent and double-edged dilemma. To be close is in many ways experienced as dangerous; though connection is deeply needed, it is also strongly resisted. Anyone using DDP as an approach will find themselves engaging moment to moment with this core fear that these children are struggling with—that is, how to have an intersubjective experience with someone when their every fiber tells them it is not a good idea. Therapists need a high level of creativity and flexibility in finding ways through these overwhelming feelings that are manageable and do not overwhelm the child to the point of dysregulation or emotional shutdown.

Furthermore, therapists working with foster and adoptive parents or with families of different cultural/racial/ethnic backgrounds than themselves must be aware that the expectations or demands from a relationship may be implicitly different between cultures. In these cases, it is imperative for the therapist to be curious about and reflect on any perceived barriers in the therapeutic process so as to invite and bring to awareness any conscious or unconscious blocks or incongruities, based on the individual's cultural background.

CASE EXAMPLE

Katherine is a fifteen-year-old foster child of Hispanic descent living in a foster home with Anne, a devoted, older Caucasian woman who has had several foster children in her home over the years. Katherine's birth father disappeared when she was an infant and his whereabouts are unknown. Katherine lived on and off with her birth mother, Tracy, until she was eight, with extensive involvement from Child Protective Services over the years. Katherine was finally removed from her birth mother's care when neighbors found her alone in her family's apartment—she had been there alone for more than two days while Tracy was out using drugs. Tracy has been visiting Katherine intermittently over the years and always promises her that she will get an apartment and "bring her home," but she never follows through. Tracy doesn't keep basic promises like attending Katherine's birthday parties. Katherine's presenting problems are that she is withdrawn and has flat affect, has a hard time setting boundaries with peers, and can be talked into doing inappropriate things by charismatic students at school. Katherine recently was suspended for trying to steal an iPad from school. It appears that she was set up by her classmates. When asked why she did it, Katherine said she wanted the other kids to like her. When given consequences, Katherine becomes very self-critical and states, "I'm an idiot, I hate myself, I'm an imbecile." Katherine's foster mom states that Katherine sometimes has angry outbursts and then will run to her room and cry, but when Anne tries to comfort her, Katherine yells for Anne to leave her room. Katherine is generally averse to touch.

Katherine and Anne meet Sally, their therapist, for the first time. Sally starts out by chatting with Katherine, full of interest and asking about what she likes to do and joining with her over their taste in music. Sally laughs easily with Katherine about Sally's poor taste in fashion when compared with Katherine. Sally is making Katherine comfortable and setting a nonthreatening, engaging tone. Then Sally shifts toward the reason why her foster mom brought her to therapy—without changing her voice tone much, still remaining engaged and with a brightness in her voice, Sally changes to a more curious tone, stating the main issues and then asking Katherine (with an inflection going up at the end of her voice), "What do you think?"

When Katherine starts talking, Sally vocalizes sounds of interest and attentiveness, like "Hmmm" with a lot of resonance, showing Katherine that she is following her.

Katherine starts talking about her mom rather dismissively, saying, "Why should I spend my time talking about her [birth mom] because she would never go to therapy to talk about me!" Sally resists the urge to ask more informational questions. Instead, Sally asks Katherine, "If she were to come to therapy, what do you wish you could say to her?" This curious tone brings the conversation in the direction of Katherine's thoughts, wishes, and feelings, which is the aim of therapy.

Katherine responds, "I would tell her that I am done being the parent and that she should be the parent and take responsibility. I tried to be mature and act like the adult, and you haven't done crap."

Sally's goal is to deepen and amplify the affect. So she responds, "OOOOOHHH, OK, I see, yes, that makes sense . . . that's what you would tell her." Sally opens her eyes wide to add meaning to her statement. Sally's next task is to reflect on Katherine's words so that she can latch on to a part of Katherine's sentiment and deepen it.

Sally understands that the emotional heart of what Katherine said was that she has cared about her birth mom but her birth mom has not shown care for Katherine. Sally must try to make meaning with Katherine about this issue. Sally continues: "Oh, wow, so you, the child, the daughter, the kid, have tried, *you* have tried, tried hard, and your *mom* hasn't done crap! Wow, so you are a daughter who has had to work hard to get her mom's attention and you've had to work hard just to have a relationship with your *own* mom?! Oh my goodness!" Then Sally pauses and waits for Katherine's nonverbal reactions so that she can shift the dialogue from leading (Sally's elaboration on Katherine's reversed role) to following (letting Katherine's feedback inform Sally's next direction).

Katherine's face changes from intent listening to a slight lowering of the head and furrowing of the eyebrows, looking sad and discouraged.

Staying with her feelings, Sally continues to explore the themes of how Katherine had to try so hard to take care of her birth mom and how disappointed she is that her birth mom has not cared enough to fulfill her role as a mother.

Katherine looks pensive and begins to talk about a phone call with her birth mom wherein her birth mom did not address the fact that she had promised to come over the previous weekend and then didn't show up. Her foster mom, Anne, reaches over and touches Katherine's shoulder and says, "I know that was hard for you, sweetie." Katherine's immediately shakes off her foster mother's touch. Katherine's face changes to one of a stone cold stare and says flatly, "That's why I am *never going to call her ever again*." Anne's face shows hurt that Katherine will not accept her comfort, and her tone becomes dismissive. Anne says, "Well, I've told Katherine that it's not her fault and Katherine knows that, right?" Katherine nods her head in agreement, but her face is still blank.

Sally notices the dynamic shift that took place when Katherine felt vulnerable and then shut down the hard feelings. Before Sally can assess whether it will be possible to return to the uncomfortable feelings, she has to accept Katherine's emphatic statement that she will never call her birth mom again. Sally matches Katherine's vitality as she repeats the words "You will never call her again! You've had enough of her lies and excuses and you don't want to talk to her!" Then Sally's voice shifts to a melodic voice of curiosity as she addresses Anne: "Wait a minute, Anne, you are saying that Katherine knows it's not her fault? You think she knows that it's not her, she's not to blame, that she didn't do anything wrong, that she couldn't have done anything different, or been a better girl to make her mom act more loving?" This expansion of Katherine's feelings while addressing her foster mom (thereby reducing the intensity for Katherine) serves to allow Katherine to return to the sadness and rejection that she was in touch with previously. "It's not fair!" Katherine announces in a childlike, dejected tone. Sally seizes this essential affective moment and amplifies it by repeating the statement with a great deal of emphasis and empathy in her voice: "It's not fair! It's not fair! You're right, it's not fair!" By matching the vitality of Katherine's statement, Sally has captured Katherine's attention and can now take her in direction of where she wants to lead. Slowing down her rhythm and softening her tone,

Sally recounts Katherine's efforts at being a good daughter and reaching out to her birth mom and the repeated broken promises and broken heart that Katherine has experienced.

Katherine's demeanor now becomes sadder as her shoulders slump, her chin lowers to her chest, and the corners of her lips turn downward. At this point, foster mother Anne's eyes are welling up with tears and she motions to touch Katherine's shoulder but then hesitates and puts her hand down. Sally takes note that Anne is sad for Katherine and wants so much to comfort her. Again, Sally will have to help Anne understand Katherine's vulnerability to being comforted in a separate session. In the meantime, Sally gives Anne a reassuring look that communicates, "I notice that this is really hard for you."

Sally's task is now to bring Katherine even deeper into her painful feelings about her relationship with her birth mom. Sally continues to expand on Katherine's theme: "So Katherine, you feel like you did everything you could and you still couldn't get your mom to show up for you and be a mom?" The curious tone allows Katherine to ponder the question and Katherine begins to reflect. Katherine then begins to talk about her sense that it might have been her fault that her mom used drugs, because she was such a troublemaker as a kid and her parents fought about her a lot. Sally harnesses this theme of guilt and again, with a rhythmic and curious voice tone, empathizes with Katherine's sense of guilt and self-reproach. For the first time, Katherine has been able to articulate the experience of feeling ashamed that her birth mom doesn't love her and care for her. Katherine's eyes fill up with tears, as do Anne's. Sally gently suggests to Katherine to look at Anne's eyes and asks Katherine what she sees. Katherine looks up tentatively and is surprised to see Anne's cheeks streaked with tears. Katherine looks puzzled. Sally, knowing that Katherine needs comforting in this state of sadness, loneliness, and shame, now shifts her focus to the relationship between Katherine and Anne. Sally asks, "Anne, can you share with Katherine why you are crying?"

"I feel sad for her," Anne says as she chokes back more tears.

One of the main principles of DDP is that healing comes from people being open to being comforted while feeling vulnerable with their negative states. Sally continues, saying to Katherine, "Katherine, do you know why Anne is sad? It's because she understands that you feel that you're to blame and she is so sorry that you've had to go through so much heartbreak at such a young age." Katherine looks deeply into Anne's eyes as Sally is speaking, and then she leans in to Anne's shoulder as she cries. Anne puts her hand on Katherine's head, and the two of them sit together in that close position for several minutes.

Sally's goals for this session have been met: she wanted to be able to connect with Katherine by showing positive regard and interest in her; she wanted to use PACE to uncover the deeper reasons as to why Katherine struggles at home and school; and she wanted to establish that Anne, Katherine's primary attachment figure, will be the one to help Katherine deal with the difficult feelings that she has stored deep inside herself.

In the subsequent sessions, Sally's goals will be to encourage Katherine to tell her foster mom directly about herself as a younger child who tried so hard to be good and who got so hurt. If Katherine cannot tell her story herself, then Sally will ask her if it would be OK for her to talk on her behalf to her foster mom. If she agrees, Sally would then use a great deal of affect in her voice and really embody that little girl, little Katherine, who was left alone, hoping, trying desperately, and waiting for her mom to get better and start caring for her.

In DDP, the therapist meets with the parent periodically to prepare the parent for the therapy process and her role in it. At this juncture in Katherine's therapy, Sally would first meet with the foster mom alone to explore the feelings that are coming up for her at this time. Sally had noted that Anne's feelings of rejection from Katherine caused her to dismiss the painful feelings underneath, so Sally would explore those feelings with Anne. One theme that Sally might explore with Anne is the effect Katherine's cultural heritage might have on her ability to rely on adults. Katherine's experience of her birth mother's failure could be embedded in a deeper sense of feeling that the world is an unsafe, unfair place where second chances are hard to come by. This needs to be first explored with Anne as one possible reason why Katherine rejects her bids for caregiving. That way, Anne could learn to be less fearful and more present in those moments when Katherine displays intense negative feelings.

CONCLUSION

The principles and practice of DDP can be used in a wide variety of ways and in many different contexts. It is an approach that can be used with people who find it hard to access other kinds of therapy support and are struggling to relate.

In the example above, a teenager is supported through the attuned, persistent, and carefully directed efforts of the therapist, to take the risk of more connected and vulnerable relating. Similarly, parents may be exhausted and frustrated, facing behavioral management issues, and may find acceptance and empathy toward the child in their care currently impossible. The strength of the DDP model is that in all these scenarios the same principles apply. With caregivers who are finding it hard to show their care, the therapist would spend time using the PACE attitude with the caregiver or foster parents. Exploring the frustration and disappointment, empathizing with their exhaustion, and sharing the emotional intensity of their experience is more likely to lead to a deepening of understanding for the child in their care than is trying to persuade them to have compassionate feelings for the child, which they currently do not have. With families, the therapist will adapt her style to find the aspects of the approach that most usefully apply from moment to moment, while keeping the overall process clearly in mind. Moments of high playfulness may follow distress and vice versa, with the therapist often moving seamlessly between different approaches to allow the child and family times of more and less intensity. Implemented effectively, DDP looks deceptively simple, like having a good chat over coffee. And when we have managed to facilitate brief times when this quality of communication is possible, we know that we are making a difference.

BIBLIOGRAPHY

Hughes, Daniel A. 2007. *Attachment-Focused Family Therapy.* New York: W. W. Norton.

Trevarthen, Colwyn, and Kenneth J. Aitken. 2001. "Infant Intersubectivity: Research, Theory, and Clinical Applications." *Journal of Child Psychology and Psychiatry* 42 (1): 3–48.

van der Kolk, Bessel A. B. 2005. "Developmental Trauma Disorder: Towards a Rational Diagnosis for Children with Complex Trauma Issues." *Psychiatric Annals* 35 (5): 401–8.

10

Slowing Down the Dance

Use of Video Intervention Therapy with Parents and Children

Karen Doyle Buckwalter and George Downing

> Face the facts of being what you are, for that is what changes what you are.
>
> —Søren Kierkegaard

William, who is six years old, was adopted from China. He has been in his adoptive family four years. As time goes on, he seems to be getting more and more out of control with his oppositional and defiant behaviors—the exact opposite of what his adoptive parents had anticipated. His parents are devoted and eager to do anything and everything they can for him. They have sought therapy services, read various books, and attended workshops for parents of struggling adopted children. They are implementing all they have learned to the best of their understanding, but nothing seems to help. This chapter will highlight how the authors' use of Video Intervention Therapy illuminated for William's parents how, despite all their good intentions and efforts, their approaches were going awry in ways they were totally missing prior to seeing themselves on video.

Film has a long history of being used in various forms of psychotherapy, but perhaps none so rich as the various ways it has been used in support of attachment theory and its clinical application. John Bowlby was able to seize the attention of colleagues when James and Joyce Robertson filmed *Young Children in Brief Separation*. This film clearly showed, despite the reluctance of the medical staff to acknowledge it, the deterioration of young children when separated from their caregivers even for brief periods of time (Robertson and Robertson 1969). Later, Mary Ainsworth's films of what would become known as the "Strange Situation" gave a clear and scientific framework for understanding parent-child attachments (Ainsworth 1969). (See chapter 1 for a more detailed explanation of the Strange Situation.)

131

There are a variety of ways in which the use of video can add potency to the therapeutic process. Watching a video clip together can enhance the therapeutic relationship, allowing the therapist and client to "be in the relationship" between the parent and child (or whoever is being filmed) rather than the parent simply reporting what is going on in their parent-child interactions.

The very experience of watching oneself on video with one's child, even without any commentary or interpretation from a therapist, allows the parent to "step back" from the interaction and view it more objectively. The use of video allows one to look at the interactions observed as many times as desired.

This chapter will explain the process and some uses of Video Intervention Therapy (VIT), a specific framework for using video in therapy. VIT is an enhanced, attachment-based form of Cognitive Behavioral Therapy, and is a versatile technique that can be used to supplement many different forms of therapy (Downing 2008).

There are numerous approaches to how parent-child videos can be evaluated and used in therapy. It is useful to highlight two distinct perspectives: video being evaluated by microanalysis, and looking at video in a more global behavioral sense.

Microanalysis is a detailed review of specific interactions, slowing and pausing the film, breaking observations down to fractions of a second. This detailed analysis allows for observation of elements such as gaze, body orientations, and vocalizations, and has been used extensively in attachment research. Global behavioral approaches (Steele et al. 2014) look at broader categories, such as maternal sensitivity, and consider larger segments of video.

VIT draws on both micro and global perspectives. Therapists learning VIT begin by working on the global level alone, then learn to supplement this with an occasional focus, when clinically relevant, on the micro level.

PREPARING FOR A VIT SESSION

In the approach to VIT discussed in this chapter, parents are asked to make videos at home, which are then given to the therapist. Recording at home allows the therapist to see clients in a familiar environment where interactions are more natural than those in an office. In a way, video allows the therapist to do a "home observation" without the additional time required to visit a family in their home.

The therapist watches the video prior to the next therapy session with the family to determine what segments might be most fruitful to highlight, and how much time will be spent on the video and subsequent discussion. In some cases only a portion of the therapy session will be used for this process; in other cases, an entire therapy session may be devoted to viewing segments of the video. It is important to note here that brief portions of the video tape, one to three minutes in length, are shown to the family. What can take varying amounts of time in the session is whether more than one segment is shown and how much discussion goes on about each segment.

There are several areas of interaction a therapist might ask a family to videotape, such as the following:

1. Play between the parent and child (preferably not a board game because the predetermined rules of the game may prevent typical parent-child interaction patterns from readily emerging)
2. Limit-setting with the child
3. A collaboration situation such as making a plan for a family outing
4. A negotiation situation such as talking with an adolescent about curfew time for a special event
5. Talking about the day's events, such as the typical chat parents have after school with their children
6. Preparing or eating a meal together
7. The typical morning or bedtime routine
8. Parent helping the child with homework

It is important for the therapist to talk with the family in detail ahead of time about how they plan to record the video and deliver it to the therapist prior to the next therapy session. In today's age of advanced technology, there are many options for doing this. The important thing is to make a plan with the family, and address any barriers they anticipate, to increase the likelihood the video will be made.

It is best if the family can use a small video camera in an inconspicuous place. This is in no way suggesting that the child should not know a video is being recorded, but rather that it's best to not have the camera where attention is more likely to be focused on it.

In some circumstances, the therapist could make the video in the clients' home. Of course, this could impact the "spontaneity" of the interactions. In a few cases where the barriers to making a video in the home are insurmountable, some institutions also regularly make videos at the institution itself. To do this, the therapist would give the parents and their child one of the specific tasks outlined above and leave the room while the parent and child complete the task. This may take approximately fifteen minutes of the therapy session. The therapist would then return to the therapy room and continue with treatment as usual with the family. Prior to the next therapy session, the therapist would view the video and make a plan of how to use segments with the family.

USING VIT IN A THERAPY SESSION

The use of VIT follows a specific procedure, and the basic steps are as follows:

1. Show the selected portion of the video to the parents. Elicit their observations and reflections regarding what they just saw. It is critical that they become actively engaged in the review quickly. The therapist may do this by asking

open-ended questions to help break through whatever discomfort or hesitancy the parents may be feeling: "What was most interesting to you about this part of the video?" "What stands out for you?" "What did you like best about what your child does?" "What did you like least about what your child does?" "What did you like best about what you do in this segment?" "Is there anything you would like to have done differently as you look at this video?"

2. Return to the video. The therapist may play again the part just reviewed or move to another segment and point out one or more positive events or patterns. Explain why these things are positive and praise and encourage the parent where appropriate. In particularly distressed parent-child relationships, it may be a bit of a challenge to find a positive pattern. The therapist may even perceive the items noted seem somewhat forced or artificial. Regardless, there must be some positive interaction patterns discovered and highlighted to the parent. Parents are in a vulnerable situation when bringing video of themselves with a child with whom they are struggling. It's important to be sensitive to this and to offer hope and encouragement. In some situations, where parents are particularly fragile, mistrusting, or defensive, the video review may stay at this open-ended discussion (step 1) and positive level only (step 2). Remember, particularly early in treatment or with therapists who are new to using VIT, the first two steps are a good start. The initial goal should be to engage the parents and get them talking about what they are seeing. Initially the therapist does not need to focus on changing anything.

3. The next step is the identification of a negative interaction pattern. Typically only one pattern is identified. The therapist must consider the most diplomatic way to talk about this, as it is important for the parent to feel supported rather than criticized. The therapist must then work with the parent to find language to describe the pattern with which the parent is reasonably comfortable. Note: Often throughout these first three steps there will be numerous opportunities for psycho-education with parents about their child's needs and behaviors.

4. Once a specific negative pattern has been identified, it can be explored in more detail. A potential framework for this discussion is the VIT concept of the "Outer Movie and the Inner Movie" The Outer Movie refers to the external behaviors highlighted in the video, and just discussing them at this level can be fruitful and rich. The Inner Movie focuses on what is going on inside the person during the highlighted sequence. Here, the therapist can look at many angles, depending on the theoretical orientation and the type of therapy being used with the family. The therapist may ask about the thoughts and feelings the client may have had during the making of the video, or the therapist may link some of what is going on in the video to the client's history and background. Regardless of what direction the therapist may go, the idea here is to explore in depth what fuels the behavior seen in the video. What is the meaning of the behavior? This step, when using all six steps, will tend to be the longest.

5. End the exploration of the negative pattern with a final focus on a specific behavior change the parent can implement in the next few days. The therapist needs to think carefully about how to break the desired behavior change down into a small, manageable step. For example, some parents tend to talk over their child or not pause to allow their children time to speak (many children with developmental trauma have delayed processing). It may be recommended that the parents agree to ask their child three questions each day and pause after each one until the child has had time to think and formulate a response. The parents should leave the session with one specific new behavior to try or a goal to build on an effective behavior they have already demonstrated by expanding on it in a specific way. It is sometimes helpful to write this down on a piece of paper for the parent to take with them.

6. Summarize what was reviewed and agreed upon related to the video, and develop a plan for making a new video, if necessary. In some cases, only one video may be made with a family, but more often it is helpful to make multiple videos. This is done not only to help parents continue to benefit from VIT but also as a way to help parents actually see progress being made with the child. Progress with children with severe problems can be slow, so it is easy for parents to miss how far everyone has come since starting treatment. The use of video allows even small changes and improvements to be highlighted and discussed.

ACTIVE PARENT ENGAGEMENT PRODUCES RESULTS

During VIT, parents will often notice negative patterns and begin to speak about them without prompting. The intervention can be more powerful when parents are given the time and space to formulate their own thoughts about what they are seeing in the video. The therapist should use restraint and not jump in with observations or interpretations before the parents have the opportunity to offer their own. After listening to what the parents have noticed, the therapist can then find a supportive way to share insights the parents may not have noted, while remaining aware of and attuned to the parents' response.

Let's go back to the case of William. William's family submitted several videos for VIT. The two primarily used were one of William's family having dinner with his grandparents and one of William having what the parents referred to as a "meltdown" when they were trying to set a limit with him.

In the dinner video, using the steps outlined above, the therapist first showed a segment at the dinner table where the father was doing a lot of very positive things with his son, who was clearly struggling to say seated and behave appropriately. The father would often glance at his son or reach over and touch his son on the shoulder. At one point, he even took his son onto his lap. Although his son was six years old, he needed much more of the type of containment that a parent employs with a younger child, including more use of touch and at times holding him to help him stay calm. The father did this naturally and gently in a way that was very calming and soothing for his son. However, until this was pointed out on the video, this father had little idea that he was doing all these helpful things for his son!

This portion of the video gave the therapist an opportunity to provide positive feedback and encouragement to parents who badly needed both. It also provided an opportunity for psycho-education for both parents. The therapist pointed out even though their son's chronological age was six years, because of the abuse and neglect in his background, developmentally he often functioned like a much younger child and needed a corresponding level of assistance from his parents. The parents then shared that they had read about this idea, but without viewing the video they were not able to really *see* what this meant for their son specifically. This kind of "ah-ha" experience is common in VIT.

SPECIFIC ATTACHMENT-BASED TECHNIQUES OF USING THE VIDEO

Within the context of the Six Basic Steps of VIT, there are some specific techniques and things to look for that can be particularly useful with children with attachment difficulties and traumatic backgrounds.

Recognize a Child's Bid for Attention

When looking at a video from an attachment-based perspective, it is common to notice times where the child is making a bid for attention from the parents. These signals from the child are often subtle and not recognized by the parents due to the overall cycle of negative interactions with the child. However, when parents begin to notice these bids and respond, this can have a strong positive effect on the relationship. Children will feel safer and more connected, and parents will feel effective and needed by their child.

Understand a Child's Worldview

VIT is a good time to talk with parents about their child's internal working model and how the noted behavior often "makes sense" if you look at it through the child's internal worldview. The use of video brings these concepts from the theoretical to the practical, and parents can actually see and understand their child's behavior in a different way. Responsiveness of parents to a child's cues is so important in building a secure relationship, but it is easy to miss these signals even in the best of situations (Wolff and IJzendoorn 1997). These attuned interactions are a strong currency for building trust with a child, and the use of video provides an opportunity for the parents to become much more aware of their child's signals.

Explore Parents' Attachment History and Reactions

Now that we have made such careful observation of the child's behavior in the video, we might also talk with the parents about how their reactions are being triggered by their child's behavior. When working from an attachment-based perspective, it is important to focus not only on the child's side of the relationship but also on the parent's response to the child. For example, a mother who constantly felt rejected and as though she did not measure up in her relationship with her own mother may be hypersensitive to any ways her own child seems to be rejecting her.

Parents who have educated themselves about how to respond to their challenging children may also get caught up in executing certain parenting strategies while losing sight of how the child is reacting to them. Video allows the therapist to "slow down the dance" the parent and child are engaged in so parents are able to *see* responses from their children that they could not see when the interaction was going on in "real time." The practice of noticing nuances in the child's behavior in VIT is also a critically important feature that then allows the parents to become more attuned to their children in everyday interactions.

THINKING ABOUT AND UNDERSTANDING A CHILD'S FEELINGS AND EXPERIENCES

Drawing more directly upon attachment theory and research, the concept of mentalization, or being able to think about what is in the mind of the other, is a critically important idea (Fonagy et al. 1991; Fonagy 2008). There are two aspects of mentalization.

The first is the ability to think about and put words to one's own thinking and feeling states and to see how they are linked to one's behavior. This has been referred to as "self-mentalization" (Allen and Fonagy 2006). The second aspect is the ability to consider and think about what others may be thinking and feeling. This is sometimes called understanding the mind of the other, or "other-mentalization," and has been linked to positive parenting outcomes (Slade 2007).

One program that has been used to enhance other-mentalization between parents and their children is the Speaking for the Baby Program (Carter, Osofsky, and Hann 1991). In this program, mothers learn to interpret their infant's cues as the therapist "talks" for the baby and describes how the baby might be feeling as the mother takes care of or plays with him or her, paying special attention to the baby's facial expression and nonverbal cues.

Adapting this concept, a VIT technique called "giving a voice" can be used when reviewing a video with parents of older children. Since an older child is probably verbally active in the video clip, hence doing his or her own speaking, the parent is asked to think about not only what the child is actually saying but also what the child may be thinking and feeling that he or she is not voicing.

The therapist chooses a part of the video to pause, giving a still image that becomes stimulus for discussion. The therapist can then ask the parent, "What do you think your child might be thinking or feeling right here?" The discussion can also broaden in other directions such as what the child might have been thinking and feeling in the seconds just before what is being seen on the screen at the moment. The therapist can suggest a few ideas to get the dialogue going, but it is critical for parents come up with their own thoughts about their child. This technique can be especially useful for parents of children with attachment difficulties because so often what the child is saying verbally is not consistent with what he or she is truly needing or wanting.

An expansion of the "giving a voice" technique is a simulation technique. The difference here is that rather than just reflecting on what the child might be thinking or feeling, the parents actually imagine being their child while a piece of video is being played.

Let's go back to the vignette at the start of the chapter and the second video William's parents made. In this video William was having a full-blown temper tantrum in response to his father setting a limit with him. He was trying to kick, hit, bite, and spit at his father, who was holding him to keep him from hurting himself or anyone else in the room. The six-year-old child was wailing like a toddler. The father was repeatedly giving the child choices and telling him he needed to calm down, make good decisions, and stop trying to hit and kick before the father would let go of him.

In the VIT session, the therapist asked the father to imagine being William in the video and what he might be saying if he was using his words rather than his behavior. The father was able to come up with "I'm so upset! I feel totally out of control and I feel terrible for hitting my dad." His father was also able to talk about how afraid and scared his son may have been feeling.

With this, a light bulb went off for the father, and he realized that with the emotional state his son was in during the video, lecturing him to calm down and asking him to make good choices was not going to be effective. His son, at that moment, just needed someone to help calm him down and keep him safe. He was not in a state of being able to make good choices.

Once the father realized this, both parents became cognizant of a pattern they both had (as do many parents)—using too many words and lecturing when a child is very upset and not in a state to gain any benefit from hearing a lot of words. The father was doing his best to incorporate what he had read in books about dealing with children with attachment and trauma issues. He was trying so hard to do it right, but he saw in the video that he was completely missing the fact that what he was doing was exacerbating the situation rather than helping it.

This is the incredible power of video. Many times a therapist can say very little, but the fact that the parents are able to watch themselves, while calm, thinking clearly, and within the context of safety, enables them to *see* negative patterns in how they are responding to their child.

A particularly powerful follow-up to "giving a voice" and the simulation is an insertion technique.

Once there has been adequate dialogue about a portion of the video and what the child may be thinking and feeling, and the parent has talked about what they see in themselves in the video, the therapist can replay the video. The therapist then stops right before the parent starts responding to their child, and says to the parent, "Based on what we just talked about, put yourself back in that moment [saying this enhances the technique and is recommended]. What could you say or do differently from what you did in the video?"

This has great impact because it allows the parents to "redo" the sequence with their child when they are not in an upset, agitated state. Many times parents can come up with worthwhile things to do and say when they are out of the "heat of the moment." This builds the confidence of a parent who may be feeling beaten down and ineffective. In addition, it gives parents the opportunity to actually practice the more effective behavior in the session, thereby greatly increasing the chances that they will be able to carry it out later with their child.

CHILDREN AND PARENTS JOINTLY PARTICIPATING IN VIT SESSIONS

There are cases with older children and adolescents where they, too, may benefit from being part of VIT. The parents and child may view the video at the same time with the therapist, or both may have a separate time to look at the video with the therapist.

One useful way to work with a parent and child viewing the video together is to ask the parent and child to pick up where the video conversation has been stopped. This allows them to talk to each other live, continuing the same conversation, but while trying one or more new skills. This is known as a continuation technique.

An example of this was an adoptive mother of a fifteen-year-old boy with some processing problems who habitually continued her part of a conversation before her son had a chance to think about what he wanted to say in response to her statements. She would ask her son something, and during the silence, when he was trying to formulate his answer, she would jump in and fill the space with more of her thoughts or what she thought he might be thinking. She also had a tendency to put a positive spin on whatever she was saying when she did this, not allowing an opportunity for her son to share difficult or painful feelings.

She thought she was being helpful and supportive, but in fact quite the opposite was true. Her son felt he was never able to really express how he was thinking or feeling about a subject. After seeing herself doing this in the video, she was able to practice giving her son the time he needed to formulate his thoughts. As a result, their conversations became much more balanced and allowed for a deeper sharing of her son's thoughts and feelings, which was something he had been working on in his individual therapy.

In this case, the parent was able to quickly and easily change her style of communication with her son as a result of the insight gained from seeing herself in the video and then practicing communicating with him in a different way. In turn, her son was able to work on skills of feelings identification and expression.

The VIT examples in this article have been from cases in both residential and outpatient treatment. VIT has also been used in foster care and early intervention programs.

CONCLUSION

The power of VIT is the opportunity for parents to step back and view their interactions with new eyes, the eyes of an observer. From that objective vantage point, they can see for themselves what is so hard to recognize in the moment or when presented as a theory in a book. Just as William's father suddenly understood that his well-intended actions actually escalated a situation, "ah-ha" moments are quite common. VIT allows parents the chance to step back, remove the emotion that may have skewed their perspective in a given situation, and see new possibilities for connecting with their child.

BIBLIOGRAPHY

Ainsworth, Mary D. Salter. 1969. "Individual Differences in Strange-Situational Behaviour of One-Year-Olds." In *The Origins of Human Social Relations*, edited by H. R. Schaffer. London: Academic Press.

Allen, Jon G., and Peter Fonagy, eds. 2006. *The Handbook of Mentalization-Based Treatment.* John Wiley & Sons.

Carter, Sheena L., Joy D. Osofsky, and Della M. Hann. 1991. "Speaking for the Baby: A Therapeutic Intervention with Adolescent Mothers and Their Infants." *Infant Mental Health Journal* 12 (4): 291–301.

Downing, G. 2008. "A Different Way to Help." In *Human Development in the Twenty-First Century: Visionary Ideas from Systems Scientists*, edited by Alan Fogel, Barbara J. King, and Stuart G. Shanker, 200–205. Cambridge: Cambridge University Press.

Fonagy, P. 2008. "The Mentalization-Focused Approach to Social Development." *Mentalization: Theoretical Considerations, Research Findings, and Clinical Implications*, edited by F. N. Busch, 3–56. New York: The Analytic Press.

Fonagy, Peter, Miriam Steele, Howard Steele, George S. Moran, and Anna C. Higgitt. 1991. "The Capacity for Understanding Mental States: The Reflective Self in Parent and Child and Its Significance for Security of Attachment." *Infant Mental Health Journal* 12 (3): 201–18.

Robertson, James, and Joyce Robertson. 1969. *Young Children in Brief Separation*. Film. Ipswich, UK: Concord Films.

Slade, Arietta. 2007. "Reflective Parenting Programs: Theory and Development." *Psychoanalytic Inquiry* 26, no. 4: 640–57.

Steele, Miriam, Howard Steele, Jordan Bate, Hannah Knafo, Michael Kinsey, Karen Bonuck, Paul Meisner, and Anne Murphy. 2014. "Looking from the Outside In: The Use of Video in Attachment-Based Interventions." *Attachment & Human Development* 16 (4): 402–15.

Wolff, Marianne S., and Marinus H. IJzendoorn. 1997. "Sensitivity and Attachment: A Meta-Analysis on Parental Antecedents of Infant Attachment." *Child Development* 68 (4): 571–91.

11

Trust-Based Relational Intervention

Karyn Purvis, Amanda R. Hiles Howard, and Casey Call

A relationship trauma can only be healed relationally.

—Karyn Purvis

Matilda and her father are out shopping. They have already been to a few shops, but her father decides to make one more unexpected stop to the hardware store. Things are going smoothly until they are in the paint section. Her father starts to become irritated because he cannot find the color he needs. After a few minutes, Matilda begins whining, saying that she wants to go home. Her father distractedly tells her to calm down while he finishes shopping. Matilda crosses her arms and rolls her eyes, irritating her father further. Soon, she begins petulantly kicking the inside of the cart. Using a very harsh tone, her father tells her to stop. Matilda begins crying, yelling, and attracting the attention of other costumers. Embarrassed and angry, her father picks her up and carries her out of the store, vowing to never take her shopping again.

TRUST-BASED RELATIONAL INTERVENTION

Situations like the one above can be frustrating and confusing even when caring for a typically developing child. However, when working with children and youth with a history of maltreatment, abuse, neglect, multiple home placements, and/or violence, caregiving in difficult situations can be even more challenging. In the course of this chapter, you will learn about Trust-Based Relational Intervention (TBRI), which focuses on helping caregivers recognize the needs of children and empowering those caregivers to do what is required to meet their children's needs in a safe, nurturing, and developmentally appropriate way. Although TBRI is specifically designed for children and adolescents from hard places, you will see that in many ways these principles apply to all children.

TBRI is composed of three interacting and synergistic sets of principles and strategies: Empowering, Connecting, and Correcting (Purvis et al. 2013). These principles help children and caregivers learn healthy ways of interacting so that both are able to play a role in the process of healing relational trauma. Empowering Principles highlight the importance of meeting physical needs and help children learn important skills like self-regulation. The Connecting Principles are based on attachment theory and research (Siegel 2012) and are focused on building trust between children and caregivers as well as facilitating attachment. Correcting Principles guide caregivers in helping their children learn behavioral and social competence. As a result, children are better able to adjust to the social world they live in.

EMPOWERING PRINCIPLES

Empowering Principles lay the foundation for behavioral change by assuring optimal conditions for the child. For example, a child who is frequently hungry has little capacity for academic achievement or exploratory play because his food insecurity overshadows his thoughts, feelings, and behaviors (Kleinman et al. 1998). Further, facilitating an environment that nurtures "felt-safety" is a crucial component in setting the stage for behavioral change (Purvis et al. 2013). This emphasizes the difference between a child *being* safe and a child *feeling* safe within an environment. Although caregivers may know with certainty that their child with a history of food insecurity will never suffer from hunger or malnutrition again, this message must be communicated in concrete and understandable ways to the child. Strategies to create this understanding could include helping the child shop for nutritious snacks (e.g., fruit, nuts, vegetables). Allowing the child to put one or two healthy snacks in her backpack may also give "evidence" to the child that she will not be hungry again. The basic idea of Empowering Principles is to enhance a child's capacity for self-regulation, decrease the likelihood of negative incidents, and increase successful "connecting and correcting" (see Purvis et al. 2013).

Physiological Strategies

The physiological strategies concentrate on empowering children internally through things like hydration, keeping blood sugar at an appropriate level, and understanding how children from hard places may have trouble processing sensory input. When the body is operating at an optimal level, it is easy to take these things for granted. However, when one thing goes off track, it can manifest somewhere that may seem unrelated, like in a child's behavior. Have you ever been very hungry and noticed that it began to show in your mood? Maybe you even had a headache, which only added to your irritability. By understanding how internal states can affect external behavior, caregivers are better able to meet their children's needs.

Blood Glucose

Unstable blood sugar often manifests through behavior. Adults may become irritable, but children may have outbursts and/or meltdowns or become aggressive or withdrawn when they have not eaten. For many children from hard places, insulin receptor sites have been dramatically altered due to malnutrition or exposure to alcohol or drugs in utero. For these children, even minor fluctuations in blood glucose can affect learning and lead to behavioral difficulties (Kleinman et al. 1998). Children with low blood glucose have difficulty regulating their behavior. Regulation is important for success, especially in school. In order to do well, children must be able to pay attention, concentrate, and resist temptations such as talking to friends or letting thoughts wander. On the surface, offering a snack to children who are having trouble may not seem like an appropriate response. However, it may be exactly what they need. To maintain proper glucose levels in the blood, children should eat every two hours. Choosing foods low on the glycemic index help keep children fuller longer because these foods regulate blood glucose over an extended period of time.

Hydration

Even at small levels, dehydration causes changes in thinking, behavior, and mood. Studies show that dehydration leads to difficulty concentrating, trouble with memory, anxiety, and anger (Armstrong et al. 2012). Dehydration also influences general health, including slower metabolism, lower quality of sleep, and decreased efficiency in the body's ability to flush out toxins (Armstrong et al. 2012). Children from hard places likely never learned to monitor their own hydration levels. Perhaps the simplest dehydration solution is to provide children with water bottles to keep on hand.

Sensory Needs

Humans rely on their senses to understand the world. When caregivers pick up their infants and hold them tenderly, stroke their cheeks affectionately, or explore their fingers and toes, the infant experiences a rich, gentle sensory bath of human affection, touch, and care. When caregivers hold, coo at, or rock fussy infants, they help prepare their child's brain for self-regulation. When caregivers hold their babies close, they provide deep muscle input, which is calming. Children who have not had early nurturing touch, or who have experienced painful touch, are at risk for sensory deficits (Warner et al. 2013). The manifestation of sensory deficits in behavior and attachment is significant, because without appropriate nurturing, children will respond inappropriately in certain situations. Being aware of a child's sensory needs can help the child be more successful. For example, children with unique sensory needs might be hypersensitive to smells and have emotional outbursts around certain odors. Moreover, due to neurological disorganization, children might perceive a peer's unintentional contact, such as accidently bumping into them in the lunch line, as intentional and overreact with aggression. Another child might brush off a caregiver's kisses or tickles because he has trouble with light touch. For children who have not received optimal care, these senses can be further developed in a nurturing environment by providing opportunities for sensory-rich activities, snacks, crafts, and learning. When these senses are reactivated, behavioral changes become possible (Purvis et al. 2013).

Ecological Strategies

In contrast to the physiological strategies, where what is going on in a child's body impacts behavior, ecological strategies help caregivers use the environment to teach children self-regulation skills. These include things like predictability, transitions, daily rituals, and scaffolding, or providing a framework for self-regulation.

Transitions

For all of us, life transitions (e.g., moving to a new town, birth of a sibling) require the support of others (Cowan and Cowan 2003). But for children from hard places, such events prove more difficult and necessitate even more support from those around them. Daily transitions also require a great amount of support. For children from hard places, moving from activity to activity (e.g., shifting from waking up to getting ready for school to sitting in a desk and paying attention) requires preparation, thinking, concentration, and mental flexibility. Making the environment and schedule predictable for children will ease daily activities and transitions. Strategies like giving several warnings prior to switching activities (e.g., "In five minutes, we will be going inside"), giving a child a pictorial schedule of the day (include a couple of "wild cards" for unexpected events), or creating a hello or goodbye ritual with the child can do wonders for their regulation and ability to learn.

Teaching Self-Regulation

A vital task for caregivers is to teach self-regulation strategies to children. It is important to understand how self-regulation develops in optimal situations (Schore 2001). Other-regulation occurs during the first year of life. Loving caregivers regulate the needs of infants (e.g., when infants are hungry, adults feed them). Co-regulation occurs during toddler and preschool years. Adults still provide much support, but children learn basic self-regulation skills and to ask for needs (e.g., "I'm hungry," "I'm cold," "I'm afraid"). Out of this system, children learn self-regulation skills that serve them well in other contexts, such as sitting still during the school day, waiting until after dinner for dessert, and handling disappointment or anger. When children have not had the experiences necessary to learn the basic skills to regulate themselves, it can manifest as having trouble sitting still, difficulties paying attention and concentrating on schoolwork, and problems waiting in line (Schore 2001). There are many tools for teaching and supporting children's self-regulation skills—for example, teaching calming techniques. Self-regulation skills can be taught through tactile and proprioceptive activities, such as fidgets and chair push-ups. Fidgets are small manipulatives that can be held and worked with one or both hands. They provide an outlet for energy that may otherwise go toward nail biting/picking, hair twirling, or lip biting. Examples of fidgets include squeeze/stress balls, tangles, or pipe cleaners. The most effective way to teach self-regulation is to repeatedly, purposefully, and playfully dysregulate children (e.g., games) and then help them to regulate themselves by practicing different strategies such as deep breathing or pushing down the wall.

CONNECTING PRINCIPLES

The Connecting Principles are based on attachment theory (Cassidy 2001; Siegel 2012) and are the "heart and soul" of TBRI (see Purvis et al. 2013). The Connecting Principles are not only important as essential mechanisms for building trusting relationships but also the mechanisms that make both the Empowering and (especially) the Correcting Principles work in practice. The Connecting Principles consist of mindfulness and engagement strategies.

Mindfulness Strategies

Mindfulness strategies aid the caregiver in being aware of what they bring to interactions with their children, such as being conscious of their own relationship histories and current emotional and physiological states (Siegel 2012). Being mindful is bringing one's complete attention to the present moment. We encourage caregivers to concentrate on feelings, thoughts, and reactions *in the moment* with their children. Perhaps the caregiver feels confused about something the child says or does. Perhaps there are feelings of anger, disappointment, or frustration. The question to ask oneself is "Is this about the child, is this about me, or is this about my history?" A caregiver's understanding of her own history, including both how it influences her behavior and how she interprets the behavior of others, is part of being mindfully aware (Siegel 2012). When she is aware of what behaviors "push her buttons" and why, it is easier to begin understanding how to be proactive in managing them. Spending time with children and using the Connecting Principles also helps adults become more aware of children's signals as well as their own (Siegel 2012). Does the child's jaw clench and breathing become shallow just before an outburst? Do the eyebrows furrow slightly when something scary happens? Adults who become at-tuned to both their own and their children's cues can meet the needs of the children in their care quickly and sensitively, which furthers a secure connection. Nurturing this type of connection can only be achieved if adults are mindful.

Engagement Strategies

Engagement strategies help caregivers connect and build trust with a child using nonverbal skills such as eye contact, behavioral matching, and playful engagement. For children and adults who have experienced relational trauma, the nonverbal chan-nels are especially potent (Schore 2001). When children come from hard places, it is difficult for them to accept emotional care and nurturing. The engagement strategies provide nonthreatening, playful ways to engage children who are not used to accept-ing care from adults.

Authoritative Voice

Implicit to successful interactions is the tenuous balance between nurture and structure. When working with children, we try to keep our voices appropriate to the situation, paying careful attention to volume, cadence, and tone. During day-to-day interactions, a caregiver's voice should be playful and melodic, such as found in "motherese" between a caregiver and infant. If behavior becomes more challenging, adults should increase their volume without yelling, slow their cadence, and adopt a firmer, more authoritative tone. Using a voice that is overly intense for the situation will signal danger and ultimately trigger a fight, flight, or freeze response, which in turn will lead to behavioral problems.

Eye Contact

An explicit goal for adult-child interaction is gaining meaningful eye contact. However, sustained eye contact might be challenging for children who suffer from depression or anxiety or have a history of trauma. If children avoid eye contact as an adaptive strategy, it is important to lead them gently toward sustained eye contact. Some basic strategies for incorporating eye contact into interactions include saying the child's name in a sentence, finding playful ways to get eye contact ("I think her eyes are pink"), or lightly touching a child below the chin. Once the child makes eye contact, adults should reinforce the behavior through praise ("I love those eyes" or "Thank you for looking at me"). Over time eye contact becomes more natural and organic.

Behavioral Matching

Behavioral matching focuses on attuning with children in meaningful ways. The art of matching develops naturally and is at the core of attachment relationships. A mother and infant who are securely attached are connected physically, emotionally, and psychologically through an attachment "dance" that is rooted in matching. In all interactions, we take great care to match children, including body position and posture, eye contact, use of words and inflections, and activities and interest. The adult might mimic the position of the child by getting down to their eye level, even down on their knees. If the child is on the floor, the adult might want to get down on the floor. As described above, eye contact is important and must be gained carefully. The adult might also match the child in inflection at the beginning of an interaction—for example, whispering if the child is whispering. After a verbal interaction, the adult might want to use an expression such as "Fair enough?" or "Yes, ma'am?" and lead the child to respond with the same words, inviting the child to continue with the back and forth of this attachment "dance."

Playful Engagement

Playful engagement produces warmth and trust between caregivers and children (Panksepp 2000). It disarms fear, promotes attachment, and builds social competence (Jernberg and Booth 1999). Mothers who engage their infants in playful interactions enhance development of attachment, socialization, and language (Montagu 1986). When working with children from hard places we encourage caregivers to play games and use imaginative play with their children. If possible, let the child lead the play and enjoy and delight in the time together.

Healthy Touch

Healthy touch is a natural part of daily life between a caregiver and an infant (i.e., holding, feeding, playing [Field 2002]). Adults tend to move away from pervasive touch as children grow out of infancy (Montagu 1986). However, children from hard places need the foundational sense of connection that healthy, safe touch brings (Field 2002). Even with children who have been wounded by abuse, it is vital to find ways to bring healing through touch so that children learn to give and receive nurturing care. It is important to be aware and respectful of a child's personal level of comfort with both giving and receiving safe touch. However, pursuing the positive results of safe touch and the trust and connection that is built through these interactions is imperative for healthy connections (Field 2002).

CORRECTING PRINCIPLES

The Correcting Principles are used to shape behavior and build social competence while maintaining connection (see Purvis et al. 2013). It is important to realize that Correcting will only be effective if it is based on a firm foundation of Empowering and Connecting. Overall, caregivers find behavioral correction easier and smoother when they have a solid basis of connection with their children. Providing a balance of structure and nurture is essential to effective correcting. In all situations, but particularly when responding to challenging behavior, caregivers must understand when to provide structure and when to provide nurture. Think of structure and nurture each as a foot—they must walk together and follow one right after the other in order to stay balanced and not fall. Giving children structure when they need nurture impedes trust. Giving them nurture when they need structure impedes growth. Balancing structure and nurture is designed to create an environment of safety. When a child has a sense of "felt-safety" he can risk abandoning old maladaptive behaviors and take his first tenuous steps toward the construction of new behaviors.

A second component of the Correcting Principles is being mindful of how high to set "the bar" for behavioral expectations. A caregiver's expectations of behavior (or the bar) should be challenging but realistic for a child. Setting the bar requires that adults be mindful in two ways: (1) remembering their child's history and (2) being aware of current circumstances (e.g., triggers in the environment, last time the child ate). For example, with children who have been harmed or abused, expect to "set the bar" low until ample trust develops in the relationship. Current circumstances such as knowing the last time the child had physical activity or food and identifying triggers in the environment like loud or crowded places are also helpful to consider. Be mindful of such situations and understand that children who have recently experienced such a trigger will need a "low bar" until they feel safe again.

Proactive Strategies

The proactive strategies are intended to teach positive social skills during calm times. When children are in a calm and alert state, their brains are optimized for learning. The best way to introduce and reinforce proactive strategies with children is through play. Play is a low-pressure time when caregivers and children can relax and connect while working together toward behavioral change and self-regulation.

Sharing Power

When children come from chaotic and out-of-control environments, they often crave control. Understanding this can help caregivers have compassion for some behaviors. Giving children appropriate levels of power over their lives is a way to build connection and allows children to feel empowered. Allowing children to practice making meaningful choices and negotiating their needs also provides them with invaluable skills to use in school, with friends, and throughout life. Sharing power is vital to building a healthy connection. This is not to say that a caregiver should give over all power. Caregivers must remain in charge at all times because children need a safe, guiding hand and should never feel that they must make all the decisions. For many caregivers, sharing power is counterintuitive, as they believe they must have all the authority However, allowing children to have some say in their own lives is important. Much like the Connecting Principles, sharing power takes two people, back-and-forth communication, and patience on the part of the caregiver.

Choices

Choices offer children appropriate levels of control over their daily lives and diffuse situations that have the potential to become challenging. In most circumstances, we suggest offering children two or three choices. All options should be positive, good decisions that will satisfy both the caregiver and the child. For example, if a child refuses to put on her pajamas, a caregiver might say, "Would you like to wear your train pajamas or animal pajamas?" In this situation, the caregiver's goal is for the child to get dressed, but allowing the child the choice of what to wear gives her some level of control. Make sure that there is no "right" or "wrong" choice. An example of an incongruent choice is "You can either eat your dinner or go to your room. Which do you choose?" Incongruent choices are not real choices for children.

Compromises

Compromises allow children to negotiate a different choice when the ones offered are not necessarily what they would like. Teaching children to ask "May I have a compromise?" allows them to practice negotiation. In the example above, the child might ask, "Can I please wear my green pajamas?" By saying yes, many adults might feel like they are giving in. However, they are teaching children the valuable skill of using their words to ask for what they want and need and building trust by honoring children's voices. In many situations, it is easy to say yes to the compromise offered. However, there may also be situations in which the caregiver must say no. In those cases, caregivers are encouraged to respond with something like "I will have to say no to that, but did you have something else in mind?"

Life Value Terms

Life value terms are guides for bringing a child's behavior back on track. These skills are taught and practiced during calm times in order to provide proactive strategies in dealing with challenging behaviors. Life value terms are short phrases with big meaning and can be woven into everyday life, even during choices and compromises. Teaching children to speak to others "with respect" and to "ask permission" helps instill character and social competence. If a child has proactively practiced these skills, these short phrases can be utilized as verbal reminders in the midst of challenging behavior. For example, if a child is playing too rough with a family pet, a caregiver could simply say, "Gentle and kind," to get behavior back on track.

Responsive Strategies

Responsive strategies provide caregivers with tools for responding to challenging behavior from children in the moment. The TBRI responsive strategies include two powerful scripts for responding in challenging situations with children: the IDEAL response and levels of response.

The IDEAL Response

The IDEAL response outlines five useful, concrete guidelines for responding to challenging behavior. These guidelines should be used simultaneously and are general parameters for responding to behavior.

Immediate: Immediate responses occur within three seconds of the behavior. The brain only holds information in the short-term memory for a few seconds. That is why when caregivers address challenging behaviors quickly children are better able to learn from the experience.

Direct: Being direct is about staying engaged and connected during challenging behavior. Remember, connection is the foundation of all relationships. There are several ways to stay engaged when children misbehave, including getting on the child's level (e.g., kneeling at the child's eye level), gentle touch on shoulder or arm, and making eye contact with the child.

Efficient: Although it is tempting to use more response than is necessary when children misbehave, this may drive children into a worse cycle of behavior. Identifying the appropriate levels of response for a situation helps ensure that the caregiver's response matches the intensity of the situation. Remember, the aim is to keep children on the behavior track without pause.

Action-based: Research shows that active, experiential learning creates new connections in the brain (Kontra, Goldin-Meadow, and Beilock 2012). We also know that action helps children learn at a greater pace and deeper level. That is why the IDEAL response incorporates a "re-do," or a chance for children to practice the right behavior at the end of an episode. Re-dos involve helping a child "go back to the beginning" of a situation and re-create things as they might have happened if the child had been regulated, using words or any other technique that applies.

Leveled at the behavior, not the child: For children from hard places, self-esteem is fragile. Adults must help them understand that their behavior is not who they are. Helping them understand that they have personal value regardless of behavior may be a long road, but using the IDEAL response in conjunction with TBRI Connecting and Empowering Principles will help.

Levels of Response

Whatever form of redirection or correction is used with a child, the most important goals are to correct the behavior as efficiently as possible and to reconnect with the child. However, knowing how much intervention to use, without using too much, is tricky. The TBRI Levels of Response are designed to aid caregivers with this challenge.

Level 1: Playful engagement: This is a relaxed, playful mode of responding that is ideally where caregivers want to be most of the time. With playful engagement, the goal is to put out a spark before it turns into a fire, so to speak. Caregivers may use playful engagement when a child is demonstrating low-level behaviors such as using a sassy/mildly disrespectful tone, talking back, speaking out of turn/interrupting, taking something without permission, or demanding something. It can be difficult to remain playful when children engage in such behaviors. However, most behavior can be successfully corrected through playful redirection. Think about this level as "redirecting with a smile." For example, if a child says, "Give me the crayons," the adult could respond playfully with "Are you asking or telling?" or "Try it again with respect."

Level 2: Structured engagement: This level requires a bit more intervention and attention. Here, adults should stop what they are doing to address the situation. Choices and compromises followed by a re-do (repeating the infringement with correct, respectful behavior and words) work well with Level 2. When Level 1 is unsuccessful and children continue the misbehavior, Level 2 is a good next step. For example, say you offer a child two choices for free time—the playground or the game table—and the child says in a demanding tone, "Go get my coloring book, so I can draw in it!" You might first try Level 1 by saying something like "Whoa! Are you asking or telling? Let's try that again with respect." Upon hearing this, the child ignores you, sits down emphatically, and says, "Go get the book!" At this point, the situation has escalated and requires a Level 2: Structured engagement response. You might approach the child gently, get on his level, make eye contact, and say something like "Sweetie, if you're asking for a compromise, I need you to use good words," followed by "I'm going to help you get what you need but you've got to use good words." In this situation, your tone should be lower and firmer than it was with Level 1. Your cadence should be slow and slightly louder, but not harsh. You have had to stop forward movement in the situation, but you will quickly be able to deal with the infraction and return to being playful. For example, when your child asks with respect to work on the coloring book, you might say, "Absolutely! Let's see if we can find the glittery markers! Aren't those your favorite ones?" The interaction ends with playful engagement and reinforces the connection between adult and child.

Level 3: Calming engagement: When situations escalate to the point that children need help regulating and calming themselves (and/or Levels 1 and 2 have not been successful), Level 3: Calming engagement responses are best. At this level, it is safe to assume that children also need help determining their needs in the situation. It is important here not to send a child away (e.g., time-out or sending a child to his room). Rather, bring the child closer so that he knows you are his advocate who will help meet his needs. Keeping a child close at Level 3 helps keep the connection between adult and child, as the situation is resolved. Often, using a "time-in" works at this level. For example, say that you have asked your child to clean up her lunch before going to the next activity. The child ignores you, so you use a Level 1: Playful engagement response to ask her again. This time, the child picks up a cracker, throws it across the room, and yells, "I'm not cleaning up this stupid food. This is stupid and you're stupid!" She then takes her lunchbox off the table and throws it on the floor. This situation calls for Level 3: Calming engagement. You might respond with something like "We do not say 'stupid' and we do not throw things. I want you to sit right here at the table with me. When you're ready to talk about what you did wrong, say, 'Ready,' and I'll be right here to listen to you." At this point, your tone should be firm, your cadence should be slow, and your volume should be intense but not loud. Be aware that, at this and the next level, children are more sensitive to sensory input. Touch (e.g., shoulder, hand) or loud volume can easily send a child into sensory overload and escalate the situation. Remember, the situation should end with Level 1: Playful engagement. In the example above, you might say something like "Okay! Let's make a game: see if you can clean up all the sweet things that were in your lunchbox. Ready . . . go!"

Level 4: Protective engagement: When children are a danger to themselves or others, a Level 4: Protective engagement response is needed. Caregivers should seek formal training in an intervention accepted in their state or regulations of their organization. While TBRI does not identify the particular method to stop aggression, it does require that a child is regulated, knows he or she is precious, and is connected to the adult before the episode is considered complete. Remember, the episode is not finished until the pair returns to Level 1: Playful engagement.

ASSEMBLING THE PIECES

Now that you know the basics of the Empowering, Connecting, and Correcting Principles, let's think about how they could apply to Matilda and her father. Matilda and her father have already been to several stores, so more than likely they have been shopping for some time. It is possible that both of their blood glucose levels are low and they are starting to become dehydrated. One simple solution is to provide Matilda (and her father) with a bottle of water and a snack either prior to going into the store or in the cart while he is shopping. By regulating her blood glucose and providing hydration, Matilda is less likely to act out. Further, Matilda might be suffering from sensory processing difficulties. She could be averse to the smell of paint or the store could be too loud and crowded. As a result of her sensory needs, she could become overwhelmed. Recognizing her sensory needs ahead of time and being proactive in meeting those needs could empower her to be successful. For example, her father could provide Matilda with earplugs or bring a soothing scent for her to smell while in the paint section.

Further, they have been through multiple transitions and this last stop is unexpected, making the transition even more abrupt. If transitions are challenging for

Matilda, her father could explain the stop prior to entering the store, so she has a better idea of what they will be doing and how long it could potentially take. One proactive solution is to have a regulation plan when they are on outings. For example, her father could have a playlist of calming music on his mobile device. Perhaps they could have one or two sensory items such as a weighted lap pad or stress ball in the car. He should also help Matilda practice recognizing her needs early and asking for help. The most effective way to reduce behavioral episodes is to teach children proactively. In this example, Matilda's father is irritated, leading him to respond in a more abrupt manner than he might in other circumstances. Further, due to his distraction, he fails to recognize the early signs of Matilda's dysregulation. By being mindful in the moment and utilizing the engagement strategies, he would have been better able to recognize both his and his daughter's subtle physical and emotional cues (e.g., whining) and appropriately intervene early. In this example, whining might call for a Level 1: Playful engagement response. Matilda has not become dysregulated and a playful response will likely stop the behavior from progressing. Her father should respond immediately and go near to Matilda when responding.

If her father did not recognize the early signs and Matilda became more dys-regulated (crossing arms and rolling eyes) or if Level 1: Playful engagement did not de-escalate the behavior, the adult would move to Level 2: Structured engagement. In this situation, he might use a firm, slow-paced voice in a moderate volume to get Matilda's attention, being careful not to sound harsh. The adult might ask Matilda to use her words or offer her choices such as "You can either sit quietly in the cart or stand beside me while I finish shopping." If Matilda's behavior continues to deteriorate (e.g., kicking the inside of the cart), her father should move to Level 3: Calming engagement. Matilda needs help to regulate herself and calm down. Her father should continue to be direct and immediate in his responses to her behavior. The adult may walk to another section of the store where the paint smell is not so strong or that is not as crowded. Once there, the adult might try to guide her through some deep breathing or another self-regulation activity that they have practiced in the past. Further, her father could offer Matilda some cold water and a snack. After she has calmed down, her father could guide her through a behavioral re-do where she uses a respectful tone to ask when they are leaving.

CONCLUSION

Children from hard places present unique challenges for caregivers that strive to provide the care and support they need. TBRI is a relationship-based model that can be administered by nurturing, insightful caregivers, and can be implemented in virtually any environment with children and youth of any age and any risk level. Holistic in nature and developmentally respectful of the impact of trauma, TBRI can lead to positive impact in the lives of children and youth who have a history of trauma.

BIBLIOGRAPHY

Armstrong, Lawrence, Matthew Ganio, Douglas Casa, Elaine Lee, Brendon McDermott, Jennifer Klau, Liliana Jimenez, Laurent Le Bellego, Emmanuel Chevillotte, and Harris Lieberman. 2012. "Mild Dehydration Affects Mood in Healthy Young Women." *Journal of Nutrition* 142 (2): 382–88.

Cassidy, Jude. 2001. "Truth, Lies, and Intimacy: An Attachment Perspective." *Attachment & Human Development* 3 (2): 121–55.

Cowan, Philip, and Carolyn Pape Cowan. 2003. *Normative Family Transitions, Normal Family Processes, and Healthy Child Development.* New York: Guilford Press.

Field, Tiffany. 2002. "Infants' Need for Touch." *Human Development* 45 (2): 100–103.

Jernberg, Ann M., and Phyllis B. Booth. 1999. *Theraplay: Helping Parents and Children Build Better Relationship through Attachment-Based Play.* San Francisco: Jossey-Bass.

Kleinman, Ronald, Michael Murphy, Michelle Little, Maria Pagano, Cheryl Wehler, Kenneth Regal, and Michael Jellinek. 1998. "Hunger in Children in the United States: Potential Behavioral and Emotional Correlates." *Pediatrics* 101 (1): E3.

Kontra, Carly, Susan Goldin-Meadow, and Sian L. Beilock. 2012. "Embodied Learning Across the Life Span." *Topics in Cognitive Science* 4 (4): 731–39.

Montagu, Ashley. 1986. *Touching: The Human Significance of the Skin.* New York: Harper-Collins.

Panksepp, Jaak. 2000. "The Riddle of Laughter: Neural and Psychoevolutionary Underpinnings of Joy." *Current Directions in Psychological Science* 9 (6): 183–86.

Purvis, Karyn, David Cross, Donald Dansereau, and Sheri Parris. 2013. "Trust-Based Relational Intervention (TBRI): A Systemic Approach to Complex Developmental Trauma." *Child & Youth Services* 34 (4): 360–86.

Schore, Allan. 2001. "The Effects of Early Relational Trauma on Right Brain Development, Affect Regulation, and Infant Mental Health." *Infant Mental Health Journal* 22 (1–2): 201–69.

Siegel, Daniel. 2012. *The Developing Mind: How Relationships and the Brain Interact to Shape Who We Are.* New York: Guilford Press.

Warner, Elizabeth, Jane Koomar, Bryan Lary, and Alexandra Cook. 2013. "Can the Body Change the Score? Application of Sensory Modulation Principles in the Treatment of Traumatized Adolescents in Residential Settings." *Journal of Family Violence* 28 (7): 729–38.

12

Using an EMDR Integrative Model to Treat Attachment-Based Difficulties in Children

Debra Wesselmann, Stefanie Armstrong, and Cathy Schweitzer

Everything's a story—You are a story—I am a story.

—Frances Hodgson Burnett, *A Little Princess*

Dillon's mother sits down with the therapist to begin the intake process. She appears angry and exhausted. "Dillon is negative, defiant, and oppositional," she states. "He argues and loses his temper, or he pretends to agree with us and then lies and sneaks around, doing whatever he wants. He has to be in control. He bosses his younger siblings. He says he has friends, but truly, no one wants to hang around him. He's too rude and controlling." She explains that Dillon was hospitalized twice last month and also two years prior for cutting on his arms and legs and for suicidal thoughts. Dillon was diagnosed with bipolar disorder and oppositional defiant disorder during his first hospitalization, at which time he was prescribed a mood stabilizer and saw a counselor. His mother goes on to say, "He admits he still wants to cut, even after being in the hospital last month. We just can't keep on going on this way."

Dillon's mother recounts his complicated history. He and his siblings were removed from their biological family due to neglect and abuse and placed in foster care when Dillon was twelve. His biological parents suffered from mental illness and drug addiction, as did several extended family members. Dillon's biological parents did not follow court orders for treatment and visitations, and the children were adopted by their foster parents after two years in foster care.

When it's Dillon's turn to speak with the therapist alone, he states, "I'm worried that I could run into some of my biological family members somewhere." He continues, "I have flashbacks about the past, and I have nightmares." He describes feeling depressed and angry. He states that cutting gives him instant relief from his emotional pain, although the relief lasts only for a brief time.

I invite Dillon's mother to join us, and I explain, "Memories of situations that are extremely upsetting and overwhelming to us become very 'stuck' in our brains, along with negative feelings and thoughts. Sometimes we have forgotten or blocked out the memories, but the feelings are still there." I turn to Dillon and say, "I believe that stuck feelings and thoughts related to the things that happened to you when you were younger are getting triggered, causing anxiety. Correct me if you think I'm on the wrong track, OK, Dillon?" Dillon nods. "When your anxious feelings get triggered, your brain probably goes straight into survival mode. The angry actions help you gain a feeling of control. Cutting may be a way to feel in control and get some relief from the anxiety." Dillon and his mother both agree that this makes sense.

ATTACHMENT TRAUMA

Children with a history of orphanage care or foster care frequently experience a cascade of traumatic events within their attachment relationships. They may have experienced some type of mistreatment by their parents, and they may suffer from intense feelings of grief over losing them. They may have been hurt by others as well.

Children residing in biological homes may also suffer from some type of attachment trauma. They may have experienced fear related to their parents' emotional problems, domestic violence, or substance abuse. They may have endured lengthy separations due to parents' medical problems or military involvement. Children with serious illnesses or surgeries may have experienced so much pain that they stopped trusting that their parents could or would help them.

Anytime children perceive their parents as the cause of their distress, they experience a deep relational wound. Traumatic, adverse events within attachment relationships leave an indelible imprint upon the developing psyche and brain of growing children.

EYE MOVEMENT DESENSITIZATION AND REPROCESSING (EMDR) THERAPY: EVIDENCE-BASED TRAUMA TREATMENT METHOD

The effectiveness of EMDR therapy with trauma-related disorders has been supported by over twenty-five randomized clinical trials, seven of which pertain specifically to children (e.g., de Roos et al. 2011; Diehle et al. 2014; Kemp et al. 2010). EMDR therapy has received a number-one rating as an evidence-based trauma treatment method by the California Clearinghouse for Child Welfare and is endorsed by the World Health Organization for the treatment of traumatic stress in adults and children. Although the majority of EMDR child research has focused on traumatic stress, there is growing evidence that it reduces broad symptoms and functional problems and disorders, including adolescent depression and behavioral problems (e.g., Bae, Kim, and Park 2008; Zaghrout-Hodali, Alissa, and Dodgson 2008). Preliminary studies have also shown EMDR therapy to have a positive effect on parent-child attachment (Gomez 2013; Madrid, Skolek, and Shapiro 2006; Shapiro et al. 2017; Wesselmann 2013; Wesselmann and Shapiro 2013; Wesselmann et al. 2012). Ongoing research indicates that children with a history of abuse and/or foster or orphanage care with internalizing and externalizing symptoms experience significant improvement in scores on behavioral and attachment measures following thirty-six weeks of integrative EMDR and family therapy treatment (Attachment and Trauma Center of Nebraska, 2011).

Eight Phases of EMDR Therapy

EMDR therapy (Shapiro 1995; 2001) involves eight specific phases and a standardized protocol for the treatment of traumatic stress. The protocol includes the implementation of eye movements or some other form of bilateral stimulation. Although the exact mechanisms by which the eye movements help resolve symptoms of trauma are still under scientific study, many experts agree that the neurological processes that take place during REM sleep may be involved.

The eight phases include (1) history taking, (2) preparation, (3) assessment, (4) desensitization, (5) installation, (6) body scan, (7) closure, and (8) reevaluation. The protocol can be adapted to meet the needs of children of various ages, as well as the specialized needs of children suffering from attachment trauma.

History taking (Phase 1) involves an interview with the child's parents to gather information about the child's problems and history with a special focus on experiences that may have been traumatic to the child, whether or not the experiences are remembered. Preparation (Phase 2) may involve both EMDR therapy components and non-EMDR therapy components that prepare the child for trauma work.

Assessment (Phase 3) involves helping the child access the traumatic memory and taking some simple baseline measures. For example, the child is asked to identify the "worst picture" associated with the memory, the "most upsetting thought," and a thought that the child would like to have instead. Rating scales are obtained by asking, "How true does that positive thought feel to you right now?" The child may point to numbers on a scale or demonstrate how true the thought feels by holding her hands wide apart or close together. The child is asked to identify her emotions about the memory and to show how upset she feels with a number scale or with her hands.

The assessment phase is immediately followed by desensitization (Phase 4), which begins by directing the child's awareness to the traumatic memory and the associated emotions and sensations and applying a set of eye movements. The therapist may simply encourage the child to watch the therapist's hand as it moves from side to side, moving at a fairly rapid pace, while staying within the child's comfort level. The length of a set depends on how quickly the child makes associations to new feelings, thoughts, or images, but it tends to last anywhere from ten to twenty-five repetitions of eye movements. For some younger children, it is easier to follow the movements of a wand, a hand puppet, or horizontal moving lights on an electronic light bar. Bilateral stimulation may also be implemented with tactile stimulation through touching or gently squeezing the child's hands or shoulders, alternating one and then the other, or through bilateral tactile pulsars placed in their hands, pockets, or shoes. A set of bilateral stimulation is followed by checking in with the child regarding any new emotions, thoughts, sensations, or images. Bilateral stimulation is then reapplied, encouraging the child to "let whatever happens happen." The processing is largely nondirective, allowing the child's natural associative processes to integrate the memory and reduce or eliminate the child's distress.

Once the emotional charge is removed, the bilateral stimulation is applied to strengthen a related positive thought during installation (Phase 5). The body scan (Phase 6) identifies any remaining somatic disturbance that needs further processing, and closure (Phase 7) involves specific steps for ending the session comfortably. Reevaluation (Phase 8) takes place at follow-up and involves identification of any new thoughts or feelings that may have surfaced or a new target for reprocessing.

The EMDR therapist assists the child with resolving past traumas as well as recent traumas or current triggering situations. The EMDR therapist also uses bilateral stimulation to reinforce images of the child's desired future actions.

Obstacles to Effective Therapy with Attachment Trauma

When infants or young children are comforted by their parents early on, the experiences become internalized and evolve into self-soothing behaviors. When children do not experience comfort from parents early in life, they have no way to develop self-soothing behaviors, and they easily become overwhelmed. Maladaptive methods to avoid an emotional overload develop naturally out of this situation.

Children who have experienced parental abuse, neglect, or loss earlier in their lives may have difficulty relying upon the adults in their lives. They may put up walls and assume negative intentions behind the actions of parents, teachers, and therapists.

Children who mistrust the adults in their lives are often compelled to protect themselves through aggression and defiance. Parents are frequently overwhelmed, hurt, and angry, and the entire family is often mired in negative dynamics and crisis upon crisis, distracting therapists from attending to the traumatic experiences driving the children's behaviors.

THE EMDR AND FAMILY THERAPY INTEGRATIVE MODEL

The EMDR and family therapy integrative model overcomes the obstacles to therapy by systematically addressing the attachment relationships and family dynamics, problems of self-regulation, underlying traumas, and current triggers (Wesselmann, Schweitzer, and Armstrong 2014a). One important role of the family therapist involves helping parents view their children's behaviors through the trauma lens and strengthening the emotional connection. The family therapist also teaches self-regulation skills to the children and writes a therapeutic narrative that becomes a road map for the EMDR therapist. The EMDR therapist provides EMDR each session, first strengthening positive affect and feelings of connection between parents and children in the office, and then working through traumatic memories and present-day triggers with EMDR therapy.

Overall, the family therapy component provides the foundational work that increases the effectiveness and efficiency of the EMDR component. The length of treatment is dependent upon the extent of children's traumatic experiences and the complexity of the family. As symptoms and behaviors improve, frequency of sessions can be decreased until therapy is no longer needed.

The integrative model can be implemented by a solo therapist, but a two-person team is recommended for children with severe symptoms and behaviors for the following reasons: (1) the EMDR and family therapy roles are more clearly delineated for the child, creating a predictable weekly structure, (2) therapists are able to strategize with one another through peer consultation, and (3) psycho-education with parents is more successful when new concepts are reinforced by a collaborating therapist. In summary, the team approach provides a more supportive atmosphere for all involved.

Ideally, EMDR therapy follows family therapy on the same day, but the sessions can be spread out if there are logistical problems or the child is unable to tolerate back-to-back sessions. Parents are involved in both family therapy and EMDR therapy sessions. Typically, therapists meet alone with parents for ten to twenty minutes at the beginning of each session so parents can share their concerns and therapists can prepare parents for the planned intervention.

Family Therapy Component of the Integrative Model

The Integrative Attachment Trauma Protocol (IATP) as applied by the family therapist includes (1) parent psycho-education, (2) mindfulness, (3) skills, (4) detective work, (5) inner child work, and (6) development of the child's story.

Parent Work

Parent psycho-education teaches parents to respond to the child's behaviors through strategies that integrate the emotional and thinking regions of the child's brain (Siegel and Bryson 2012). Parents are encouraged to implement four ingredients of secure attachment: physical affection, emotional attunement, a secure holding environment, and shared pleasure and play. The use of consequences is minimized and emotional attunement is emphasized. The strategies can be taught through a formal class and informally throughout the family therapy sessions (Wesselmann, Schweitzer, and Armstrong 2014b).

Mindfulness, Skills, and Detective Work

The family therapist models a nonjudgmental, curious, matter-of-fact approach toward investigating the triggers, feelings, and beliefs that are driving the challenging child behaviors. The therapist encourages parents and children to become a "team" with the therapist, with all members working together to understand what is happening and solve the problems. The family therapist opens communication between children and their parents and improves skills for expressing, listening, and validating feelings.

As children feel more supported and understood, they become more capable of accessing vulnerable feelings and memories for trauma work. The family therapist also works with the children to help improve their ability to identify their own thoughts and emotions.

The Smaller Child Within

The family therapist explains to children and their parents, "We all carry feelings and thoughts from when we were much younger inside of our hearts." To convey this concept, the family therapist brings out a set of nesting dolls, lining them up from smallest to biggest and says, "These littler dolls on the inside of the bigger doll are very much like the littler parts of you inside your heart."

The therapist and child assign each doll an age, and the therapist asks, "Which of these little ones might be the most hurt?" The therapist explains, "Many of your upset feelings and reactions are coming from these littler hurt parts of you. We will help each little one on the inside feel calm and safe, and we will help your 'most grown-up self' become stronger."

Timeline and Therapeutic Story

Traumatic memories are stored in an unprocessed form, leading to reactivity and disorganized thinking. The family therapist helps organize the child's memories by creating a simple timeline on a large piece of paper, noting important events, both positive and negative.

Next, the family therapist uses the timeline to create a therapeutic narrative as conceived by Lovett (1999). The narrative is relatively brief and begins with positive elements of the child's current life followed by a brief sequential description of important events that happened throughout the child's life, both positive and negative. The story identifies the child's negative feelings and beliefs along with helpful factual information to counter the child's negative beliefs.

One child's therapeutic story began as follows:

> There is a lovable young girl who lives with her grandmother. She likes to draw and ride her bicycle. Like all children, she had some happy things and some confusing things happen in her life. One happy thing was that she was born with a healthy body, a pretty

smile, and a smart brain. One confusing thing was that her mother had a problem with alcohol that made her brain foggy. She couldn't take good care of her baby girl. The baby girl felt sad and scared, and if she could have put her beliefs into words she might have said, "There must be something wrong with me. I must be doing something wrong." The truth was that the baby girl was fine just the way she was, and the situation was not her fault at all.

After describing some happy things, such as moving in with a grandma who loves her very much, the story ended like this: "Today, the little girl still struggles with believing she is lovable, safe, and loved, but her grandma keeps her safe and she loves her, each and every day. The truth is, the young girl is lovable and special, through and through."

EMDR Component of the Integrative Model

The Integrative Attachment Trauma Protocol (IATP) as applied by the EMDR therapist includes customization of the eight phases of EMDR therapy to overcome obstacles related to emotional dysregulation and dissociation. Important components include EMDR exercises to strengthen attachment security and inclusion of parents for emotional support during trauma work.

History Taking (Phase 1)

History taking involves meeting with the parents to identify traumatic experiences, triggers, and symptoms. Next, the therapist encourages the parents to begin hypothesizing about the child's beliefs, based on the child's behaviors and traumatic experiences. For example, the parents of a young girl adopted from an overseas orphanage thought about their daughter's history and current symptoms and realized that she believed "I can't trust others to take care of me" and "I have to be in charge of getting what I need or I will die." Identification of the young girl's belief system helped the parents feel more compassionate toward her and make sense of her stealing and hoarding behaviors.

Preparation (Phase 2)

The EMDR therapist may choose from many EMDR preparation activities to help the severely traumatized child build inner resources by strengthening positive memories, images, and feelings. Tactile bilateral stimulation is often chosen for these activities, as it tends to have a calming effect on children. One twelve-year-old girl held the tactile pulsars as she thought about the safe feelings associated with sitting in a treehouse in the middle of a beautiful forest. Later, she held the pulsars as the therapist asked her to think about her "most grown-up feelings" related to reading to her younger "reading buddy" in the kindergarten class.

The IATP EMDR component includes a customized Attachment Resource Development method in which experiences of closeness are created in the therapist's office and deepened with slow bilateral stimulation. For example, in the "messages of love" exercise, the parent and child are encouraged to sit together, provided they remain comfortable. The parent is asked to describe the traits the parent enjoys about the child as well as favorite memories of the child. As the parent makes affirming statements about the child, bilateral stimulation is applied to deepen the child's positive feelings and sense of connection to the parent. Tactile stimulation, applied slowly, appears to have the additional benefit of relaxing the child.

The inner child concept, introduced in the family therapist's office, is utilized for development of a "safe place" for the child's hurt, younger self. The therapist may suggest the child depict the safe place in a drawing or sand tray. The child's present-day parents are drawn into the safe-place picture. The therapist applies slow tactile stimulation while calling the child's attention to details about the safe place. Next, the parents are encouraged to describe what they might be doing to care for the "little one on the inside." Seven-year-old Sammy drew a safe place nursery for "baby on the inside." He enjoyed beginning most sessions by listening to his adoptive mother talk about various ways she was caring for "baby Sammy" while the therapist applied slow, alternating taps on the child's palms to strengthen the feelings of connection and trust with his mom.

In another Attachment Resource Development activity, the therapist guides the child in visualizing a "beautiful, magical cord of love." This cord is made up of a beautiful light (in a color chosen by the child) connecting the parent's heart to the child's heart. The therapist says, "It is magical because even when you are in different places, the cord stretches and stretches so that you are always connected." As the child pictures the cord and experiences another moment of closeness with the parent, the therapist applies alternating taps to deepen the experience for the child. Attachment Resource Development is repeated periodically throughout the child's treatment in order to further strengthen and maintain the child's sense of connection with his parents.

Trauma Work (EMDR Phases 3 through 8)

Trauma work may be conducted with eye movements or tactile stimulation. The trauma work is most effective if the bilateral stimulation is implemented at a fairly quick pace, with an eye to the child's comfort level.

To begin the trauma work, the therapist asks the child to describe the most upsetting picture related to the disturbing memory. Some children have difficulty with a mental picture, in which case they can be encouraged to draw a picture of the trauma or create the picture in a sand tray. Then the child is asked to describe the most upsetting thought, and together the therapist and child identify the thought the child would prefer to have. The child is also asked about emotions and body sensations.

By nature, attachment trauma is associated with extremely vulnerable, intense emotions. Parents are invited to stay present in order to provide silent but compassionate support during EMDR trauma work. In some cases, another supportive adult may be chosen to provide emotional support. Children often sit close to their parents during trauma work, and young children often want to sit on the parent's lap.

As sets of bilateral stimulation are applied, the child is instructed to "let whatever happens happen," and the child begins processing the memory by associating naturally to new thoughts, emotions, sensations, and pictures. The therapist must stay alert to any important deficits in the child's knowledge base. When children lack the knowledge they need to make sense of early events, the EMDR therapist provides the missing information through a brief question or statement, termed a "cognitive interweave." It is important that interweaves are brief, so as not to interrupt the flow of the child's processing.

The EMDR therapist may utilize the therapeutic story to initiate EMDR trauma work. Initially, the story is read from beginning to end, adding bilateral stimulation to begin overall desensitization to the story. But when the child is ready, she is asked to listen to her story and raise her hand as soon as a part of the story feels upsetting. The upsetting part of the story is then targeted and processed with the standard EMDR therapy procedures, customized as needed. The child may identify an experience that happened preverbally, in which case the child is asked, "What did you picture in your mind when I read this section?" The child's imagined picture related to the preverbal event is then targeted and processed. It is not necessary for a child to have conscious memory in order to achieve adaptive resolution with EMDR therapy.

DILLON, FIFTEEN YEARS OLD

Dillon and his mother met for family therapy and EMDR therapy on a weekly basis. His father attended sessions intermittently. The family therapist provided psychoeducation to the parents, described the smaller child within, and wrote a therapeutic narrative during the first four sessions of family therapy. The EMDR therapist implemented Attachment Resource Development and other resource development work during the first two sessions and then began the desensitization and reprocessing procedures to help change Dillon's reactions to present-day triggering events involving behavioral corrections from his mother in the third and fourth sessions. As EMDR processing moved forward, the intense feelings of anger and mistrust were eliminated, and Dillon's thoughts shifted from "My mom is against me" to "She wants the best for me."

In the fifth EMDR session, the EMDR therapist read the part of Dillon's therapeutic story that Dillon found the most upsetting. This part described how Dillon's biological parents had left him for an extended period in the care of his grandmother and her boyfriend. Dillon described hurt, fear, and anger, and the negative belief that "I wasn't meant to be. I'm insignificant."

Following is an excerpt from the EMDR session. The symbols <<<<< represent the eye movements.

Dillon: "Gramma's boyfriend had knives. He threatened to cut off my nose and fingers. This went on for a long time. I was really scared."

<<<<<

Dillon: "We were in the boathouse later, and I was supposed to open the door, but I couldn't. He threatened to throw me in the water."

<<<<<

Dillon: "Scared and upset in my chest, my stomach, and my arms."

<<<<<

Dillon: "I wasn't meant to be. My parents didn't want me. They would leave me for days at a time. My grandmother hated me."

<<<<<

Dillon: "They left me so many times."

<<<<<

Dillon: "Sad, shaky."

<<<<<

Dillon: "They wouldn't stop using drugs. I was always afraid they would inject me with the drugs."

<<<<<

Dillon: "Nothing else came up."

Therapist: "Can you go back to your original picture and notice what comes up?"

<<<<<

Dillon: "Why would they treat me that way?"

<<<<<

Dillon: "I didn't do anything wrong. I didn't deserve to be treated like that."

<<<<<

Dillon: "Every baby is a blessing."

<<<<<

Dillon: "If Mom [referring to the adoptive mother] had given birth to me, I would have had everything I needed."

<<<<<

Dillon: "I have a loving and caring family who takes care of me now. God doesn't make mistakes."

By the end of the session, Dillon stated he had no remaining distress related to the memory, and he believed "I am meant to be and I deserve love."

This excerpt illustrates how EMDR therapy jump-starts the child's natural processing system, integrating the traumatic memory with adaptive information in the brain. During the processing, Dillon associated with several memories of abuse, which reduced emotions related to all of the memories simultaneously. This generalization effect is common during EMDR therapy. As the memories were integrated with adaptive information stored in Dillon's brain, his disturbance was eliminated and he shifted to a more rational perspective in his thoughts about the events.

During EMDR therapy, several more triggers and memories were processed, including a memory of making poor choices along with his negative belief that "I am not my [adoptive] parents' son, because I am a bad person." He gained insight into his own behaviors and came to believe "I am a likeable person," "I was meant to be born," and "I am my parents' son." He also shifted to a more compassionate view of his biological parents' problems.

After completion of nine EMDR therapy sessions and nine family therapy sessions, both Dillon and his parents reported that Dillon was making good choices and no longer experiencing intrusive memories or feelings. His mood was good, and he was getting along with his family, friends, teachers, and classmates.

ANN, SIX YEARS OLD

Ann had been exhibiting aggressive meltdowns at home in which she screamed, hit, kicked, and destroyed things. Ann had primarily lived with her great aunt the first three years of her life, due to her mother's addiction to drugs. At that point, her great aunt decided that Ann should be adopted by a younger couple. A willing couple was found, and they agreed to maintain contact with the great aunt. After the adoption, however, the great aunt moved to another state, and she had visited Ann and her new parents only about three times per year. The therapist theorized that Ann's meltdowns were primarily driven by grief and feelings of abandonment, leading to mistrust of her adoptive parents and low self-esteem.

The family therapist provided psycho-education and worked with Ann on communicating feelings with words. She created a timeline and a therapeutic narrative.

Following is a partial transcript of an EMDR session. Ann had drawn a picture of her great aunt driving away and said, "She left me." Ann sat next to her adoptive mother throughout the processing. The symbols <<<<< represent the eye movements.

Therapist: "So think of her driving away and just notice those sad feelings."

<<<<<

Ann: "I miss her." (Ann starts to cry.)

<<<<<

Ann: "Just sad." (Still crying)

Therapist: "Where do you feel the sad?"

Ann: "In my heart."

Therapist: "Just notice that."

<<<<<

Ann: "Still sad." (A little tearful)

<<<<<

Ann: "Why didn't she keep me?"

Therapist: "So, Mom, tell us what you know about that." (The therapist encourages Ann's mother to provide adaptive information as an interweave, thus reinforcing her role as expert and as a source of comfort.)

Mom: "Your aunt loves you a lot. She wants you to have a mommy and a daddy, and she feels she can't give you the care you need because she is getting older and her body is slowing down. She still wants to come and see you when she can."

Therapist: "Think of that."

<<<<<

Ann: "Sometimes I ask her, 'Do you love me?' And she says yes."

<<<<<

Ann: "She loves me."

<<<<<

Ann: "A little sad but a little happier."

Processing continued until Ann reported feeling relaxed and comfortable. Two more sessions were devoted to processing other triggers related to grief and loss. Several current triggers were also reprocessed with Ann, including her mom saying no, her mom telling her it is time to go to bed, and her mom telling her to pick up her room. Ann's parents role-played with Ann, helping her rehearse new, positive behaviors, while Ann held the bilateral pulsars and noticed how she felt in her "most grown-up self."

As treatment progressed, Ann's aggressive rages steadily decreased until they were eliminated. Ann completed therapy after thirteen EMDR sessions and thirteen family therapy sessions.

BEN, FOURTEEN YEARS OLD

Ben was accompanied to therapy by his biological mother. Ben was developmentally delayed. He exhibited autistic features and suffered from epilepsy and other medical conditions. During the week, he resided in a group home for autistic boys, which provided him needed structure and supervision. He stayed at his family's home each weekend and one week night each week. He entered therapy with symptoms of defiance and aggression, primarily directed toward his mother, but also toward staff and teachers. He had damaged windows, doors, and furniture in fits of temper.

During the history taking, the therapist learned that at the ages of four and nine, Ben had experienced seven surgeries related to a congenital medical problem. He continued to have frequent doctor visits and medical interventions. The therapist hypothesized that the medical traumas could have had a negative effect on the quality of his attachment with his mother.

The family therapist worked with Ben and his mother to provide psycho-education and social and emotional skills, develop Ben's story, and identify important memories and triggers. The EMDR therapist implemented three sessions of Attachment Resource Development. Next, Ben's memories of his surgeries were processed with EMDR. Ben remembered waking up in pain and seeing his mother's face after each surgery. He verbalized the negative beliefs that "Mom is mean. Mom caused it. Mom doesn't love me." Over three EMDR sessions, the distress related to his surgery memories was eliminated, and Ben came to believe "Mom loves me and helps me stay alive."

Several other adverse early events were processed over the next several sessions, including memories related to other painful medical interventions as well as teasing and rejection from classmates. The course of therapy was interrupted twice when Ben had to undergo more difficult medical procedures. Afterward, these adverse events were processed with EMDR therapy.

Ben and his mother attended thirty-six sessions with the EMDR therapist and eighteen sessions of family therapy over eighteen months, attending less frequently as behaviors improved. By the end of treatment, Ben was attending medical appointments without anxiety. He was cooperating at home and school, and the aggressive episodes had ceased. He appeared more relaxed and affectionate with his mother. The final sessions were devoted to reinforcing and maintaining the positive gains.

CONCLUSION

Many children with attachment difficulties have experienced trauma within their earliest attachment relationships. The stored, unprocessed trauma causes them to operate out of fight-or-flight and to have difficulty with trust. Children with a history of attachment trauma present with symptoms and behaviors that interfere with progress in therapy, such as poor self-regulation, mistrust of adults, frequent crises related to the child's behaviors, and parent frustration.

EMDR therapy is an evidence-based trauma treatment method. An integrative EMDR and family therapy model is designed to help overcome the obstacles to therapy and strengthen attachment security, resolve traumatic memories, and eliminate reactivity to current triggers. The model can be implemented by a solo therapist, but a two-person team is recommended with more challenging cases in order to provide increased structure for the child, increased support for parents, and the opportunity for peer consultation. The collaborative EMDR and family therapist team allows our most vulnerable population of children to benefit from this powerful trauma treatment method.

BIBLIOGRAPHY

Attachment and Trauma Center of Nebraska. 2011. *EMDR Integrative Team Treatment for Attachment Trauma in Children: Treatment Manual.* Omaha, NE: Author.

Bae, Hwallip, Daeho Kim, and Young Chon Park. 2008. "Eye Movement Desensitization and Reprocessing for Adolescent Depression." *Psychiatry Investigation* 5: 60–65.

de Roos, Carlijn, Ricky Greenwald, Margien den Hollander-Gijsm, Eric Noorthoorn, Stef van Buuren, and Ad de Jongh. 2011. "A Randomised Comparison of Cognitive Behavioural Therapy (CBT) and Eye Movement Desensitisation and Reprocessing (EMDR) in Disaster-Exposed Children." *European Journal of Psychotraumatology* 2: 5694–704.

Diehle, Julia, Brent C. Opmeer, Frits Boer, Anthony P. Mannarino, and Ramon J. L. Lindauer. 2014. "Trauma-Focused Cognitive Behavioral Therapy or Eye Movement Desensitization and Reprocessing: What Works in Children with Posttraumatic Stress Symptoms? A Randomized Controlled Trial." *European Child and Adolescent Psychiatry* 24 (2): 1–10.

Gomez, Ana. M. 2013. *EMDR Therapy and Adjunct Approaches with Children: Complex Trauma, Attachment, and Dissociation.* New York: Springer.

Kemp, Michael, Peter Drummond, and Brett McDermott. 2010. "A Wait-List Controlled Pilot Study of Eye Movement Desensitization and Reprocessing (EMDR) for Children with Post-traumatic Stress Disorder (PTSD) Symptoms from Motor Vehicle Accidents." *Clinical Child Psychology and Psychiatry* 15: 5–25.

Lovett, Joan. 1999. *Small Wonders: Healing Childhood Trauma with EMDR.* New York: Free Press.

Madrid, Antonio, Susan Skolek, and Francine Shapiro. 2006. "Repairing Failures in Bonding Through EMDR." *Clinical Case Studies* 5: 271–86.

Shapiro, Francine. 1995. *Eye Movement Desensitization and Reprocessing: Basic Principles Protocols, and Procedures.* New York: Guilford Press.

———. 2001. *Eye Movement Desensitization and Reprocessing: Basic Principles Protocols, and Procedures.* Second edition. New York: Guilford Press.

Shapiro, Francine, Debra Wesselmann, and Liesbeth Mevissen. 2017. "Eye Movement Desensitization and Reprocessing Therapy (EMDR)." In *Evidence-Based Treatments for Trauma-Related Disorders in Children and Adolescents*, edited by Markus A. Landolt, Marylène Cloitre, and Ulrich Schnyder, 273–97. New York: Springer.

Siegel, Daniel J., and Tina Payne Bryson. 2012. *The Whole-Brain Child: 12 Revolutionary Strategies to Nurture Your Child's Developing Mind.* New York: Bantam Books.

Wesselmann, Debra. 2013. "Healing Trauma and Creating Secure Attachment through EMDR." In *Healing Moments in Psychotherapy: Mindful Awareness, Neural Integration, and Therapeutic Presence*, edited by Marion Solomon and Daniel J. Siegel, 115–28. New York: W. W. Norton.

Wesselmann, Debra, Meghan Davidson, Stefanie Armstrong, Cathy Schweitzer, Daniel Bruckner, and Ann Potter. 2012. "EMDR as a Treatment for Improving Attachment Status in Adults and Children." *European Review of Applied Psychology* 62 (4): 223–30.

Wesselmann, Debra, Cathy Schweitzer, and Stefanie Armstrong. 2014a. *Integrative Team Treatment for Attachment Trauma in Children: Family Therapy and EMDR.* New York: W. W. Norton.

———. 2014b. *Integrative Parenting: Strategies for Raising Children Affected by Attachment Trauma.* New York: W. W. Norton.

Wesselmann, Debra, and Francine Shapiro. 2013. "EMDR and the Treatment of Complex Trauma in Children and Adolescents." In *Treating Complex Traumatic Stress Disorders in Children and Adolescents,* edited by Julian Ford and Chris Courtois, 203–24. New York: Guilford Press.

Zaghrout-Hodali, Mona, Ferdoos Alissa, and Philip Dodgson. 2008. "Building Resilience and Dismantling Fear: EMDR Group Protocol with Children in an Area of Ongoing Trauma." *Journal of EMDR Practice and Research* 2: 106–13.

13

Family Attachment Narrative Therapy

Todd Nichols, Melissa Nichols, and Denise Lacher

Every man's life is a fairy tale, written by God's fingers.

—Hans Christian Andersen

The Carlson family adopted seven siblings, adding to their already busy household of five. Raising twelve children is challenging and hard work every day. The special needs of these adoptive siblings were beyond what any education or training could have prepared them for. Ranging in age from thirteen years to eighteen months old, each child had a distinctive set of problems and each required unique strategies to integrate into the family. All seven were born to birth parents with borderline intellectual and adaptive functioning. The birth parents themselves had been abused and neglected in their childhood. Child Protective Services were involved with the birth family off and on for years due to severe neglect and unsanitary conditions of the home. When they were finally removed, authorities reported piles of garbage both inside and outside of the home, infestations of mold and bugs, and the presence of raw sewage in the basement. The children did not attend school regularly or receive medical and dental care. It is likely that birth parents left them unattended for long periods of time, the older siblings caring for the younger. They were malnourished and all were demonstrating significant developmental delays. All seven children were subsequently diagnosed with micro-encephalopathy and some with other genetic abnormalities.

The children's adjustment to their new family was complicated by intense loyalty to their birth parents that consistently undermined the Carlsons' parenting and attachment work. Older children often told their younger siblings that their new mom and dad were "horrible" and "mean." Brian and Sue Carlson described the sibling group as behaving like untamed animals—a "bunch of raccoons." They were hyperactive, impulsive, and unable to communicate their most basic needs or wants. They lacked self-care and domestic skills but clearly were survivors. Adept at foraging for food and stealing, they were not going to starve ever again. Some of the siblings were charming and overly friendly with strangers—seeking attention in any way that they could. Some were withdrawn and guarded; they isolated themselves from the family that wanted to connect with them and help them create a new story and a new future.

FAMILY ATTACHMENT NARRATIVE THERAPY

Our earliest experiences shape how we perceive, and in turn how we interact with, the world. Without a solid foundation grounded in nurturing, loving, and supportive care, the world seems like a very dangerous place. The children and adolescents referred to the Family Attachment Center have complex issues stemming not only from attachment disruptions but also from multiple other sources such as abuse, neglect, neuro-developmental disorders (sensory processing, alcohol and drug related disorders), and genetic abnormalities.

Family Attachment Narrative Therapy is a structured process of connecting and healing stories, created by parents for the special needs of their unique child. Discovering, and understanding, a child's internal working model allows parents to create stories that challenge their child's mistaken beliefs and restore their hope and trust in the world. Simple to learn and fun to use, hundreds of parents have successfully employed this methodology to create bonds, heal past trauma, and teach new skills to their child, teen, or young adult.

Stories are found in every culture, society, and family around the world. Oral accounts chronicle our history, traditions, values, and everyday ways of life. Our parents and grandparents told us their parents' and grandparents' stories, passing on family lore that is found nowhere else. Life stories help us make meaning of everyday joys, triumphs, and suffering. Using therapeutic stories to form connections with a child struggling to attach to new parents makes practical and clinical sense. Redoing a child's story can create new meanings and shift negative beliefs about self and others. Narratives of trauma may help the victim understand and process a frightening, life-threatening event (Cohen, Mannarino, and Deblinger 2006).

The success of Family Attachment Narrative Therapy depends on discovering and examining every facet of the child or adolescent's internal working model. This set of beliefs or expectations about self, others, and the world shapes an individual's development and relationships and drives everyday behavior (Bowlby [1969] 1982; Sroufe et al. 2005). Discovery of this model is the cornerstone of constructing a successful narrative. The internal working model is complex and made up of nonverbal impressions of interactions with a primary attachment figure, subsequent life events whether traumatic or nurturing, and developmental issues. The internal working model can be thought of as three separate, partially overlapping spheres.

Each sphere—attachment relationships, life events, and development—influences the meaning the child or adolescent makes of early experiences. The quality of inter-

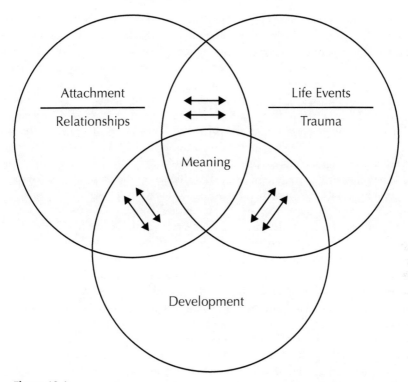

Figure 13.1.

actions between first caretakers and the child determine the patterns of attachment behaviors he or she will use to relate to others as they go through life. Ambivalent, avoidant, or disorganized patterns are created when caretakers are inconsistent, unavailable, or abusive and neglectful. Life events, especially those that cause traumatic stress, affect the security of a child's attachment and their future reactions to stress. Development may be altered by attachment disruptions, traumatic stress, and neurodevelopmental issues.

Internal working models change and shift, constantly being updated as life unfolds. However, those first preverbal, subconscious impressions are paramount. They establish the basis for our interactional attachment patterns. In other words, our first mental model is how we do life. Some models seem simple: "I am bad and bad things will always happen to me." But the vast majority of children and teens in care have many facets or layers that make up their model. The meaning of behavior is different for each child. Like diamonds, once cut no two are alike.

The child's internal working model is discoverable through observations by the parent and therapist, records of the child's history, and assessments. Documentation of past history and testing might lead to a diagnosis, but much more is needed to root out the underlying belief system of the child. It is our belief that parents are the experts regarding their child. Their knowledge of the child's history, stories, day-to-day behavior, and mood cannot be matched by any professional. Many adoptive or foster parents feel stumped because nothing seems to be working, but they are in the best position to put the pieces of the model together, or at least to create the best hypothesis about the child's internal working model. The information they need is standing right in front of them (or perhaps sitting in time-out).

The child's model inevitably appears shortly after placement in a new family. Children and adolescents act out the pattern or blueprint for interactions that was established a long time ago with their first caretakers. Not only do they play it out, but they also skillfully engage their new parent in the drama. The parent does not audition or even get a script, but he or she is the star of the show. Each scene that is successfully reenacted reinforces the model, showing the child again and again that "I am bad and bad things will always happen to me." So many parents have confided, with a great deal of guilt, that they get so angry they want to "hit him," "lock her in her room and throw away the key," "take away every possession and privilege he has," or "pack up and check into a hotel for a few days." Unsurprisingly, as we dig deeper, we find that child was hit, that girl was locked away, he had nothing as a child, and her parents left her for days at a time. Understanding the clues contained in these scenarios can be a painful process, but once a parent recognizes that they have been pulled into their child's model, they can start to rewrite the script or story.

Parent-created narratives are used to challenge and shift the model and negative beliefs to something that is more positive, or at least neutral, so the individual can develop and maintain healthy, long-term connections with others.

Change the story—change the model. Can it really be that easy? Yes, it can. The neuroscience of narrative therapy suggests that the brain processes a story similar to how it processes an experience (Cozolino 2002). Sophisticated brain scans of a listener reveal activity in every part of the brain, not just the area responsible for processing verbal language. In terms of neurological activity, it is as if the listener is having the experience! Family Attachment Narrative Therapy is a "backdoor" into the individual's internal working model, the cluster of mistaken beliefs. It does not require the child or adolescent to tell their story or even talk about their feelings or "bad" behavior.

Family Attachment Narrative Therapy consists of four types of narratives: claiming, trauma, developmental, and successful child. The narratives are created to re-do early life experiences, opening the door to new possibilities for beliefs and a different way of viewing people and the world. Claiming narratives are designed to increase the security of attachment within the caregiver-child relationship. The parent lovingly describes what it could have been like if the child had been with them from the beginning. This is the ideal in parenting. It is a chance for the caretaker and the child to jointly experience something that they both missed. Some parents begin prenatally, others start at birth or at some later point in life, but the common theme is that from the beginning the child deserved to be cherished and cared for by responsible adults. Care is taken to be respectful of birth families. Many children and teens in foster care or adoptive homes, including the Carlson siblings, are intensely loyal to their birth family. Bad-mouthing previous families seldom helps and usually only serves to deepen their defenses against bonding to a new family.

Trauma narratives are created to help the child or teen understand and process previous life events. Often the story is done in the third person. This perspective effectively gives the parent "literary license." No one can fully know the child's internal and external experience of trauma. The third-person perspective allows the parent to fill in the gaps with well-educated guesses based on the child's documented history, the stories they tell over time, and the observations of day-to-day behavior. A compelling narrative captures the child's attention, pulls them in, and allows them to experience and process the events and emotions along with the protagonist.

Many of the kids we see are oppositional. In the first person, children and teens often interrupt to argue a fact or jump in to defend their birth family, a previous placement, orphanage, or country of origin. The third-person perspective avoids these obstacles. Further, the use of the third-person perspective assures parents that the trauma narrative will not trigger their child's trauma and overwhelm the child with memories and feelings. Most children know on some level that the narratives are about them, but the stories allow them to think, feel, and process in a safe way. Trauma narratives can be done in the first person as well. Parents seem to intuitively know that first person will work best with a very young child who has not mastered symbolic representation or an older child who has heard and told their story so many times. Some children, especially those who crave attention, want all the stories to be about them, and in some cases, teens object to a third-person story and prefer a story that is "real."

As stated above, within the context of the narrative, the storyteller takes care to respect the birth family. However, the child needs to know certain facts to dispel mistaken beliefs about those past traumatic events. Beliefs such as "It was my fault" or "I should have done better, been smarter, faster, and tried harder" are common. The themes of trauma narratives are that what happened back then was not the child's fault and that the past does not have to define the future. Every individual has the chance to make different choices and to interact with others and live life in a new way.

Developmental and successful child narratives are designed to teach skills and remediate behavior problems. They are similar, but where the successful child narrative focuses on changing a challenging behavior, the developmental narrative assumes that the cause of a problem behavior is simply that the child does not know how to behave appropriately. The key to creating both narratives is having a clear understanding of the child's internal working model. For example, poor hygiene skills could be a problem of obedience—"I'm not going to do it." However, in a home with garbage-filled sinks and no toothbrushes, the child might not know where to begin. Most children learn these basics as infants and toddlers. As parents bathe, toilet, groom, and dress them, the child learns how each of those tasks is done. Without that care, children behave, as the Carlsons described, like they have been raised with wild animals. Developmental narratives teach new skills by describing how children learn to do personal care, develop social skills, manage strong emotions, and use parents as a secure base. In first- or third-person perspective, parents detail how infants, toddlers, preschoolers, seven-year-olds, and fourteen-year-olds grow and learn age-appropriate skills.

Successful child narratives separate a behavior from the child or teen. Typically told in the third person, the character is not bad, but is making bad choices for very good reasons. Usually those behaviors helped the child survive in an abusive, neglectful environment. And as such, survival behaviors can be difficult to change with simple behavior management techniques. When the consequence of not stealing food is hunger or maybe even death, stealing is a useful skill to have. Successful child narratives make talking about behavior (otherwise known as lecturing) more enjoyable and even fun for both the parent and the child or teen. Using characters the listener will identify with, such as animals, aliens, superheroes, the kids down the street, movie stars, and sports idols, the story introduces possibilities for new behaviors. The protagonist has similar problems, gets into all kinds of trouble, and needs to figure out a new way of behaving. The character can even do things far worse than the child has ever done so he or she can judge the character and at the same time, learn from the character's mistakes. Parents' own stories of misbehavior in their childhood are often the favorites. The themes interwoven into the stories are that the child's behavior does not define who they are and that they deserve to be loved, no matter what.

CASE EXAMPLE

The Carlsons used Family Attachment Narrative Therapy with all of their newly adopted children, but only four of the seven children came into the therapist's office (the remaining three were told stories at home). Once families learn the therapy, they frequently use the technique with their other children. The purpose of this case study is to describe the process as it was used for one of the children. Irene, age fourteen, attended five narrative therapy sessions. Each session lasted between two and two and a half hours. In each session, a team of therapists worked with Irene and her parents to uncover her unique model and craft stories to shift negative beliefs, strengthen the parent-child bond, and help Irene integrate past experiences of neglect and loss. In addition to the narratives, several other adjunct therapies were used, including Eye Movement Desensitization and Reprocessing (EMDR) (Shapiro 2001), audio-visual entrainment, play therapy, and others. However, the material in this case study focuses on the narrative portion of the therapy, which is the workhorse of our program.

Prior to beginning therapy, background information revealed the extent of Irene's complications, a portion of which is presented here. Irene was a Fragile X carrier, had been diagnosed with micro-encephalopathy and failure to thrive, was short in stature, had dysmorphic features (including webbed toes), and displayed learning issues. Her biological parents were charged with criminal neglect and their parental rights terminated. Irene and her six siblings were placed in different foster homes for four months prior to their joint placement in the Carlson home eight months prior to the beginning of treatment. Irene was intensely loyal to her birth parents. The Carlsons found that she had secretly kept contact with her biological parents via a cell phone that was slipped to her during a home visit. Irene reported to them information about each of her siblings and then communicated the biological parents' instructions back to her siblings. One of their instructions was not to trust the new parents. Brian and Sue Carlson initially felt that this loyalty fueled her behavior. Irene acted withdrawn in her new home, often retreating to her room instead of interacting with other family members. She also acted as an instigator in the family, pitting child against child in an attempt to create chaos in the home. Irene stated she was confused as to why she was placed outside the care of her birth parents. She said she was not hit or hurt—she didn't think her life was so bad. When she came to therapy, she acted like an uncomfortable guest in the presence of her adoptive parents. She was pleasant but distant. Her eye contact was poor, she seldom spoke, and she stated that she did not like hugs.

Day One

Each day, Irene first met with a play/individual therapist while her parents met with a lead therapist. The purpose of Irene's meeting with the therapist was primarily diagnostic, to gain information about her internal model.

On the first day Irene chose to play Don't Spill the Beans and Operation. Both of these games are designed for younger children, and Irene's selection of these games suggested delayed development. Irene then taught the therapist a card game called Trash. Although Irene initially presented as shy and quiet in the sessions, she opened up as time progressed. She refused help initially but eventually asked for some assistance, displayed curiosity, and was cooperative. She did not struggle emotionally when she lost a game and seemed to be empowered by teaching a game to the therapist. All of these insights were reported to the family therapist and the Carlsons to aid in their understanding of Irene's internal working model and the formation of the stories.

While Irene engaged in play therapy, her parents discussed with the family therapist her adjustment to their home, her behaviors, and her interaction with her siblings, both biological and adoptive. They talked about her immaturity compared to their same-aged biological daughter. Irene seemed to connect better with their eight-year-old, as they had similar interests and skills. They also talked about her status in the home. According to her parents, Irene's younger sister and brother were the primary caretakers in the birth home and Irene had spent most of her time sequestered in the back room watching television. In the conversation, Brian and Sue began to see ways her current behavior mirrored her behavior in her birth home. They also noticed that her actions seemed similar to those of her birth mother, the person to whom she was most loyal. They speculated about Irene's thoughts, feelings, and beliefs that might be fueling her behaviors, and how to use the narratives to combat the mistaken beliefs that she had formulated. With the guidance of the family therapist, her parents prepared a claiming narrative to address these distortions. The narrative emphasized how Irene would have been welcomed and celebrated as a baby in their home, and how Brian and Sue would have provided loving and effective care for her.

During the family session, Brian and Sue used a book titled *Happy Birth Day* to introduce to Irene how they wished they knew her as a baby and what it might have been like if she had started her life with them. They described in detail how they would have cared for her prenatally and after birth. They told how her older siblings might have reacted to the news of another baby—how she would have been welcomed by the entire family, grandparents, aunts, uncles, and cousins. Irene was initially uncomfortable being so close to her parents, but she seemed to soften as the story progressed. She occasionally added a comment that indicated her loyalty to her birth parents—"My mom said I was like that." Sue acknowledged her comments, often incorporating her ideas into the story. This acknowledgment seemed to calm her, indicating that Brian and Sue would not be ruffled by her input but appreciative of it. At the end of the session the therapist gave homework to Irene and her parents of "cuddle time" together. This time was to be decided by her parents, could be five to ten minutes in length, and involve being physically close to each other and talking or retelling the claiming narrative.

Day Two

In the next session Brian and Sue reported that Irene was open to completing the assigned homework and was willing to be physically close to them at home rather than withdrawing to her room. Candidly, Sue spoke about her difficulties attaching to Irene. She expressed frustration concerning Irene's negative reaction to her in comparison to her more open treatment of Brian. Sue perceived Irene as constantly pushing away her attempts to provide nurture. The one exception to this behavior was when she made food—Irene thought she was a good cook!

They discussed Irene's early environment in her birth home, including the birth parents' mental health and skill set. According to documentation and information given to the adoptive parents by case workers, the birth mother seldom cooked food for the children. Instead, she relied primarily on McDonald's or microwaveable items to feed them. When she made food, she often did not make enough. She ate first, and the children divided the leftovers among themselves. Reports indicated that the birth mom spent much of her time in her room sleeping and watching television, leaving the care of her younger children to their older siblings. If she did intervene, it was to tell them to "shut up." Due to the birth father's experiences in foster care, where he was treated in a harsh, insensitive manner with many restrictions, he refrained from giving his children discipline. He sometimes played with the children but did not provide care or correct them. In addition, the parents displayed poor boundaries, often engaging in sexual activities in the children's presence.

Reviewing her early experiences assisted the team to better understand Irene's internal model and to begin thinking about how to form a trauma narrative, to be used when the time came. It was hypothesized that due to her passive temperament and significant gaps in her intellectual functioning, she was overshadowed by her bold, bright, and determined younger sister, who made decisions for the sibling group. Her parents and the therapist began to strategize how, given her temperament, past experience, processing issues, and needs, she might better fit in the hierarchy of siblings at home. Sue stated that she had been trained years ago as a cranial sacral massage therapist. They talked about how to incorporate her knowledge of massage at home to aid Irene in becoming more attached to her and decrease her defensiveness to her environment. They also talked about possible beliefs that drove Irene's behavior, including her conflict regarding her placement and feelings of inadequacy within her current and previous families. Possible beliefs began to emerge: "I am defective and incompetent"; "what I have to say does not matter"; and "I do not belong."

Based on these possible mistaken beliefs, her parents and the therapist talked about the importance of claiming and developmental narratives to provide Irene with a sense of belonging in their family. They discussed the purpose of these stories to instill the idea that she would have been loved and cherished no matter what. In the second narrative session Irene listened to a story about what her first year of life would have entailed if she had been with the Carlsons. They talked about the close proximity in age to their other daughter and how the girls would have been like twins. (Since Irene admired her newly adoptive sister, this idea of being her twin was well received.) Due to the extensive neglect in her previous home, her parents emphasized that she would not have been hungry, would have been kept safe, and would have seen the doctor whenever she was ill. Sue also mentioned her unwillingness to leave Irene with anyone and spoke about her protectiveness of her "babies." Brian discussed his role in the care of the children, which included getting up in the middle of the night. Both parents talked in detail about normal developmental milestones and how each would have been celebrated and recorded with pictures and video. Irene smiled throughout the session. At the end of the session, cuddle time was given again as homework. This time, massage by her mother was also given as a homework assignment.

Day Three

The following day, Sue reported that Irene was very receptive to the massage. Brian stated she was talkative and appeared to engage more with the family, and Sue agreed. Brian and Sue continued preparing for the trauma narrative by identifying a hero and sketching the contents of the story. After Brian compared the children to wild animals, they decided that using raccoons as the lead characters would hit home. They considered what details to incorporate, where to begin and end, and how to offer a resolution that would be acceptable to Irene.

During the third narrative session, Irene listened to a story about what it would have been like if she had been with the Carlsons for her first five years. Included in the story were family rituals such as special foods for holidays, birthdays, and the beginning of school. They described Irene's reactions to entering kindergarten—how excited she would have been. She would have taken her parents' hands and walked to the neighborhood school to meet the teacher. Her siblings would have excitedly shared their first day experiences. Her parents expressed how they would have prepared her for school so that she would not be afraid. They spoke about how she would have already known her colors, letters, and numbers and even how to write her name. Irene soaked in the words from the story. She smiled and nodded at certain parts, indicating that she could imagine what they said. Again, the threesome was assigned homework of cuddle time and massage.

Day Four

On the fourth day of the intensive session, Irene completed assessments including the Kinetic Family Drawing (KFD) and the Children's Sentence Completion (CSC). On the KFD, she drew her current family of fourteen playing at the park, and herself playing catch with a sister. While this indicated some connections in her current family, the CSC gave contradicting information. For example, her answer for the story stem of "It would be funny" was "if this was all a dream." When asked what "all of this" signified, she responded that it meant her adoption, therapy, foster placement, change in school, and new family. She went on to describe how she had a premonition in kindergarten that she would be adopted, so she stole a picture of her birth mother, which she still keeps. She further stated that she also felt fear that she would be adopted when her birth mother would yell at her to "clean the house or the cops will come."

During her parents' time with the family therapist, Brian and Sue talked about the change in Irene's behavior. She sat by Sue and waited for Brian to come home so she could "do her homework." Her parents reported that Irene discussed their upcoming family camping trip. Brian and Sue stated that this was the first time they had seen her excited about something. They expressed amazement over her progress.

During family therapy, Brian told a trauma narrative about a family of raccoons. In the story, the young raccoons were taken away from their home when the parents were away. The young raccoons were found alone, hungry, cold, and dirty and placed with another family. The story related the thoughts and feelings of the young, including their fear and confusion at being taken from their parents (which mirrored Irene's thoughts and feelings about the situation). The story included reasons why the raccoon parents left their babies and emphasized that the baby raccoons did not do anything wrong. In the conclusion of the story, the little raccoons continued to miss their mom and dad but grew to love their new family that helped them learn the skills that they needed to grow up and provide for their emotional and physical needs. Using EMDR during and after the story helped to solidify the messages to

Irene. She was asked to think of a happy memory, and she chose one about her birth mother. During EMDR, Irene talked about feeling happy and sad at the same time while thinking of her memory. The therapist compared this to a patchwork quilt of someone's life. She said that the rule of making a beautiful quilt is to include some ugly fabric because it enhances the beautiful cloth. She gave Irene a journal and asked her to draw both her good and her bad memories in her birth home and adoptive placement for homework. She asked Irene to dictate her recollections to a parent, who would write them down on the backside of the picture. The parent was to read it back to Irene, and she could correct it until it was right. This homework was given in addition to the massage and cuddle time.

Day Five

In the fifth and final session for Irene, her parents discussed the transformation in Irene at home. She voluntarily sat by Sue on the couch and interacted with everyone more frequently. She even asked to ride with Sue as she dropped off some of the kids at the pool. Her parents reported that she grimaced less frequently and seemed more relaxed with them. Sue stated that she had thought about the story for today and would like to tell a successful child narrative about a friend who died. She thought Irene might benefit from realizing that she understands loss and how to go on in life after someone leaves your life.

In family therapy, Irene chose to lie on her parents' laps and listened to the story about the death of Sue's friend, how she misses her, and how she was able to move on in life. Her parents gently suggested that Irene might have similar feelings about not living with her birth parents. She participated in EMDR again and revisited the memory of saying goodbye to her mother—how her mother had grabbed her hand and said she would always love her. We reviewed her journal and discussed her good and bad memories concerning her birth family. Irene and her parents read a poem about adoption aloud. The poem talked about the love of a birth mother and an adoptive mother for a child. Brian was enthusiastic and stated that it should be prominently displayed in their living room. Irene carefully placed it in her mother's bag. The therapist talked about the good work Irene had done in therapy. She appeared happy and proud as she left the clinic with her parents.

The next week, Sue reported that a family friend had commented that Irene chatted the whole car ride—she was more bubbly and positive than she had ever seen her. Brian and Sue remarked that she continued to seek them out and appeared more content in their home.

It was hypothesized that Irene's behavior was due to anxiety that adults might not be available to care for her in a sensitive or effective manner. Coupled with her conflicting feelings toward adoptive parents, she was displaying ambivalence toward her caregivers. Her behaviors toward her parents were often mixed—that is, she might be helpful but deceitful in her interactions with them, guarded in her words and actions but still desiring a hug. Family Attachment Narrative Therapy was successfully used with Irene to shift her distorted cognitions and related behavior based on a faulty internal model she had developed in response to her developmental and attachment history.

As this case illustrates, Family Attachment Narrative Therapy provides a springboard for deepening the attachment relationship between parents and their adopted child. It is a technique that effectively taps the empathy of the parent and their knowledge of the child, and provides a vehicle to begin the process of healing. Stories have the ability to change the viewpoint of the listener as well as the teller. By creating narratives for their child, parents have to understand the turbulent home, the heartbreaking neglect, and the disappointment of their child as he or she attempts to trust new parents. In short, they have to walk in their child's shoes, and in doing so they begin to be amazed by the child's journey and ability to survive. With this understanding, true claiming and healing happens as they protect and provide sensitive care for their child.

BIBLIOGRAPHY

Bowlby, John. (1969) 1982. *Attachment and Loss, Vol. 1. Attachment.* New York: Basic Books.

Cohen, Judith A., Anthony P. Mannarino, and Esther Deblinger. 2006. *Treating Trauma and Traumatic Grief in Children and Adolescents.* New York: Guilford Press.

Cozolino, Louis. 2002. *The Neuroscience of Psychotherapy: Building and Rebuilding The Human Brain.* New York: W. W. Norton.

Shapiro, Francine. 2001. *Eye Movement Desensitization and Reprocessing (EMDR): Basic Principles, Protocols, and Procedures.* Second edition. New York: Guilford Press.

Siegel, D. J. 1999. *The Developing Mind: How Relationships and the Brain Interact to Shape Who We Are.* New York: Guilford Press.

Sroufe, L. Alan, Byron Egeland, Elizabeth A. Carlson, and W. Andrew Collins. 2005. *The Development of the Person: The Minnesota Study of Risk and Adaptation from Birth to Adulthood.* New York: Guilford Press.

III

KEEPING IT REAL

14

The Voice of the Adoptee

Faith Friedlander and Melanie Chung-Sherman

One of the most common fears is that of being abandoned. Abandonment is the dominant theme in child myths.

—Harriet Machtiger

INTRODUCTION

Karen Doyle Buckwalter

So often when working in the field of adoption as professionals we can get caught up in reading articles and going to various seminars to learn about "adoption issues." In this process it is easy to think we know and understand what is *really* going on for adoptees. How could we not as we eagerly read books and educate ourselves about adoption? A great deal is written about the need to support parents and understand how hard it can be to parent a child with "attachment issues." But do we sometimes forget what it must be like to *have* the attachment issues? Are we so busy thinking we know why adopted kids may be doing what they are doing, and explaining this to their parents and others, that we forget the voice of the adoptee? After we ask adoptees so many questions and get "I don't know" as an answer, do we become even more convinced that we know? Might we get so caught up in executing our evidence-based practices that we forget to truly listen to the story right in front of us? The purpose of this chapter is to remind clinicians that we must never forget to truly listen. And remembering this is not as obvious as it sounds. The two stories shared in this chapter are complex and reflect years of working out how to truly express one's narrative in a coherent way. The stories are a reminder for us as clinicians to remain open and curious, to never be certain of knowing, and to work hard to create the safe haven and secure base that will free those we work with to allow their authentic stories to come forth.

The unexpected highlight of asking these two professionals to write this chapter together was the relationship that developed between Melanie and Faith, both adoptees but with very different stories. As they listened to each other, they each understood the complexity of the adoption experience and how it had impacted their respective lives. Both chose to become professionals in the area of trauma, and they are passionate about building emotionally safe relationships between caregivers and children. This chapter is about their personal experiences of growing up as adoptees. What they want professionals to know is that although adoption is a lifelong process and not a discrete event, adoptees are not broken because of this life experience. Although they agree it is important to understand evidence-based practices and to keep fine-tuning one's skills as an attachment-based trauma-informed therapist, they believe the best clinicians work on their own attachment histories and do not pathologize their patients. What adoptees want and need is to be seen and understood by their parents in safe, authentic relationships, and by clinicians who are there to help them and their families to heal.

REFLECTIONS OF AN ADULT ADOPTEE

Faith Friedlander

> I believe the greatest gift I can conceive of having from anyone is to be seen by them, heard by them, to be understood and touched by them.
>
> —Virginia Satir

From my earliest beginnings, being adopted has impacted my life and continues to do so. At sixty-nine, I am still integrating parts of my own personal adoption experience. The story I am about to tell has taken a lifetime to develop. As a child I knew very little about my adoption. Most of what I have learned about my birth parents and my earliest beginnings was gleaned in bits and pieces throughout my lifelong quest to know where I came from and how I came to be.

I was born in New Orleans on October 30, 1946, and named Valerie Anne by my birth mother, Kitty. Upon arriving in Los Angeles ten days later, I was renamed Faith Ann. I was named Faith after my adoptive mother's favorite cousin. (From here on, I'll simply refer to my adoptive mother as "mother" or "mom.")

I often wondered how I came to be born in New Orleans, since my birth mother was from Pennsylvania. I have also wondered what those ten days were like for me in the hospital. Did anyone hold me or cuddle me? What about Kitty? Was she scared and alone when she birthed me, or did she have support? How was Kitty treated by the medical staff? Historically, 1946 was a time when unwed mothers were scorned and shamed. As a child, I was full of questions and, to this day, I have a longing to know the intimate details surrounding my birth.

When I became pregnant with my first child at twenty-five, it dawned on me that I knew nothing about my biological roots. I realized that my husband had a long line of relatives with whom he could connect our child, but all I had of my ancestry was me. I wondered if my child would look like some relative of mine or have talents and skills that came from my side of the family. I felt sad that I would probably never know, and sadder that everyone would focus on my husband's genetic family since we knew nothing about mine. I briefly worried about what medical conditions there might be in my family history, but I let go of that concern quickly because I had been healthy most of my life. My instincts told me that my baby would thrive, and I was correct.

As the family story goes, when I was ten days old and weighed less than six pounds, I traveled by airplane across the country. It was a stormy day and the flight was long and turbulent. I turned blue, and it was necessary to give me oxygen.

Waiting at the airport was my new family, which consisted of my adoptive mother and father; their biological daughter, Janet, who was almost five; and my older adopted brother, Leon (from another family), who was almost a year and a half. I have no conscious recollection of this early time, but I imagine it was stressful for me because when I was a month old I got pneumonia. I'm sure that my arrival was disruptive for my sister and brother as well, but no one in the family seems to remember much about that time.

When I was two, my mother discovered that she had tuberculosis and was sent to a sanitarium for a year. I did not see my mother at all during this time, and I did not seem to remember her when she returned home. It wasn't until years later that I even addressed the fact that by the time I was three, I had already navigated through two major losses, though they were never discussed or labeled as losses within our family.

I grew up always knowing that I was adopted. I was full of questions. My parents assured me that they were my "real" parents and that, although my birth mom loved me, she couldn't keep me. I wasn't sure why she couldn't keep me, but I was always careful not to ask my mom too many questions about my adoption at one time. I knew, intuitively, that asking too many questions was being disloyal to my adoptive parents. I felt confused and ashamed about needing and wanting to know so much.

In those days, life began with adoption and no one wanted to address the adoptee as being connected to a birth family. As a child, no matter how much I attempted to accept that being adopted was no different from being born into the family, deep inside I felt this was not true. In my heart and in my head, I felt connected to this mystery woman known to me as my birth mother, and I wondered if she ever thought about me. I longed to share my thoughts, concerns, and feelings with my adoptive mother and to have her understand the importance of my questions. However, living with the belief that my life began with my adoption, my mother and father perpetuated the myth that there was no difference between being adopted into a family and being born into a family. I believe my parents saw "difference" as synonymous with "less than," which was also the message implied by society. It makes total sense to me that my parents did all they could to protect themselves and their children from feeling different in a society that did not value differences.

Attempting to accept this myth of "sameness" was probably one of the most destructive and painful parts of my childhood. On the inside, I felt confused, ashamed, and alone. I loved my adoptive parents. Growing up, I believed they were meant to raise me, and yet I yearned to know about my birth mother. I wanted to share with my adoptive mother my ongoing internal questions and concerns. Due to my mother's discomfort and my shame, however, my questions dwindled over several years, but my "need to know" remained protected and persistent deep in my soul.

My teenage years were troubling for me. Out in the world I was a compliant child, but at home I often felt frustrated and I verbally fought with my mother. I was struggling to find my own identity, which was made more complicated by being an adoptee. Although I was vocal about my upsets, I lived in fear that my mother would abandon me if I didn't live up to her expectations. I had internalized society's message that I should be forever grateful to my parents for adopting me, and yet I continued to ride an emotional roller coaster. My mother was the primary target of my emotions. For me, my dad was much easier for me to get along with during my teen years.

At fourteen, I asked my mother if I was born out of wedlock. She was uneasy as she answered me: "Yes." She followed up by saying that my birth mother had made a mistake. Although not my mother's intention, I took this to mean that I was a mistake. Although we never talked about it directly, I sensed my mother feared I might repeat my birth mother's experience. I believed, beyond a shadow of a doubt, that if I had gotten pregnant and had not been married, I would have been rejected and abandoned by my parents. Holding all of this fear and shame within deeply impacted my sense of isolation and loneliness. My self-esteem was low, and I felt like damaged goods because I could not simply be grateful that my parents had adopted me and given me a good life, and that I couldn't be compliant. I was not sexually active during this time, but just beginning to experience my sexuality within, and this was turbulent and troubling for me since there was no one to help me to make sense of this intense time.

From as early as I can remember, I wanted to be a mother. My first marriage happened when I was twenty. By the time I was twenty-five, I had my first child, who was planned and wanted. Later, I had two more children, also planned and wanted, with my second (and current) husband.

During the early years of my firstborn son's life, the two of us spent many hours with my parents. CJ was their first grandchild, and they enjoyed having him around. I wasn't working outside the home, and I had time to spend with my parents. My father had a degenerative disease and was having difficulty walking and talking, but he and CJ had a special bond, and I wanted them to have lots of time together. While spending time with my parents, I began to dialogue again with my mother about adoption. I could tell she continued to feel threatened. She feared that I might eventually search for my birth mother, and I knew that she was adamantly opposed to this idea. However, the more we talked, the more forthright she was becoming with information about my earliest beginnings.

One afternoon, while sitting in my parents' family room, I remember saying to my mother, "Mom, you weren't adopted; you don't know how it feels. Please understand that my experience is different from yours." She seemed to really hear me that day, and it was in that moment that she shared with me that my birth mother had named me Valerie Anne. Having my mother give me that information directly was a greater gift than she ever knew.

Mom and I were beginning to converse in a much more open and relaxed way, and I was feeling emotionally closer and safer with her than at any other time in my life. Although I don't remember this directly, my mother told me that when I was little and playing, I sometimes pretended that my name was Valerie. Mom would watch my play in amazement, since no one other than my mother and my father knew of my previous name. What I do remember as a little girl was being enthralled with women's military uniforms. I was particularly attracted to those of the navy. The same day I found out my birth name was Valerie, I discovered that my birth mother, when first pregnant with me, had been a WAVE (Women Accepted for Volunteer Emergency Service) in the navy during World War II.

During my twenties, my life went through changes. My first marriage ended in divorce, and I met and married my current husband. Through it all, I grew closer to my mother. Shortly after our marriage, I became pregnant with my second child. Excitedly, I shared the news with my parents. By now, my father was quite sick and emaciated, and I was coming to grips with the knowledge that he was dying. My pregnancy was an exciting bright spot for all of us. However, the focus of the excitement of my early pregnancy was short lived when, two weeks later, my mother died suddenly and unexpectedly of a heart attack. Mostly, I was in shock, and my sister and I turned our attention to our ailing father; there was no time to grieve over the loss of our mother.

My father died eight months later when my daughter was ten days old. Before my thirtieth birthday I had lost both of my parents. Because of the suddenness of my mother's death, I felt particularly abandoned by her. In the safety of therapy, I began to fully experience and process my grief. What I discovered inside was a preverbal rage and a preverbal grief that went back to the loss of my birth mother. Opening up to these intense feelings enabled me to understand more fully the depth of that loss that is a part of the adoptee's legacy.

Four years after the death of my parents, and shortly after the birth of my third child, I knew that I was emotionally ready to search for my birth mother. I started slowly as I built up my courage to find Kitty. My husband, who was helping me with the search, was sometimes more enthusiastic than I was. David came to understand that I had to be thoroughly ready before I made first contact and that I was often on an emotional roller coaster. Through military records and cross-references, we eventually found Kitty.

My first contact with Kitty came in 1982; we had a brief phone conversation. Kitty was angry that I had searched for her. I managed to stay calm and let her know I wasn't out to harm her or compromise her secret. I only asked her one question: "Did you ever think about me on my birthday?" She said that she had often thought about me when I was a younger child and admitted that those early years had been difficult for her. Kitty told me that as time went on she had made peace with God and had found a way to move forward with her life. Kitty did not volunteer any other information, and I knew better than to ask more questions.

In a last-ditch effort to maintain a connection with Kitty, I asked if I could send her a paper I had recently written about my need to search. I promised to send it to a general delivery post office. I enclosed pictures of myself and my children in the hope that seeing these pictures might begin to moderate Kitty's initial anger toward me, and perhaps lay the groundwork to build a bridge.

Years came and went, and I never received a response of any kind. I wondered if she ever received the package I had sent. Because I had since moved to a new city, I considered that maybe Kitty didn't know how to find me. It was now the late 1980s and adoptees were speaking out loudly to the media. Many wanted their original birth records opened. The TV was filled with reunions between adoptees and their birth families, and I wondered if any of this was impacting Kitty. My life was nourishing and fulfilling, and yet I continued to feel the pain of this forced cutoff.

During 1991, after facing a series of major challenges, I decided to attempt to contact Kitty once again. By now I had discovered that Kitty was married and had a grown daughter and two grown sons. I wrote her a letter and gave it to a private investigator with the instruction that the letter be delivered discreetly. It was never my intention to hurt Kitty or to disrupt her current family by revealing her secret. My letter requested two things: that she respond to my letter by letting me know that she received it, and that she be willing, once in my lifetime, to allow me to sit in her presence so we could share about our lives.

A month passed before my letter was delivered, and another month passed before I finally received a response from Kitty. The letter arrived with no salutation. She simply began by informing me that I was ruining her life by attempting to track her down. She appreciated my discreetness, but she felt she would forever live in fear that I might attempt to contact her at any time. Kitty did not think it was wise for us to meet. She saw no value in it for either one of us. She requested that I leave her alone and allow her to live her remaining years in peace. There was no name or signature at the end of the single typewritten page.

I read and reread Kitty's letter more than a dozen times. During the first several readings, I was enraged. I couldn't understand how she could be so insensitive to my needs when I had done all that I could to protect her privacy. I couldn't relate to her not wanting to know me or share with me when I had felt so connected to her for so many years.

In spite of my tremendous support system, I felt pain and disappointment over Kitty's reaction to my letter. However, with time and distance, I was able to see how fearful and threatened Kitty must have been by my existence. I began to feel sadness for Kitty instead of anger. I realized that processing my various feelings throughout the years had given me the opportunity to work through much of my pain and grief. Kitty, however, was stuck in her shame and suffering. I valued my letter to Kitty and the risk I had taken: I had shared openly and honestly what, specifically, I wanted from her. Kitty was unable to give me what I wanted, but I now knew that this was the consequence of Kitty's inability and not about my personal worth. Although I didn't like the tone of Kitty's response to my letter, I appreciated that she had responded and that she was clear about what she wanted. The fact that Kitty responded at all helped me gain a sense of momentary closure.

In spite of a life filled with loving connections, I have continued to want contact with my birth family. Often, I would fantasize about making contact with my biological half-sister. I knew there were two half-brothers as well, but reaching out to a sister seemed less risky. As the years went by, I was aware of feeling angry that I was going to go to my grave as a family secret. I hadn't caused the secret, but I was the product of the secret, and I continued to have waves of pain around my forced cut-off because society had shamed women for having children out of wedlock and had determined that all I really needed was the adoptive family that had it in its heart to provide me a good home. This was never enough for me, and I finally allowed myself to speak my truth—even if my birth mom and my adoptive mom saw it differently.

In my sixty-eighth year, my husband and children were talking about how it might be time to reach out to my half-sister. I had always been hesitant about this because I didn't know if I could handle being responsible for revealing a family secret after so many years. I felt sure that none of my siblings had ever been told about me, and I worried about how this would impact their lives and, possibly, their relationship with Kitty if she was still alive. Additionally, I knew I wasn't ever going to be willing to initiate the first contact with my sister after such a thorough rejection by my birth mother.

On the weekend of Mother's Day 2015, my daughter decided to reach out to my half-sister and sent her a priority letter that began "Dear Judy, as I write this, I feel extremely nervous as to how it will be received. I am also very aware that the information I have is most likely shocking and definitely life changing." My daughter went on to share the facts of my birth, including that it had been Kitty's desire not to have contact with me but that I had always wanted to make contact with my siblings, especially my sister. The letter was written respectfully and only requested an acknowledgment that it had been received. My daughter expected that the siblings would need time to process such big and shocking news.

My sister, Judy, was in shock, and she shared with me later that she read the letter over and over before reaching out to our brother Ricky, who was convinced, almost immediately, that it was not a scam. Kitty had died the October before my daughter made contact. On her deathbed, she did not reveal the secret of my existence. However, as rejecting as Kitty had needed to be of me, my sister and all the family chose to embrace me fully, with open arms! Judy had spent her entire life wanting an older sister!

In August 2015, I traveled to Pennsylvania to spend several days with my sister, Judy, alone—sharing life stories and being together. Having this special time allowed for more healing. I asked to go to the cemetery where Kitty was buried. I left flowers and felt my heart open as I was able to genuinely just send love to Kitty for giving me life and doing the best she knew how. I continue to have a close relationship with my bio sister. We have many similar mannerisms and are both invested in our love of family.

At the end of this year I will turn seventy. I hope in the near future to have a reunion that will involve all generations of my adoptive and birth families. Due to my own life experience, I am invested in building healthier adoptive families that promote connections rather than cutoffs. I believe I'm a member of a triad that connects me to both my birth and my adoptive families forever.

RELEASING

Melanie Chung-Sherman

> Compassion is not a relationship between the healer and the wounded. It's a rela-
> tionship between equals. Only when we know our own darkness well can we be
> present with the darkness of others. Compassion becomes real when we recognize
> our shared humanity.

> —Pema Chödrön, *The Places That Scare You*

When I was five years old, I packed two suitcases to run away from home. One
was for my little brother and the other was for me. I carefully put our piggy banks
filled with coins into the bottom of each suitcase along with my security blankets,
his favorite shirt, toothbrushes, and a change of clothes. We walked down the stairs
dragging our suitcases behind us while our adoptive mother watched us leave in
stoic silence. Our little legs walked out into a bright, temperate, and clear Minnesota
afternoon. Alone and with a twinge of excitement, I remember looking back to see
if my mom would come after us, but she never did. There was a McDonald's on the
outskirts of our neighborhood that we walked to because we were hungry. We sat
on the curb while I opened a suitcase and pulled out coins to feed us, though I had
no idea how to count money. A lady approached us, and my four-year-old brother
informed her that we were running away. Her face turned from smiling to concern.
We did not know what to do, and terror swept over me. We had been found out.
The lady put us in her brown, two-door car and instructed me to tell her where we
lived. I have no explicit memory beyond that point, besides the voiceless anxiety I
felt in the presence of my adoptive mother. I do not remember being comforted,
sought after, or even disciplined by either of my adoptive parents after our escapade.
We were left alone in our rooms until my parents decided to open their doors to us
emotionally. It was a game I learned to navigate from a young age. That was one of
the many traumatic memories associated with growing up in an emotionally neglectful and unstable adoptive home.

My story feels like an outlier. But perhaps not so much, because as hard as this was
to write, I know that I am not alone. I choose to speak to the hearts of those who feel
they will not be believed or understood due to childhood abuse and neglect by biological, foster, kinship, or adoptive parents. My story is also about hope, resilience, and
transformation. It is not necessarily the positive adoption story that papers the walls of
memes and blogs. It is my truth, and it has taken me decades of healing, professional
support, and the love of so many to be ready to share openly. It is meant to encourage
others to do the hard work of addressing their past to break the chains of loss and pain.

I now know, after years of effort to piece together my story, that I was adopted
from South Korea in the late 1970s at the end of the first generation of Korean
adoptees following the armistice of the Korean War. I was eight months old when I
was adopted. Korea has placed more than 225,000 adoptees throughout the Western
developed world. My younger brother (born to a separate birth family) and I were

a part of Korea's adoption diaspora. During the time we were placed for adoption, unethical and unregulated child welfare practices were rampant. Without regulated screening or accountability, there was room for marginal prospective parents, who might not have been approved to adopt under today's tighter adoption regulations, to be approved to adopt Korean children. Both of my adoptive parents had suffered grievous losses shortly before my placement. There was a history of unresolved trauma and mental health challenges that went unaddressed, while my adoptive father actively battled alcoholism. Their home study was less than four carbon-copied, type-written pages. Their inner turmoil, pain, and unresolved grief became my known and familiar world for decades.

My birth mother delivered me with the help of a midwife, Ms. Kwon. Without protective checks and balances overseas, the midwife's in-laws posed as my birth parents and relinquished me to the orphanage without question. I was assigned a case number, C-1942, and placed in two foster homes before being escorted to the United States. Two weeks before I came to the United States, my adoptive mother tragically miscarried her fifth child. I arrived into a grief-filled home, tapped out of emotional and psychological energy, and was left to cry it out separate from any regulated adult. I learned at a very tender age to quiet my needs. My lived experience had already suggested that expressing too many needs leads to psychological abandonment.

I am the oldest of three siblings. My brother was adopted from Korea approximately one year after I was placed. My youngest brother was born to my parents three years after I was adopted. He was born following five miscarriages, which had been the impetus for my parents to adopt. My adoptive mother constantly reminded my other brother and me that he was "the blond-haired, blue-eyed child" she always wanted in the first place, while my adoptive father remained silent. I internalized the message that adoption is a placeholder until parents had "real kids." There was constant fear that my adoptive mother would leave my brother and me because she finally had the child she wanted. Though I could not change my Korean-ness—my dark hair, slanted eyes, dark skin, and the visage of all their losses—I desperately tried to with innocent futility. I prayed that God would change whatever was so burdensome and different within in me that caused both mothers to reject me.

When I was in the first grade, we moved to an all-white, working-class community in Texas. We were one of the only Asians as well as "Yankees" in our neighborhood, place of worship, and school. The racial teasing and bullying intensified. On one occasion, I was accused by an English teacher of stealing a book. She marched me up in front of the class and I was instructed to apologize for something I did not do. My parents failed to do anything, and she went on to be Teacher of the Year. I thought it must have been something about who I was. My adopted brother brought a gun to school to protect himself from extreme bullying (to which our parents turned a blind eye), resulting in his suspension. I closed more of my emotional world off from my parents. Despite the overt racism we faced, my parents sent us to a high school that flew the Confederate flag and played the "Spirit of Dixie" at football games. We were without protection, support, or guidance to navigate the racial intolerance and discrimination we experienced from both adults and peers. It was not until adult-hood that I exposed myself to literature and historical understandings related to racism and racial disparity.

Formulating my sense of identity as an Asian woman and adoptee, without any racial mirrors or mentors, left me alone in a world filled with the antithesis of my Korean heritage. My mother was not available to help me navigate the passage into womanhood. I was surrounded by white, voluptuous, blond-haired, blue-eyed models of beauty and was keenly aware of my mother's desire to have a white child. As a result, I attempted to become as white as possible. In an effort to be the "perfect girl," my anxiety became so elevated that I came home with migraine head-aches, which I hid from my parents. I bit my fingernails and toenails, and when that did not soothe my aching heart, I started pulling my hair out, such that a portion of my head went completely bald. Concerned, my beautician pointed this out to my mother. That was the last time I ever saw the beautician, and nothing more was spoken about my hair. Feeling invisible, I ripped myself apart through self-harm in an effort to be seen.

During adolescence, the contempt in my adoptive home intensified under the weight of so many unspoken things. There were few boundaries or rules in my home, but the most significant, yet unspoken, rule was "do not talk about emotions, and pretend everything is fine." I believe my parents divorced psychologically during that time. My father went through their savings and retirement on fast-money schemes, while my mother worked as an elementary school teacher. The financial instability in our home resulted in an increase in hoarding and disorganization. There were moments when I feared we would lose the house.

My adopted brother was the scapegoat and caught the brunt of my adoptive par-ents' ire. It was not until adulthood that I learned he was repeatedly sexually abused as a child by friends of the family, with no protective adults in his life to intervene. As my brother grew, he fought back. He eventually dropped out of school at the tender age of fourteen and ran away from home. He quickly spiraled into an abyss of drugs and alcohol. As a sibling, coupled with being adopted, my greatest fear was that my adoptive parents would emotionally abandon me as they did my brother, so I placated my adoptive parents' emotional states in an attempt to evade pending rejection. Caught up in my own survival, I retained very little explicit memory of my youngest brother. He held a firm place in the family by virtue of being a biological child. Sadly, he was constantly ill. Looking back, I speculate that he absorbed the trauma into his young body, which manifested into autoimmune deficiencies, severe asthma, and digestive issues.

In an attempt to distance myself from the chaos and gain predictability, I ran headlong into perfectionism through academics, books, the arts—anything to avoid going home—although I struggled with dyscalculia, a math learning disability, and felt inadequate at school work. I had little support or encouragement to complete academics, but there was always spark within me that kept pushing because I knew that in order to escape I needed to go to college. After seeing a high school play, where the director was the first Asian American teacher I had ever met, I was encouraged to audition for future productions. Looking back, it was no surprise that I excelled in the performing arts and music because I had been performing my entire life. Theater provided me with a way to find my voice and be seen by others, as well as a path to college.

I put myself through college while working three jobs and taking out countless student loans. I graduated with my bachelor's degree in theater. Upon college graduation, I was approached by a family friend about an overseas Korean adoptee tour. My maternal grandmother loaned me money to travel. Boarding the plane, I saw a Korean family with a little girl in pigtails, and I thought to myself, "How odd—when Koreans keep their children, that is what it looks like." I wondered what it would have been like had I remained with my birth family. To be culturally Korean. To belong somewhere. To be beloved by those who might understand me. While on the tour, I met sixty Korean adoptees from around the world. It was my first real exposure to Korean food, culture, and language. It was a watershed moment in my life. For the first time, I felt connected to others who shared a similar narrative. I felt understood and empowered. I also began to allow the enormity of everything left behind when I was adopted to sink into my bones. In every corner of Korea—the subway, open markets, and restaurants—I looked for someone looking for me.

Following my first trip to Korea, I made the decision to search for my birth family and more answers. I became actively involved within the adoption community and took a job in post-adoption work. I slowly pieced together aspects of my life and built up the courage to search. My referral papers stated that I was "illegitimate" and was left at the hospital soon after my birth. As a child, this created a deep yearning to know where I came from, why I was left, whom I looked like, and what happened to my birth mother. However, I dared not explore this with my adoptive parents because I knew that they could not hold my pain, my questions, or my yearning.

Over a twelve-year search, I discovered that I was born to an intact birth family as the fifth daughter and was subsequently "switched" for an infant boy who was raised in my stead while I was placed for adoption. I learned that my birth father was a violent man who had threatened my birth mother if she brought another daughter home. Due to the level of secrecy and shame involving my relinquishment, my birth mother refused any contact with me because no one in my birth family knew that I existed. During the course of the search, I also learned that an older birth sister was placed for adoption a year before me. As I reflect on that painful time, it was then that I began to release the idealized picture of a "mother figure" in my life. I was seeking not just my birth mother but also a mother who would finally see me. When I realized that would not happen, I had to reconcile my picture and my reality of what "mother" and "being mothered" meant. During that process, I discovered my strength, determination, and heart through the love and support of other secure figures who had been part of my life. Those secure figures encouraged me to finish my master's in social work and moved me along a path to meet my husband.

For decades, I did not have the words, or the courage, to fully make sense of what happened in my adoptive home. On reflection, many of my behaviors, as well as my adopted brother's behaviors, were too easily dismissed by outsiders and professionals as "adopted child issues," genetic abnormalities linked to our birth families, prenatal trauma or exposure alone, or attachment disorders. My brother and I would go to strangers, seeking comfort from any adult because there was not a secure attachment figure in our home. This was compounded by our early trauma before we were placed. It is interesting that the stability and mental health of our adoptive parents was never questioned, despite the fact that my adopted brother was sent to numerous professionals and in-patient hospitalization for medication and interventions to "fix him." As a young girl, I quickly internalized the message that parents should not be questioned, particularly adoptive parents who "rescued my brother and me from the streets." The truth was that we lived in a home fraught with addiction, rage, and unpredictability. Our behaviors reflected the chaos in our home, and how we coped. Quite frankly, under the circumstances we were pretty ingenious and creative!

When I became a mom, I realized what I had been denied throughout my own life. Throughout both pregnancies, I wondered what my birth mother experienced as she carried me. I became aware that the precious lives inside of me were the only human beings biologically related to me I would ever know. There was minimal guidance from my adoptive parents after the birth of both of our sons, but due to trainings and seminars I benefited from as a social worker, my husband and I were committed to parent with attachment and attunement in mind. When my oldest son turned eight months old, I fell into a deep depression. The timing correlated with the age I was placed into my adoptive family. Depression was an unlikely gift that led me to seek professional support, and to learn how to readily ask for and receive help. My husband and I miscarried our second child, and my mother's response was "Now you know how it feels." I recognized from her extreme lack of empathy the depth of her mental state, and this gave me permission to peer into my past more intentionally.

The "looking back" was a loving anthem to integrate what had been compartmentalized, silenced, and shame-filled inside my heart. It was time to confront the generational bondage of disconnection and fracture from two family systems, my birth family and my adoptive family. The responsibility for my difficult beginning was not mine to bear, but it was my responsibility to break the cycle for my children and the generations to follow. My parents' mental illness and the resulting family dysfunction did not allow room or safety to explore our adoption, losses, transracial impacts, or identity outside of responding to their unmet psychological needs. Compassionately, I recognize that my parents did not have a road map to parent us, but the difference between me and my past is an awareness and a desire to do things differently. Over the years, I made the difficult decision to limit contact with my adoptive family based on their repeated refusal to seek help or grow in awareness. I chose to love them from a distance and, more important, to love and protect my children by honoring what I know to be true in my heart. I have been blessed with a chosen family who seeks us with love and acceptance with no strings attached. It takes profound courage to acknowledge a painful past and resolve to build a brighter future for those we love. This journey is necessary to heal the past and provide an authentic and intimate relationship with loved ones today.

Today, I must make an intentional choice to emotionally engage and be with my children, and I recognize that it does not come naturally to me. Though I may not have had a consistent and nurturing mother figure in my life, I know I am not relegated to the same fate as either of my mothers. I can proactively and thoughtfully seek to be intentionally present as a mom, wife, and friend. It is no longer about perfection, though I recognize that I will always fight that ghost script. It is about being authentic, real, and owning my mistakes in the face of parenthood with my boys. My boys ask about their birth grandparents and wonder why anyone would have to leave their mommy. Though I do not have answers, we are not afraid to talk about those heavy feelings and deep questions. Their understanding of adoption and Korea can only be as integrated as I can communicate both implicitly and explicitly, so I must continually remain aware, imperfect, open, and vulnerable.

I'm thankful for the professional exposure to attachment theory, the psychodynamics of grief and loss, and incredible mentors and teachers along the way who influenced how I parent my children and my inner child. Years of hard work have helped me further integrate my history and embrace it all with loving kindness, forgiveness, and grace. That is daily work. Daily forgiveness. Daily releasing. Daily faith. Despite the circumstances within my adoptive family and birth family, I believe in the power of adoption. I will purposefully choose not to slide into bitterness, hate, rage, or vitriol. Though there have been plenty of days filled with pain, anger, and betrayal, those emotions will not define me. Adoption is not about rescue or salvation. Nor does adoption offer immunity from parental accountability and awareness. In fact, the very essence of adoption places greater responsibility for the adults to understand (and, if necessary, make peace with) their past. Adoption is about committed and tender parenting with a unique and intentionally defined skill set.

My motivation to enter social work—more specifically, adoption—was not altruistic. No, in the beginning I entered to make sense of my life, as many who choose helping professions do. And like many, for me that pull evolved into an awareness regarding what brought me into the field and how that experience will impact those I serve. For too long, I shied away from sharing my truth as not to appear mentally ill, viewed as the "angry adoptee," or infantilized by other professionals and triad members questioning my competence. Now I own every lovely and excruciating part of my narrative.

There is an unspoken myth that adoptees' successes are a direct result of successful adoptive parenting. Humans are multidimensional and resilient. We must begin to view the adoptive family, birth family, and adoptee holistically and as an interdependent system. It is important to consider how these histories between adults and children who have experienced trauma might collide, and be resolved. Discussing insecure attachment–related issues with adoptive parents, much less abuse or neglect issues within adoptive homes, is often considered taboo, but it is readily discussed regarding adoptees and birth families. We must level that playing field gracefully and honestly. There is an overrepresentation of adoptees in counseling, many of whom come with stacked diagnoses, which makes sense, as adoptees have unique layers to uncover and have already endured the trauma of separation from at least one caregiver early in life. Conversely, for every adoptee taken to therapy, adoptive parents and/or caregivers are underrepresented. The subversive message this sends to adoptees is one of patronizing inadequacy and the continual need to be saved, rescued, or redeemed by those who "know better."

Professionals must do their internal work in order to truly see each client holistically, not pathologically, or in terms of their trauma or adoption singularly. We are all more than our past, but it is our past that we must make sense of to be present with others today. We cannot journey with others along a path of healing if as professionals we have not done intentional work. I firmly believe the best therapists and professional helpers are those secure enough to seek help from others. Before we, as professionals, label or interpret individuals, we need to explore their strengths, their supports, their experiences in their adoptive family, as well as early history and how their race has played a role. Not one of us is more healed than another. Not a one. When we view each other as equals in this journey, we find the relaxing curve of healing and releasing. The beauty is that it is never too late to enter in.

15

A Parent's Note to Therapists

What We Really Want You to Know

Lori Thomas

Let others see their own greatness when looking in your eyes.

—Mollie Marti

Sarah walked into the therapist's office, hopeful that she was on the path that would lead to some healing in her family. Sarah and her husband, Abe, had taken a new child into their home a few weeks ago and could not believe how much despair they felt in such a short time. This child, Stefan, was seven years old, and unfortunately the child had been living in an orphanage for most of his life. He seemed so happy and sweet for a few days after he arrived, and then he started to change. He began to pinch and squeeze the family dog. He always stopped when directed, but then he would begin the behavior again once his parents weren't looking. He was really rough with their other children. He would hit or kick, and when Sarah or Abe spoke to him about hurting his new siblings, he seemed almost happy as he said he was sorry. He frequently had episodes of rage and refused to look his parents in the eyes when they talked to him about their concerns. Stefan did not like to be hugged by these new parents, but they were understanding and tried to be patient. This week, Sarah caught him taking money from her wallet. He did not seem to have any boundaries and often took things that did not belong to him. Sarah once saw him hide them under his bed.

As Sarah and Stefan opened the door to the counseling office, they entered a waiting room with hard plastic chairs, a table with a few tattered books for children, and a sign-in sheet. Sarah didn't feel welcome there, nor did she think Stefan would look forward to repeated trips to the counselor. Although this did not give Sarah a warm feeling, she remained hopeful that therapy would help her new child find his way and become a happy member of their family. Something needed to change!

Prior to this appointment, Sarah had filled out a questionnaire by e-mail with some of Stefan's history and a checklist of behaviors. She was glad that the therapist had that information already, thinking that it would be easier to get started with that background information out of the way.

As Sarah was thinking about these things, Stefan was fidgeting in his chair, looking at one of the books, and glancing around almost constantly. He looked like he wanted to jump out of his own skin. Poor kid. Sarah felt sorry for him at moments like this, moments when she had the time to observe him without the need to jump in to protect the dog or stop Stefan from hurting the other kids. Just then, the therapist opened the door to his office and stepped out. He introduced himself to Sarah, and then asked Stefan to follow him into the office. "Should I come, too?" Sarah thought that the therapist would want to get her input about what was happening at home, and maybe even include her in the therapy. "No," the therapist answered, "I have all the information I need on the questionnaire you filled out for me. I like to work alone with my client." Stefan looked at Sarah, smiled his strange smile, and turned away. With that, the therapist and Stefan walked into the office, leaving Sarah feeling bewildered and a bit disenfranchised. This did not feel like a good start.

As Sarah related this story to me, I reflected on similar events I had experienced with my own adopted children. I had requested that, whenever possible, I would be part of any therapy that involved my children. After all, my goal was for me and my family to establish a strong attachment with each adopted child. I asked Sarah how things worked out with Stefan and his therapist. She shared with me that things did not improve. When Stefan came out of the counseling sessions, Sarah anxiously quizzed the therapist for feedback. The therapist described some of the session, stating that he used the session to observe Stefan and get to know him. He stated that many such sessions would be needed to begin to change behaviors. Unfortunately, he never included Sarah, and after several months and no change, they decided to find a new therapist. Similarly, things did not work out with the second therapist. Or the third. The work done in therapy didn't seem to impact life at home. Stefan's attachment disorder left him largely uninterested in working on his relationships or behaviors. Sarah would leave each session with hope but would be unequipped to deal with the challenges her family faced upon returning home.

Many families with children like Stefan suffer as they continue the search for help, and it costs them dearly. It strains marriages, children, and finances. Then they show up in your office and hope you are the one who can finally help them. You are taking the time to read this book, so I can conclude that you probably are a therapist who *can* team with these families and give them hope. Many of you will intuitively know the things that are shared in this chapter. Others will have worked with families who are struggling, and will have learned these lessons along the way. Even so, my hope is that the thoughts shared here on behalf of these families will reinforce and validate these important lessons. These are some things that many adoptive families have in common, experiences they share, and things they would like you to know. This chapter invites you, their therapist, to consider some of the parents' thoughts on the therapeutic process.

Help us as we attempt to help our child. We entered this parent-child relationship with high hopes. We were going to pour a lot of love into our child and were certain he would become a happy member of our family. We planned to live happily ever after. Those hopes were quickly dashed. Our child has behaviors that scare us, and that drive away our neighbors and friends. When one child tried to burn the dog, or his brother, or the house, that scared us. When another child began to masturbate in front of his sibling's friends, our house was put on the "I'm sorry, but our children cannot come to your home to play" list. That is understandable, but hard on the siblings. This child kicks us, hits us, spits at us, and does not make eye contact. He seems to reject everything about us, and all we want is to help. We have been told that our child has ADHD by one doctor, and Reactive Attachment Disorder by one of his past therapists. Obsessive Compulsive Disorder was discussed as a possibility, and one therapist said we need to be on the lookout for a personality disorder. We understand that it is important to have a diagnosis, but this is our child, and we want you to see him as such—not as a set of symptoms or a diagnosis, but as a child who needs your help. We know something is really wrong. We have done some reading about these conditions. We understand that his past is showing up in the present through his behaviors. Our child was beaten by his first parents. Our son was abandoned in an alley. Our daughter was abused physically, emotionally, or sexually. Is there any hope for these children? For their families? For their relationships? We all need to figure out what comes next. How can we help our children begin to trust us? The parenting skills we use effectively with our other children are not working. Who can help us get to the place where we can parent these children differently and have success?

Each child has a story. Emily, a six-year-old girl adopted from foster care, had been in her family for two months. She wanted a pet, and the family decided that a kitten would be a comforting companion for their new daughter. This family helped Emily set up a little bed for the kitty, a litter box in the bathroom, and then went shopping at the animal shelter. They found a sweet little eight-week-old kitten, and Emily named her Boots. Boots came home, and Emily's parents taught Emily how to care for such a little one. Emily was super excited and, after showing that she could be sweet and gentle with the kitten, convinced her parents that Boots should sleep in her room. Mom tucked Emily into bed, checked on little Boots curled up on her blanket, and went to bed herself. In the middle of the night, Emily began screaming, and ran into her parent's bedroom with a lifeless kitten, Emily was crying hysterically, shaking the kitten and yelling, "Wake up, wake up!" over and over. Mom intervened, took the poor kitten from Emily, and sat down with her to find out what had happened. Emily shared that Boots had awakened in the night, and Emily woke up and decided to play with her. Emily said that she was holding Boots like a baby, singing to her, when Boots scratched at her face and jumped out of her arms. Emily ran after Boots and snatched her up. Apparently, Emily then shook the kitten forcefully and told her that she was not allowed to run away like that. Emily told her mom that she was mad at Boots and that Boots was a bad kitten because she ran away and didn't want to play. Then Emily began to cry. "Why didn't Boots like me? Why wouldn't she play with me? I thought she would love me forever and never, ever leave me!"

Emily's mom, Ruth, is in our parent support group. She shared this story with me one evening, tears running down her face. She realized, she said, that she should not have allowed Emily to have so much responsibility with a pet. The loss felt by this family over the death of this little kitten was clear. However, Ruth shared a wonderful side to this tragedy. The day after the death of the kitten, Emily and Ruth went for their weekly therapy. Their therapist was well versed in attachment disorders. As Emily shared the sad story, the therapist listened carefully, and then he began to explore the feelings of loss and abandonment that Emily had experienced in her first few years. This therapist helped Ruth see that Emily was responding to the feelings of rejection when Boots clawed at her and ran away. Emily was not an evil kitten killer, but rather a child who had a complex background and who needed her behaviors to be heard as cries for help.

Sometimes similar situations call for different responses. Another family was fostering a thirteen-year-old boy. He was playing with the family dog in the garage and came into the house earlier than expected. After calling for the dog to no avail, Betty went looking. She found the dog's body in the garage, under a table. This felt like a completely different level of behavior, a greater disruption to the family, and needed a careful response. With the help of their therapist, some respite, and Jimmy's social worker, the family worked to understand what had happened and why. The family had questions. Was the child a psychopath? Was he purely impulsive and caused the death accidentally? Did he care? Those are questions that they had to work through.

Each of our children have unique histories, with a complex combination of experiences and memories. My child might have an attachment disorder that, on paper, looks a lot like the next kid's. However, I know some of my child's triggers and am learning more about him every day. Together, maybe we can help my child make sense of his story.

Each parent has a story. Each of us had different childhood experiences. Some of us entered adulthood with secure attachments, while others had adverse childhoods, with abuse, neglect, or medical conditions that affected our own attachments with our parents or other caregivers. These early attachments affect our parenting. I know that now, but I did not consider it prior to adopting. Parenting this child sometimes brings out the worst in me. I knew that I had some issues, but I discussed all of that with a counselor years ago. My problems with my temper resolved and did not reappear until this child began to push my buttons. You will pick up on that in the therapy office, I am sure. If you feel the need to talk about my past, to help me understand myself and my triggers, please explain the process to me. If you want to complete the Adult Attachment Interview with me, let me know that this is not because I am not good enough, or because you think I can't parent my child, but that you are teaming with me to help me process my past and understand why I am being triggered. I tell my child that I am on his team, working with him. Please do the same for me. Making sense of the past is part of the ability to deal in a healthy way with the present. Help me to see that in a way that affirms me and gives me hope.

Sometimes we need some prompting to realize what is behind our reactions. Marilee, a local mom, shared her concerns. Raised by emotionally present parents, she was sure that she had no trauma in her history. Even so, she thought that her reactions to her new son were a bit extreme. She wondered what it was in her history that could possibly be part of such a reaction. Maybe she just was not a very good mom, she asserted. She had no excuse, no trauma history, no reason to have strong reactions to this new teenaged son who was showing some sexualized behavior. We began to talk, exploring a bit of her story after childhood. She had a first marriage, she told me, and within that marriage, she suffered some pretty bad treatment. That included a husband who was aggressive emotionally and sexually at times, and then physically and emotionally absent at others. That marriage produced a daughter, and she loves that daughter, so she cannot regret the marriage. However, after a few years, the marriage ended. As we spoke of the abusive nature of the marriage, it reminded this precious woman of some other things that had occurred in her teen years. There were some traumas, things that none of us want to happen to our teen daughters, that affected her. However, they did not amount to abuse to the extent that she felt she needed to report the incidents or receive counseling to heal. This early marriage, and the events of her teen years, still affected Marilee. As she spoke of them, she looked at me and whispered, "I guess I have suffered trauma! I never thought of it before, but maybe there are some things that happened to me that might be part of my reactions to my son." Therapists, sometimes we forget, or we don't see the connection between the past and what is happening now. Ask the probing questions so that we can see that these things do matter, now, to our own parenting. It is easy to understand that my child's behavior is, at least in part, due to his trauma history. Help us understand that our own history affects our responses. Help us work out our stories, to make sense of them. Only then will we be free to make decisions to honor our histories, yet not have them rule our reactions.

We are his family, and we would like to be part of the healing process. The work you do with our children is vital to their healing, and we are so thankful that you chose this occupation and are there to help. My child, with his history of trauma and issues with attachment, may be different from many of your other clients. He sure is different from our other children! If you have not worked with a child like him before, please consult with others who have. If you don't know much about attachment disorders, please take the time to learn or refer us to someone with this knowledge. We have already figured out that our child must be parented differently from our other children. He might need a different type of therapy, too. As you consider his treatment plan, please keep us in mind. We want to be part of this process, so that his healing can continue at home. You are with us and our child for a few hours each week. We leave your office full of hope and high expectations, which are often dashed within minutes. Please help us to learn how to take your wisdom home with us, how to apply the therapeutic stance with our child, to become parents that can build healthy attachments with our children and help them to heal. Give us homework. Tell us to read good books, like *Building the Bonds of Attachment* by Daniel

Hughes, so that we can see examples of therapeutic parenting. Give us a list of movies to watch with our child that might enhance dialogue around tough subjects or that might create warm, healing moments. Once I went to watch a movie with my children. I don't even remember what movie it was, but I know it evoked warm feelings for my son. This child had a difficult time with eye contact and resisted touch. After the movie that day, we walked outside to a beautiful crisp sky and a gentle wind. Walking along the sidewalk, my son suddenly took my hand, looked up into my eyes, and said, "I love you, Mom." The way he held my hand, with a little squeeze and a twinkle in his eye, made my heart skip a beat. Something in that movie stirred an emotional reaction in my child, and he was responding! I was able to tell him that I loved him too. If I had not been at a place, due to guidance and hard work, where I could respond to his unexpected overture, the attachment that subsequently built up between us would likely never have happened. Help us as parents to be ready to recognize and respond when that moment comes.

Believe us when we tell you what we see at home, even if our children do not exhibit those behaviors in your office. Please don't minimize the behaviors I describe or try to tell me that they are "normal" childhood tantrums. Listen to our stories about our child, his behaviors, and his interactions with others. He works really hard to triangulate his parents. Some days, he gets the other children so frustrated that they complain that they can't stand to be around him. In the office with you, he might work really hard to be on his "best behavior." I suppose, in a way, we want you to affirm us, to hear us as we tell you what we observe. Most of all, we want to make it work.

Please take time to listen to us and to really hear us. We often feel very alone in this parenting process. Not many people understand us, and this very different parenting that we are doing. When we arrive at your office, we want to know that you are listening, that you hear us, that you care enough to really tune in. When we go to a therapist who doesn't appear to have read all the paperwork they asked us to complete, asks us to repeat the same information each week, and does not seem to remember much about our child from visit to visit, we are dismayed. We have placed a lot of our hopes, along with our time and money, in our visits with you. We need to know that you care, that you hear, and that you are paying attention to us and our precious child.

Talk to us when our child tells you incredible stories that seem out of character or context. I know that our son just told you that we forced him to kill a wild rabbit and cook it for dinner. You might be required to report that to social workers, but please also talk to us and get our perspective. You might learn that he actually did kill animals and eat them in his birth home. He has shared that story with us, too. The truth is we tend to buy our meat from the great selection at the local grocery store. Did our daughter tell you that dinosaurs come to her window each night and that she has to feed them cookies to keep them from harming her? We wonder if you can help us sort out the true, sometimes dimly remembered events from those that are purely fanciful. We wonder if you can help us dig out the implication of each to our child and to us.

We seemed pretty happy and normal until this child entered our lives. We were nice, and the neighbors liked us. We had friends who invited us to dinner. When it was time for holiday get-togethers, we were included by our extended family. Now all of that has disappeared. Back then, we were not maniacs. We did not yell, and it was rare for anyone to yell at us. Boy, has that changed!

Just yesterday, while watering the flowers, an enraged neighbor stomped across my yard. "Keep your child away from my property! If you let him pee on my roses again, I might have to call the police and report it."

Another family had their own story to share. At a gathering of a group of friends, ten-year-old Dan started acting out, disturbing everyone there, it seemed to Jennifer. Her husband, Jack, quietly told the family to get their coats on, that they were going home. When the host saw them preparing to leave, he said, "Please wait," and asked Jack and Jennifer to come upstairs, where he gathered all the adults. He told everyone there that he thanked God that Jack and Jennifer were willing to do the hard work with little Dan and led the group in a prayer for the whole family. That event not only encouraged Jack and Jennifer but also involved all there in seeing the adoption as a blessed event and resulted in support over the coming years.

Please encourage those with whom you come into contact to be part of the extended support structure needed by all those dealing with these challenges.

We wanted this child. We really did. In fact, we gave up a lot in order to bring him into our family. We made a decision to add to our family through adoption. We spent months, and thousands of dollars, completing a home study. We waited for a referral. We got excited when this child's file was offered to us. We traveled to meet him. Time and money kept flowing away from us. We were happy to make the sacrifices in order to adopt him. Know that *we are doing our best.* Sometimes we respond to our child in ways that are not intended or that are not healthy for the child or for us. We know that we could be handling things better, but we don't yet know how. In fact, sometimes we feel like we are on the right track, only to get caught in a terrible cycle. Our child does not trust us, so we work really hard to gain his trust. Then, when we see him calm down a bit and respond, we become afraid. You see, whenever there has been a calm period with our son, it isn't long before he explodes into a rage. So we see this calming down period, and rather than enjoy it and experience it in a positive way with our child, we tense up out of fear. We know that chaos is coming. Then our child senses our tension and responds to that. Is his inevitable explosion due to our tension, or was it truly coming anyway? Help us to expect the difficult behaviors, and to see them for what they are, with compassion and even with a sense of humor.

Please don't become his hero. Instead, help us to fill that role. We want him to learn to trust us, to see us as important in his life, and to want us! It would be easy for our child to get confused about all of that, especially if he finds someone else to fit his perceived needs. As you build a trust relationship with our child (and with us!), we can sense good things happening in our home. We are so happy for your influence. We just want to become the most important people to our child, to be the ones who are trusted. We all know that he needs us. Help him to know that, too, and work with us as parents.

This child is ripping our family apart. Our other children feel abandoned by us, as we spend so much of our time and energy helping this one very needy child. Before our newest child entered our home, we sat down with the other kids and explained that there was a child who needed a family. We even asked for their input as we came to the decision to adopt. We did not ask them, however, if they wanted to have to hide their toys or risk getting them destroyed. We did not ask them if they would be okay spending lots of time at Grandma's house, while Mom drove long hours to therapy with their new sibling. We did not ask them if they understood that this new child would be so needy that they would feel that they were suffocating in her presence. We did not ask, because we did not know. Arleta James wrote an excellent book on this topic; *Brothers and Sisters in Adoption* is a great resource to help families prepare for a new adopted child or to navigate some of the pitfalls that can occur once the child is placed.

Our spouses feel neglected, too. How can we take the time to calm this new child when he is scared each night, after spending the day running all over the place for all of our kids, and still have energy for a romantic relationship? In fact, sometimes the evening is a time when the primary caregiver gets out to do the grocery shopping, and he or she might just stay out a bit longer than necessary in order to get a break. Finding time for the spouse, or maybe time for a date, seems like a stretch. We must find the time and energy, of course, but it is not easy.

One mom told me that the stress of dealing with their son has resulted in her husband, Stan, developing sexual dysfunction. She said she was at her wits' end. What had been an important part of their life was now a train wreck. Was it only the stress, or did he blame her for pushing for the adoption? Didn't he love her anymore? Now a whole series of new issues has risen.

Therapists, help us to know that as parents we need to form a united front at all costs—our relationship must be top priority. Our extended family does not always understand what we are doing. Some of them are swayed by the superficial charm that our son exhibits. Others have cautioned us that we are in over our heads, that this child is destroying us, and that we must give her back. We once picked up a grandparent from the airport after she arrived to visit and get to know the newest grandchild. By the time we arrived at our house, fifteen minutes into the visit, we were told that this adoption was a grave mistake. However, the next day we had therapy and invited Grandma to join us. This gave her a glimpse of the inner pain our child experienced, of the traumatic past that haunted him, and it forever changed her view of him and our adoption. As tears flowed down her cheeks, she stated that she could not believe a child could have been treated so badly, and of course we should continue with the adoption and help this precious child. She became his greatest advocate. Thank you for understanding the needs of the extended family and including them in the therapeutic process when appropriate.

I share this information with you, our therapists, so that you can know the outside pressures that we feel. If you help us navigate these different relationship struggles, it will benefit the child who is your client but who is also part of this extended family that needs support.

This child is very important to us, but we also have other responsibilities, other family members, and other things that we hold dear. Remember those other children who need some of our time and attention? Do you know that our other sons and daughters have really big feelings about this new child? They get angry at the amount of time and attention we spend trying to help one child, and feel that we are doing this at their expense. They lost the family that they loved, and they are now sharing us with someone who is still a bit of a stranger to them. We need to find a way to balance everything. We also have jobs. We belong to the PTAs at school and are expected to volunteer with some of the events at church. We would like to see our friends (the ones who still talk to us) from time to time.

We asked you to give us homework, to help us figure out how to make life work with this new child. Sometimes you give us that homework, only to find out that we did not get much of it accomplished last week. Our intentions are good, and we will keep trying. It might just be that this week, all we could handle is trying to survive from day to day. Hopefully, next week will be better.

Can we be honest about this? Really, truly honest? Sometimes we have regrets. Regrets about parenting. We mourn the independence we had before taking on the responsibility of children. We might have regrets about adoption. This does not feel like the life we signed up for! We have regrets as we mourn the life we had and are challenged by the life we now have. Then we feel guilty about those regrets. Tim and Anne told me they would not have made it, separately. That is, one day Anne would be ready to give up on the whole adoption thing, and the next Tim would be at the end of his rope. Help us to remember to lift each other up when we are down.

We are exhausted, physically and emotionally. Really, truly exhausted. Some days, we don't even want to wake up. However, we do. We get up because we know that we must, and things will really get bad if the parents stay in bed! So we get up and begin each day hoping to survive. When we share these feelings with others, we often get great advice: "Get away for a break with your spouse." "Take time for yourself." Get a hobby." We know that this advice is good, as far as it goes. However, sometimes it just does not seem possible. Today, for example. Get up at six to get two children fed, dressed, and off to the school bus by seven. Then spend time with another child, who needs to be at the therapist's office by ten. Unfortunately, the therapist's office is two hours away. Be prepared for the drive, to try to avoid a meltdown in the car. Healthy snacks, headphones, good books, soft stuffed animals, a change of clothes—these and many other things need to be packed into the car for the drive. It is a challenge to gather enough items to keep this child occupied and calm for the drive but also choose things that are soft enough that they won't knock me out if she throws them at my head in a rage. Get to therapy in the nick of time, and after therapy, grab lunch together and head home to be back before the other children get off the school bus.

Try to keep all the children regulated, to some extent, after school. Make dinner. You get the idea. Some days, it does not seem like there is a minute to breathe. We just want you to know that, so if we arrive at your office seeming a bit frazzled, we probably have a good reason. Please bear with us.

We are here. In spite of our fears, our exhaustion, our occasional regret, and our failure rate with other therapists, we are here. We wake up each day, hopeful for a bit of progress, and take a deep breath. We get out of bed. Take another deep breath. Then we say a prayer, take another deep breath, and head in to check on our child. We tell him we are happy to see him. We try to convince ourselves that this is true. We tell him that we love him. We do, you know. We try to begin each day with a fresh start, a bit of optimism, and still hold our expectations in check. Some days, we remember to take this journey, to be present and available to this child, one hour at a time. We are here, even if just for this hour. Then we are here for the next hour. There are times when that is all we can promise. To be here, right now, in this moment.

We don't plan to give up. We love him. We really do. We adopted him because we knew he needed us. Boy, it is clear that he needs us now! When he looks at us, when we have the rare opportunity to see into his soul, we see that he is crying out for security. He needs to be loved, in spite of the truth that he does not currently know how to accept that love or to love us in return. We feel a sense of mission, we know why we are doing this, and we plan to continue. This is not easy, so we don't make this commitment lightly. However, we won't give up.

Sally told me about a therapist who worked with her daughter for six weeks, then told her that all her issues were resolved. "Are you kidding me?" Either he wasn't trying or he was done dealing with her daughter, who would say whatever she thought the therapist wanted to hear. It seemed, to Sally, like the therapist was just giving up.

Please don't give up on us. This child could use some consistency in his life. After five families, six therapists, and countless schools, it would be nice if a few things in his life could be predictable. Our child would benefit from a team of people who will stick with him, and with us. He isn't the only one who needs you. We do, too. We really could use some support, encouragement, and consistency, too.

Affirm us. When we do things right, please point that out to us. We might be feeling pretty darned drained from the daily grind of parenting this child, and a bit of encouragement goes a long way. When we could do better, please let us know, but do it gently. We want to get this right, we really do, and we will do our best to learn better strategies as you show them to us. We will affirm you, too, and are truly thankful for your efforts!

Acknowledge us as part of the team. We spend more time with our children than anyone else. We know our children as well as they can be known. More than that, show us you value our input. Jennifer told me her therapist asked her to repeat the same background information. She said, "It seemed as if he had never met my child." That makes us believe we are an afterthought, and it certainly doesn't reflect a growing and valued relationship.

Give us tools to work with. Train us. Help us take the strategies you teach us into our homes. In addition to teaching us strategies for helping our child, could you please help us to understand and take ownership of our responses?

Sometimes we wait too long to seek professional help. We start out talking with family. Then, when things don't improve, perhaps we move to support groups. Those help a lot but do not substitute for intensive therapy, both individual and family. We seek a therapist who is both nearby and affordable. That is a tough one! There are so many potential pitfalls involved in working with and transforming our family and, at the same time, responding to the needs of an often very troubled child.

Our high hopes can become a catastrophe caused, in part, by unmanaged expectations. Even when we are warned of the challenges ahead, we fall into denial—we are certain love will be enough. When we arrive at your door, we often feel abused and uncertain, and we are searching for eight main things:

1. Help us as we attempt to help our child. We are your client as much as our child is your client!
2. Our child is a distinct individual and needs an individualized approach, within the parameters of your therapeutic approach. Please learn and understand our child's story.
3. Both the parents and the family are unique, and we truly desire that our child's therapist understand the context of each relationship. Understand our many pressures, and be encouraging.
4. These connections need to be part of the big picture, so please include the whole family in the healing process.
5. If you give us, as parents, the benefit of the doubt, giving us both respect and a key role in therapy, outcomes will improve.
6. If we are at the place where our family is in the process of breaking, give us guidance and referrals to therapeutic help that is needed to stabilize the situation.
7. Help us get through second thoughts, even when we are too exhausted to continue.
8. We know our child can get there. As you equip our child and our family to succeed, believe in us. We are thankful for your efforts.

Thank you for taking the time to hear us, to listen to our thoughts, and to learn more about attachment disorders in general and our child specifically. Thank you for including us, for working with us as a family. Thank you for your presence, your patience, and your professionalism. Thank you for sharing our hope and for joining us on the healing path. We are happy to have you on our team.

16

Incorporating Attachment-Based Models within Organizations

Debbie Reed

The man who moves a mountain begins by carrying away small stones.

—Confucius

Sue was excited to finally be able to attend a three-day training on a specialized attachment-based intervention. Budgets were tight in her organization, and clinicians, especially those new to the organization like she was, rarely had the opportunity to add to their therapeutic toolbox with this type of out-of-town training. It had taken months of persistent advocacy on her part to gain approval, and she planned to make the most of this opportunity.

The training was amazing, and Sue could immediately identify opportunities to shift her organization's approach to benefit the children and families with whom she worked. Throughout the entire trip home, Sue's mind was bubbling over with new possibilities based on what she had learned, and she looked forward to sharing her ideas with her supervisor and discussing how to implement them.

The following week, Sue's meeting with her supervisor was a bit like slowly letting the air out of a balloon. Every suggestion was met with "That's an interesting idea, but I'm not sure it fits with our approach," or "Whoa there, let's not get ahead of ourselves. I like your enthusiasm, but something like you are suggesting would first have to go before our clinical review committee," or "I'm not sure that could be considered a billable service." Sue left the meeting deflated, frustrated, and wondering why the organization sent her to the training in the first place if she wasn't going to be able to implement what she learned.

While this is a fictional recounting, we have heard from many "Sues" in the weeks and months following attachment-based training. They leave the training so excited about the impact this new technique can have on their kids and families, and they

213

are at first baffled, and then discouraged, by the roadblocks and apparent lack of support they seem to receive within their organization. Or perhaps, for independent practitioners, the treatment technique doesn't fit within the guidelines of funding contracts, end of discussion. In either case, it may feel like pushing against a brick wall. Isn't everyone supposed to be working together to help kids and their families?

Full disclosure: I am not a clinician. I spend a lot of time with clinicians and have even been told on occasion that I think like a clinician, but I am actually a "them." My positions have all been on the operational side of my organization. And it is from that vantage point that I offer the following considerations that may be helpful as you work to influence the powers that be on the importance of attachment-based therapies.

Before you start to worry that you really don't know much about how to approach management, I'm going to let you in on a little secret: the same basic concepts you use with your clients also work with organizational leaders. Sure, the popular business press describes the process a bit differently, but if you look past the vocabulary, the core concepts are basically the same. For example, one classic leadership guide identifies the five practices of exemplary leadership as (1) Model the Way, (2) Inspire a Shared Vision, (3) Challenge the Process, (4) Enable Others to Act, and (5) Encourage the Heart (Kouzes and Posner 2002). Is that really all that different from how a clinician supports a client? Another best-selling business book talks about the dividends of high levels of trust and the tax of low levels of trust—that work happens more quickly and easily (and therefore costs less—that is, the dividend) where there are high levels of trust (Covey 2006). Do you not already, intuitively, do a lot of listening, understanding, and validating (building trust) before you put forth a gentle challenge to your clients? Yet another business book talks about resonant leaders being attuned to their people's feelings, and gifted leadership occurs where the head and heart meet (Goleman, Boyatzis, and McKee 2002). Really, these are from the business section of the bookstore. The takeaway is that you know how to do this stuff. If you bring the same level of observation and attunement to your organization's operations that you do to the client relationship, there are lots of clues as to how to most effectively move an idea forward.

While I will give examples of how to effect change inside an organization, the same steps apply if you are an independent practitioner working with external funding sources. In some ways it may be a bit more of a challenge to get external funders to take a chance on something different, but that's the double-edged sword of working on your own—you can practice the way you like, but you still have to find a way to fund your efforts.

So, where do you start in your quest to gain support for incorporating attachment-based therapies into your work?

Look for what is going on underneath the behavior. You are good at looking for the root cause of behavior with your clients. Are you using those same skills to facilitate change in your organization? As a general rule, supervisory and management staff don't say no just to be difficult. Managers' core responsibilities center around systems, processes, consistency, and stability—not as an end to itself, but as a means to efficiently, effectively carry out your organization's mission.

What may seem like no big deal from a clinician's standpoint can have ripple effects that challenge the processes and stability that managers (a) have established to meet a myriad of expectations and requirements and (b) are held accountable to, often both internally and externally. Have you considered that you might not be the only one asking to do things differently? Imagine having twelve, or twenty, different clinicians who all want to do their own thing in their own way. It's not that managers don't share your commitment to children and families; however, their role is designed to facilitate serving kids and families by making sure the agency is meeting licensure requirements and payroll. (And really, as aggravating as that may be at times, aren't you glad they are taking care of those things so you don't have to?) While you are focusing on the one thing you want to do, your manager may be looking at the eight things that one change would impact.

Another consideration that may impact a supervisor's response is the agency's strategic goals. Do you know how your suggestion fits into or flies in the face of industry trends or the direction the agency is headed? What may be a great idea when considered in isolation may not be a fit for the course the agency has charted. How much easier do you think it will be to get a "yes" if you present your request within the context of moving the agency forward toward its goals? External audiences, such as funders or state agencies, have goals, too. Are you framing your ideas/suggestions in a way to support their efforts?

It is all about looking at the big picture and being strategic in how you present your request. Before you start to think that sounds manipulative, do you not approach a five-year-old differently than you would a fifteen-year-old? Same concept. Don't try to impress finance people with your grasp of clinical terminology (they won't be impressed). Talk to them about the bottom-line impact of this opportunity, especially if you're asking for a short-term investment to achieve a long-term gain. If you're talking to an external funder, it helps to know that they are probably looking at replicability. If you present your idea in that context, you will have a much better chance of success. And for those of you who are thinking this sounds like too much work, my response is that you probably give this same kind of consideration to your work with an individual child. Isn't it worth a little extra effort to be given the green light to move forward with an intervention that could benefit many children?

Once you have taken some time to consider what factors are going on underneath a manager's (or funder's) behavior, you can take steps to respond to the "why" of their actions (their goals/requirements/expectations) instead of the "what" (their behavior that appears to be creating a roadblock to what you want to do). When you get back from that training, tell them you appreciate the investment the agency has made in your professional development, and how excited you are to maximize that investment by applying what you have learned to your work with kids and families. Ask them to help you figure out the best way to do that. Listen to them. Wonder with them. Make them part of the team. They will know, probably far better than you, if there is a way to get over, around, or through the regulations or expectations that are currently blocking your path. They might even suggest an alternate path that you had never considered. Sometimes no doesn't mean no—it means not yet or not in that way. Is your first attempt at breaking through to a child always successful? It may take the same type of tenacity you use to connect with a child to find a path forward for attachment-based work in your agency. Take a deep breath, keep your focus on the "why," and it is likely you will find a way around the barrier of the "what."

Baby steps. You don't expect to get from Point A to Point G in one fell swoop with your clients. Sure, sometimes it happens, but that is not the norm. Nor is it the norm to make sweeping changes within an agency because of one clinician's good idea. Baby steps. Change in organizations typically happens in a series of predictable phases and usually requires considerable time (Kotter 2012). Research has shown that transformation (yes, one idea or treatment approach well planted can lead to organizational transformation) is a process of buildup, where there may be little visible progress, followed by a breakthrough (Collins 2001; Gladwell 2000). I'm trusting that by this point you can see the obvious correlations to clinical work.

Can you work with your supervisor/manager to find a way to test, to pilot, your idea with one child who has not responded to other interventions? As long as what you are suggesting isn't going to hurt the child, it's a small bet—a low-risk way to (a) help a child and (b) demonstrate whether this new approach can improve the effectiveness of your work. Don't start out trying to change the entire system. Just like with your clients, if you try to go too far too fast, you will get resistance. Start small. Document the impact of your efforts. What worked, what didn't work, what would you like to change? Share what you learned with the powers that be, repeatedly. One of the reasons that change efforts fail is that they are under-communicated by a factor of ten (Kotter 2012). Be a broken record. (Does one conversation usually change your client's behavior?)

Some days it will feel like you are taking two steps forward and one step back. Okay. Don't give up. When setbacks happen in therapy, you don't immediately decide your client is impossible or ridiculous just because they failed to embrace your great idea. You stick with it. Or when one strategy doesn't work, you try another. Systems, like clients, are wired to resist change. It takes multiple repetitions of the new, more effective experience for a different behavior to stick. And under times of stress, both clients and organizational systems tend to resort back to old, more familiar ways of responding. It's not personal; it's not a lack of desire for things to be better; it's what feels safe. You foster change one baby step at a time.

Find a point of connection. With a client, it might be a shared interest or favorite activity that opens the door to more rapid progress. Organizationally, you're looking for a "champion" who shares your excitement and will open doors on your behalf. Champions may or may not be in your direct line of supervision in the organizational hierarchy (which can be tricky, but more on that later). They tend to be bilingual—that is, they understand the language of both the clinical and the operational aspects of the organization. They are people who have taken new ideas and run with them. That doesn't mean they're an easy sell, but if you can show how your idea will help further the organization's mission/goals/strategy, they will help you get there. In some situations, they may help you by providing wise counsel, while in other cases a champion may play a more active role in the change effort. Don't expect a champion to do the work for you. They open doors, they offer advice or perspective, they may pave the way, but you still have to walk through the doors they open.

Start with your supervisor when looking for a change champion, or, in the case of an independent practitioner, start with your primary funder contact. Do your homework first to identify a possible point of connect. Are they looking for specific client results? If so, how will what you are suggesting impact those outcomes? Does involving the parent in treatment provide better long-term results, and does that justify any upfront costs associated with only being paid for the child but actually working with the parent-child dyad? (There is plenty of research to back up this concept. Find it and use it to make your case.)

If you get a no, ask why. Listen to what is being said, and what is not being said, in the answers. Ask for alternate solutions. Learn from the feedback, formulate a response to the objections or build on the suggestions, and try again. The second no is the point at which many clinicians throw up their hands in frustration: "All 'they' care about is the bottom line. Don't 'they' want to do what is in the best interest of the child? 'They' wouldn't know a good idea if it bit them in the backside!"

Again, look at the situation through your clinical lens. A child often resists the changes you are trying to facilitate because the outcomes of their current coping mechanisms are predictable and feel safe. Even if the results aren't optimal from your perspective, the response is succeeding to some degree to achieve the child's primary survival goals. Organizationally, systems and processes are designed to maintain the status quo, to create consistency and predictability—"safety," if you will. Thus, it should not be surprising that a challenge to the system will likely be met with resistance—not because those managing the system don't want to improve, but change means risk and systems are designed to minimize risk.

Some of you may be reading this and thinking that it would be easier to just do what you want and "beg for forgiveness" after the fact. As a general rule, I advise against that, and here's why. It gets you labeled as a rebel/troublemaker/one of those "free spirits" who will go off and do whatever you want, and as a result "the system" (that is the supervisors and managers whose responsibility is to maintain stability within the organization) will work even harder to clip your wings, so to speak. Even your great ideas may be taken less seriously because you will be seen as a threat to the stability of the system. Why do something that is going to make it even harder to achieve your ultimate goal when there is an easier way?

Similar to many clinical interventions, if you can "sideswipe" the system rather than directly confront it, your likelihood of success increases significantly. Can you work with your champion to get an exception, or carve out a small trial, without attempting to change the larger system? If that is successful, increase the size of the pilot effort, *without trying to change the larger system*, thus avoiding the systemic push to maintain the status quo. If you are tracking the data and can show that what you are doing is working, you will eventually reach a tipping point that will impact the larger system (Gladwell 2000; Collins 2001). Yes, this is using the baby-step method to sideswipe your way into finding a point of connection via the path of least resistance. And just like with your clients, it works.

If you have tried to work with your supervisor to champion your efforts to incorporate attachment-based therapies into your work to no avail, you may choose to look to other individuals in the organization to assist with the change initiative. Just realize that sidestepping the organizational hierarchy may bring additional layers of resistance, with possible pushback from both a systems and a process standpoint, so it is always better to work within the organizational structure, if possible. When that is not possible, however, where do you start in searching out a possible champion?

Sometimes those who can most influence the system may not be in the "logical" places in the organizational chart. Look for enthusiasm and a track record of being involved in projects that have moved forward in the organization. People, not positions, make change happen. Is there someone on the operational side of the organization that you have just "clicked with"? That is probably a good place to start. Enthusiasm is a powerful lever, and even if your kindred spirit isn't in a position of authority, he or she may be able to connect you with just such a person that you otherwise may not have considered.

Do your homework. Identify the agency's strategic goals, and consider how your desired treatment approaches can help impact those efforts. Where do you see changes taking place in the organization? Who or what is happening quietly behind the scenes to facilitate that change? There is no one right approach that works every time in every situation, so you have to listen and observe (i.e., use your clinical skills). There will be clues regarding the most likely path to effect change in the organization. You simply have to look for them and follow where they lead to find your most powerful point of connection.

Trust the process. Behaviors sometimes escalate during the course of treatment. How do you respond clinically? In some cases, you back off temporarily; in other cases, you choose to push through the resistance. Regardless of the specific approach, there are usually some rocky patches, and the clinician has to stick with it, to trust the process, to shepherd the client to the healing on the other side of the pain. By now you know where I'm going, right?

Change brings resistance, and the amount of change being sought usually corresponds to the level of resistance to be expected. As a skilled clinician, there are many things you can do to anticipate, plan for, and minimize the resistance, but it is also important to recognize that resistance is part of the process. Do you walk away from treatment the first time your client resists your attempts to help them change? Even though, to you, the change you are requesting may seem quite small? Have you ever noticed that what seems so very logical to you may not seem at all logical to the person you are working with? Sometimes you have to put your sense of logic in a box, with clients and with organizations. You have to start where they are at, find a path forward from there, and trust the process.

Feel like you don't understand the business side of the process enough to trust it? Perhaps perusing the business press a bit might boost your confidence. I would suggest John Kotter or Jim Collins as a good place to start. Both have written a number of (approachable and interesting!) books and articles that are directly relevant to accomplishing your goals. Kotter focuses on change, management, and leadership. Collins is more research based and focuses on overall organizational success. I believe that both will expand your understanding of how transferrable your clinical skills are to effecting change in the organizations. In other words, I think they will help you gain the confidence to trust the process.

That's it. Look for what is going on beneath the behavior, take baby steps, find a point of connection, and trust the process. You knew how to do this all along. Sure, there are hundreds of business books out there that will use different words or frame it in a different way, but the change process is pretty much the same regardless of the environment or individuals involved. That's not to say it's easy. Change never is. But if you have gotten this far reading this book, I'm guessing you're not a status quo kind of person.

So find a path to incorporate attachment-based interventions into your work. It may not be the well-paved one you hoped for, but that doesn't mean there is no path. Some clinicians find a way by going it on their own. Others seek out organizations with cultures that embrace new ideas and place a high value on learning, growth and change. Still other clinicians choose to grow where they're planted and challenge their organizations to become the best version of themselves, thereby impacting even greater numbers of children and families, along with the systems designed to care for them.

Just as there is no one attachment-based intervention that is the ideal solution in every situation, and often it is the combining or layering of techniques that brings the best result, so, too, there is no one way for clinician to impact the larger systems in which they work. At its core, impacting changes within an organization, like good clinical work, takes passion, commitment, and a determined resourcefulness to find a way.

BIBLIOGRAPHY

Collins, Jim. 2001. *Good to Great: Why Some Companies Make the Leap and Others Don't.* New York: HarperCollins.

Covey, Stephen M. R. 2006. *The Speed of Trust: The One Thing That Changes Everything.* New York: Free Press.

Gladwell, Malcolm. 2000. *The Tipping Point: How Little Things Can Make a Big Difference.* Boston: Little, Brown.

Goleman, Daniel, Richard Boyatzis, and Annie McKee. 2002. *Primal Leadership: Learning to Lead with Emotional Intelligence.* Boston: Harvard Business School Press.

Kotter, John P. 2012. *Leading Change.* Boston: Harvard Business School Press.

Kouzes, James M., and Barry Z. Posner. 2002. *The Leadership Challenge.* San Francisco: Jossey-Bass.

Appendix

Additional Resources

Association for Training on Trauma and Attachment in Children (ATTACh)
ATTACh is an international coalition of professionals and families dedicated to helping those with attachment difficulties by sharing our knowledge, talents, and resources.
Website: www.attach.org

Attachment and Trauma Center of Nebraska (ATCN)
Offers specialized team treatment for attachment and trauma in children and professional workshops for the EMDR/Family Therapy Integrative Model.
Website: www.atcnebraska.com

Attachment and Trauma Network (ATN)
The Attachment and Trauma Network (ATN) is the nation's oldest parent-led organization supporting families of traumatized children. ATN provides both online and on-location training in therapeutic parenting; operates private online support communities with experienced therapeutic parents moderating; maintains a database of worldwide therapists and resources; and provides support, education, and advocacy for those raising traumatized and attachment-disordered children.
Website: www.attachmenttraumanetwork.org

Chaddock
Chaddock is on the cutting edge of residential treatment for children who have experienced severe abuse, neglect, or other trauma in their early years of development, and is nationally respected for the excellent results demonstrated in our Developmental Trauma and Attachment Program (DTAP). Chaddock also offers and Intensive In-Home Program to families anywhere in the United States.
Website: www.chaddock.org

Child Trauma Academy
The Child Trauma Academy is a not-for-profit organization based in Houston, Texas, which works to improve the lives of high-risk children through direct service, research, and education. The academy provides training in the Neurosequential Model developed by Bruce Perry.
www.childtrauma.org

Children's Research Triangle
CRT is located in Chicago, Illinois, and provides diagnostic and therapeutic services related to fetal alcohol spectrum disorders and other developmental disabilities.
Website: www.childrensresearchtriangle.org

Daniel Siegel
Daniel J. Siegel is a well-known child, adolescent, and adult psychiatrist. Much of his career he has spent studying family interactions with an emphasis on how attachment experiences influence emotions, behavior, autobiographical memory, and narrative. His website has a variety or resources related to these topics, including his books.
Website: www.drdansiegel.com

Developmental Attachment-Based Psychotherapy
The website for Developmental Attachment-Based Psychotherapy includes useful education materials about the model.
Website: www.attachmentskills.com

Donaldson Adoption Institute
The Donaldson Adoption Institute's mission is to provide leadership that improves laws, policies, and practices—through sound research, education, and advocacy.
Website: www.adoptioninstitute.org

Dyadic Developmental Psychotherapy (DPP)
A worldwide body that promotes Dyadic Developmental Psychotherapy (DDP) and provides information about the therapy, parenting approach, training, and resources.
Website: www.ddpnetwork.org

Empowered to Connect
Offers a wide array of resources for adoptive and foster parents. Helps parents create strong and lasting connections with their children in order to help them heal and become whole.
Website: empoweredtoconnect.org

Eye Movement Desensitization and Reprocessing International Association (EMDRIA)
The EMDR International Association (EMDRIA) is a professional association where EMDR therapy practitioners and EMDR therapy researchers seek the highest standards for the clinical use of EMDR. This website provides information to

the greater EMDR community, including clinicians, researchers, and the public that our members serve.
Website: www.emdria.org

Family Attachment and Counseling Center
Training in Attachment and Narrative Therapy that offers distance and onsite training opportunities.
Website: www.familyattachment.com

Infant-Parent Institute
Founded in 1986 by Michael Trout, the Infant-Parent Institute has been a private clinical practice, consultation, and training facility dedicated to understanding the relationship between early social experiences and how our lives form. Excellent array of training materials available.
Website: www.infant-parent.com

International Association for the Study of Attachment (IASA)
The International Association for the Study of Attachment (IASA) is a multidisciplinary association of mental health professionals. A focus on how humans cope with danger, how attachment relationships affect this, and how later adaptation to life circumstances draws on these experiences.
Website: www.iasa-dmm.org

Kids and Families Together
Innovative agency committed to bringing the best of guidance and resources to foster, kinship, and adoptive families. Sponsors and provides training about understanding the adoption triad and attachment-based models of therapy for California and beyond.
Website: www.kidsandfamilies.org

Lifespan Learning Institute
Cutting-edge conferences for mental health professionals with a special focus on attachment and trauma. All conferences are recorded and recordings are available for purchase.
Website: www.lifespanlearn.org

Melanie Chung-Sherman
Ms. Chung-Sherman provides adoption-sensitive counseling to individuals, couples, and families in the Dallas/Fort Worth area. She encourages anyone touched by adoption who desires support, assistance, and counsel to contact her regardless of age, gender, sexual orientation or identity, marital status, disability, religious affiliation, socioeconomic status, or method of adoptive placement.
Website: www.mcsadoptioncounsel.com

National Child Traumatic Stress Network (NCTSN)
National Center for Child Traumatic Stress works to advance a broad range of effective services and interventions by creating trauma-informed developmentally and

culturally appropriate programs that improve the standards of care for traumatized children. The website has many free resources and fact sheets about trauma.
Website: www.nctsn.org

North American Council on Adoptable Children (NACAC)
Founded in 1974 by adoptive parents, the North American Council on Adoptable Children is committed to meeting the needs of waiting children and the families who adopt them. Annual conference with adoption-related training and resources.
Website: www.nacac.org

Sensorimotor Psychotherapy Institute (SPI)
SPI is a professional educational organization that designs and provides trainings and services to mental health practitioners and the public at large related to Sensorimotor Psychotherapy and Somatic Psychotherapy.
Website: www.sensorimotorpsychotherapy.org

Society for Emotion and Attachment Studies (SEAS)
SEAS is devoted to the dissemination and use of reliable and valid attachment measures for the betterment of research and clinical work aimed at understanding and promoting security in children, families, and society. The prevention of child abuse and respect for diversity in family forms are vital to the SEAS mission.
Website: www.seasinternational.org

STAR Institute for Sensory Processing Disorder
STAR Institute is the premier treatment, research, and education center for children and adults with Sensory Processing Disorder (SPD). This includes feeding disorders and other disorders with sensory issues such as autism and ADHD.
Website: www.spdstar.org

The Family Place
The Family Place, located in Wales, features a multidisciplinary team with a wide range of experience and skills. The team specializes in interventions with foster and adoptive families and their support networks. All team members have significant training in attachment and trauma to provide a coherent approach.
Website: www.thefamilyplace.co.uk

Theraplay Institute
An international training institute that provides training for mental health professionals, parents, and teachers, both locally and off-site around the world, in the Theraplay model.
Website: www.theraplay.org

Trust-Based Relational Intervention (TBRI)
TCU Institute of Child Development offers training in the TBRI for therapists, caseworkers, foster and adoption care specialists, occupational therapists, medical professionals, counselors, CASA representatives, and early childhood and development specialists.
Website: child.tcu.edu

Video Intervention Therapy (VIT)
Information, resources, and dates of seminars related to Video Intervention Therapy.
Website: www.vit-downing.com

Zero to Three
Zero to Three works to ensure that babies and toddlers benefit from the early connections that are critical to their well-being and development. Offers many resources about attachment and child development.
Website: www.zerotothree.org

Index

227

Editors and Contributors

EDITORS

Karen Doyle Buckwalter, LCSW, is director of program strategy at Chaddock, a multiservice agency providing a range of residential, educational, and community-based services for youth, birth through age twenty-one, and their families. While at Chaddock, she has been instrumental in the development of an innovative residential program for adolescents, ages eight to sixteen, with attachment disorders and complex trauma. One of the only programs of its kind serving older adolescents, Chaddock's Developmental Trauma and Attachment Program (DTAP) has served youth from thirty-three different states in the United States originating from eighteen different countries.

Karen has presented at numerous national and international conferences. She has coauthored journal articles and book chapters as well as articles that have appeared in *Adoption Today* and *Fostering Families Today* magazines. She is also a Theraplay therapist, trainer, and supervisor.

Karen has more than twenty-five years of experience working with children, adolescents, and families, the last twenty-three of which she has been at Chaddock. She has a BS in individual and family studies from Pennsylvania State University and a master's in social work from Temple University. She has completed a two-year post-master's training program in family therapy at the Menninger Clinic.

Debbie Reed is president/CEO of Chaddock, a multiservice agency providing a full continuum of community-based, educational, and residential treatment services for children, birth to twenty-one, and their families. While at Chaddock, Debbie has championed the development of several programs and services specifically designed to meet the needs of children and their families struggling with trauma and attachment disorders.

In addition to fostering the growth of these specialty programs, Debbie led efforts to diversify and expand Chaddock's mission reach at the national and international levels. With thirty years of marketing, strategic planning, innovation, and organizational leadership experience, Debbie has trained, consulted, and served on a range of nonprofit boards and councils at the national level. She has also developed a nonprofit leadership development program and writes a weekly leadership blog, *Reed about Leadership*.

Debbie has a BA in journalism and mass communications from Drake University and a master's in leadership from Bellevue University, and she is currently pursuing a PhD in organizational leadership from Concordia University.

CONTRIBUTORS

Stefanie Armstrong, MS, LIMHP, specializes in treating trauma resolution and attachment problems in children and adolescents. Before she cofounded the Attachment and Trauma Center of Nebraska, she spent ten years working in the public school system as a school counselor. She is EMDR certified and is an EMDR consultant. She has presented her expertise nationally to numerous parent and professional groups.

Jonathan Baylin, PhD, is a clinical psychologist and coauthor of *Brain-Based Parenting* (2012) and *The Neurobiology of Attachment-Focused Therapy* (2016), both in the Norton Series on Interpersonal Neurobiology. He is an international presenter on the integration of neuroscience and psychotherapy.

Phyllis Booth, MA, is clinical director emeritus of the Theraplay Institute in Chicago. She collaborated with Ann Jernberg in developing the Theraplay method for helping children and families with attachment, trauma, and relationship problems. She received her training at the University of Chicago in Human Development and Clinical Psychology; at the Tavistock Centre, London, under John Bowlby and D. W. Winnicott; at the Anna Freud Centre, London; and at the Family Institute at Northwestern University, Evanston, Illinois.

Casey Call, PhD, is the assistant director at the TCU Institute of Child Development and a passionate advocate for vulnerable children and families. Her responsibilities include research, training, and outreach connected to Trust-Based Relational Intervention. Casey has earned advance degrees in elementary education, counseling, and developmental psychology, which contribute to her passion for bringing trauma-informed interventions into systems of care, especially educational systems.

Melanie Chung-Sherman, LCSW-S, LCPAA, is a licensed psychotherapist specializing in attachment, trauma, and adoption-related issues. Melanie is also an adjunct professor of social work through Collin County College and a guest columnist for the popular magazine *Adoption Today*. She and her brother were adopted internationally from South Korea in the 1970s. She is happily married with two wonderful children.

Gloria M. Cockerill, LCSW, is a registered play therapist-supervisor and certified Theraplay trainer and supervisor. She has worked extensively with children and their families impacted by abuse, neglect, issues of abandonment, and the traumatic separation from family as well as a broad range of emotional and behavioral problems.

George Downing, PhD, an American psychologist, lives in Paris, where he is on the teaching faculties of Salpêtrière Hospital and Paris University VIII. He also teaches clinical seminars at the universities of Munich, Heidelberg, and Padua and the New School for Social Research, New York. He is the author of numerous articles on video intervention, child development research, and other aspects of psychotherapy.

Faith Friedlander, LMFT and cofounder/vice president of Kids & Families Together, which was established in January 2000, is a wife of forty-plus years, mother, and grandmother. The agency was born out of Faith's strong desire to celebrate diversity and her value of healthy relationships. The mission of Kids & Families Together is to strengthen relationships and provide safe, supportive help and education to emotionally connect families that have been brought together through adoption, foster, and kinship care as well as birth family support.

Amanda R. Hiles Howard, PhD, is an assistant professor of psychology at Samford University, an affiliate of the TCU Institute of Child Development. Her work focuses on understanding interpersonal processes underlying quality of life and applies research to practice for youth in nontraditional care.

Angel Knoverek, PhD, LCPC, ACS, is an international trainer who has been working with children and adolescents for more than twenty-two years in a variety of environments, including schools, residential programs, foster care, and outpatient counseling.

Denise Lacher, MA, LP, is the Family Attachment Center's director of attachment programs. Ms. Lacher has received extensive training in attachment theory, posttraumatic stress disorders, and parenting. She came to the center in 1994 and specializes in EMDR, Family Attachment Narrative Therapy, and Trauma-Focused Cognitive Behavioral Therapy. Ms. Lacher has authored several publications and presented nationally on attachment and treatment of attachment disturbances.

Dafna Lender, LCSW, is a licensed clinical social worker and a certified Dyadic Developmental psychotherapist, trainer, and consultant. She is the program director for the Theraplay Institute in Evanston, Illinois. Dafna's main interest is in combining DDP and Theraplay to heal trauma and create healthy connections between children and their caregivers.

Sandra Lindaman, MA, MSW, LSLP, LCSW, LISW, is a certified Theraplay therapist, supervisor, and trainer, and the training advisor for the Theraplay Institute (TTI) in Evanston, Illinois. Sandra has been with TTI since 1990, training professionals around the world and writing about Theraplay.

Bonnie Mark-Goldstein, LCSW, EdM, PhD, is the director of the Lifespan Center for Psychological Services, offering integrative treatment through the lens of Sensorimotor Psychotherapy, Interpersonal Neurobiology and Attachment, and the dynamic interaction of group psychotherapy. She is an adjunct professor at the USC School of Social Work and coeditor of *The Handbook of Infant, Child, and Adolescent Psychotherapy, Vols. 1 and 2* and *Treating Attention Deficit and Hyperactivity Disorder in Children and Adolescents*, and she has published numerous professional papers.

Kenny E. Miller, LCSW, is a clinical social worker in full-time private practice with Esperero Family Center of Tucson, Arizona. He has for twenty years trained agencies and clinicians nationally in understanding and treating developmental trauma. He has long sought a "unified field theory" for helping victims of attachment trauma and loss, and he gets closer every day.

Evangeline Munns, PhD, CPsych, RPT/S, TTI/ST, CACPT/ST, is a certified clinical psychologist who is a registered supervisor and trainer for three national play therapy organizations: The Theraplay Institute, APT, and CACPT. She is a popular presenter and currently teaches workshops all over the world. She has edited two books on Theraplay and written chapters in numerous other books. In 2016 she received a lifetime achievement award from the Canadian Association of Child and Play Therapy.

Melissa Nichols, MA, LMFT, has been at the Family Attachment and Counseling Center since 1997 and specializes in working with children, adolescents, and their families who have suffered early trauma. She is the originator and author of several programs and books, including *First Steps for Strengthening Adoptive Families* (program and DVD), *Parenting with Stories*, and *Connecting with Kids*. Ms. Nichols is trained in Eye Movement Desensitization and Reprocessing (EMDR) and Trauma-Focused Cognitive Behavioral Therapy (TF-CBT). Ms. Nichols has presented nationally and internationally on topics of attachment and adoption.

Todd Nichols, PhD, LP, has been executive director of the Family Attachment and Counseling Center since 1997. He teaches graduate students in a counseling program and has authored several journal articles and books. Dr. Nichols is trained in multiple approaches to working with children and adults, including Eye Movement Desensitization and Reprocessing (EMDR) and Trauma-Focused Cognitive Behavioral Therapy (TF-CBT).

Vivien Norris, DClinPsy, DipMusicTh, is a UK-based consultant clinical psychologist providing specialized therapeutic interventions for children and families with histories of severe and complex trauma. She is a qualified DDP practitioner and consultant and a certified Theraplay practitioner, supervisor, and trainer. Vivien is clinical director of The Family Place (UK).

Pat Ogden, PhD, is a pioneer in somatic psychology and the founder of the Sensorimotor Psychotherapy Institute, an internationally recognized school specializing in somatic-cognitive approaches for the treatment of posttraumatic stress disorder and attachment disturbances. She is a clinician, consultant, international lecturer and trainer, and first author of *Trauma and the Body: A Sensorimotor Approach to Psychotherapy* and *Sensorimotor Psychotherapy: Interventions for Trauma and Attachment.*

Karyn Purvis, PhD, was the Rees-Jones director and cofounder of the TCU Institute of Child Development. The late Dr. Purvis cofounded Trust-Based Relational Intervention, a holistic, research-based approach for healing children from traumatic backgrounds through building trust and meaningful relationships. Her work and research continues to flourish at the TCU Institute of Child Development, where her team is fiercely committed to carrying her legacy forward.

Michelle Robison, LCSW, has more than twenty years of therapeutic experience working primarily with adolescents and children with severe trauma and attachment issues. Michelle was a key player in the development and implementation of Chaddock's Developmental Trauma and Attachment Program, where she was the lead therapist and later the associate director of clinical services. Michelle is a certified Theraplay therapist, trainer, and supervisor.

Marcia Ryan, MS, has more than twenty-seven years of experience working primarily with children and adolescents who have severe trauma and attachment issues. Marcia was a key player in the development and implementation of Chaddock's Developmental Trauma and Attachment Program (DTAP). She currently serves as a parent coach in Chaddock's In-home Intensive Program. Marcia is certified in TBRI and Reality Therapy/Choice Theory.

Cathy Schweitzer, MS, LMHP, is cofounder of the Attachment and Trauma Center of Nebraska and has specialized in treating attachment trauma for nine years. Ms. Schweitzer is a certified EMDR consultant. She conducts research, presents nationally and internationally, and has authored articles and two books related to attachment and trauma.

Lori Thomas, BS, is the coauthor, with Michael Trout, of *The Jonathon Letters*, a book about caring for and adopting a child with reactive attachment disorder. She has seven children through a combination of birth and adoption and is an active advocate and public speaker on children's issues. She lives in Northern Virginia with her husband, Paul; their youngest child; and two dogs.

Michael Trout completed his specialized training in infant mental health at the Child Development Project, University of Michigan School of Medicine, under Professor Selma Fraiberg, and now directs an institute engaged in research, clinical practice, and clinical training related to problems of attachment. He has written extensively in the field, but he is better known for his fifteen documentary films, including four films on the unique perspective of babies on divorce, adoption, loss, and domestic violence. After forty-six years, he retired from clinical practice in the summer of 2014.

Debra Wesselmann, MS, LIMHP, is cofounder of the Attachment and Trauma Center of Nebraska and has specialized in treating attachment trauma for twenty-seven years. Ms. Wesselmann is a member of the faculty of the EMDR Institute and is on the editorial board for the *Journal of EMDR Practice and Research*. She conducts research, presents nationally and internationally, and has authored articles, chapters, and books related to attachment and trauma.

Made in the USA
Middletown, DE
06 January 2021